RIDING SO HIGH

THE BEATLES AND DRUGS

JOE GOODDEN

First published in 2017 by Pepper & Pearl.

ISBN (paperback) 978-1-9998033-0-8

For Ellie, Ted and Rosa. Always.

I remember we had dinner one night – just a friendly dinner, just bein' mates – and I remember John saying he was thinking of having this trepanning thing done: drilling a hole in the skull. The Romans or the Greeks or somebody used to do it, so that gave it a validity in John's mind, I think. And he said, 'Would you be up for that? Do you fancy doin' that? We could go and get it done.' I said, 'Why?' He said, 'It relieves the pressure on your brain.' I said, 'Look, you go try it, and if it's great, you tell me, and maybe I'll do it.' That was the kind of stuff that was floatin' around then. I just feel very lucky to have said no to those things. 'Cause at the time, I felt bad about sayin' no. I thought, 'Oh, here I go again, look at me, unadventurous, I'm always the one, they're gonna make such fun of me.' I mean, I got such pressure when I wouldn't take acid the first time. I got a lot of pressure there.[1]

— PAUL MCCARTNEY

CONTENTS

INTRODUCTION

The flow of drugs runs throughout the Beatles' story. From the long, late nights wowing crowds in Hamburg aided by the rush of speed pills, to the LSD-fuelled creative breakthroughs that came with *Revolver* and *Sgt Pepper*, and onto harder drugs as the 1960s stumbled to a close, those illicit chemicals helped change their music, personalities, style and beliefs.

John Lennon, Paul McCartney, George Harrison and Ringo Starr may have been reluctant leaders at times, but they were in the vanguard of change in that most revolutionary of decades. The Sixties saw a new British social movement which threw out deference to the upper classes, allowing anyone with enough talent and determination the opportunity to influence culture, the media, books, music and more. Events and attitudes which had been largely inconceivable a decade earlier became commonplace, from the sexual freedom that came with the Pill to debates in parliament and the press on the dangers of drugs and the newly permissive society.

For the most part, drugs provided the Beatles with stimulation, escape, or distraction from the pressures of performing and being in the public eye. We can never know if they would have been the same group making the same music had drugs not been a part of their lives, yet it is undeniable that they used them much as they seized upon any new stimulus throughout the 1960s: taking what they could, then moving on when they ceased to deliver.

Occasionally, as with the Beatles' manager Brian Epstein's chaotic final months and John Lennon's addiction to heroin, the drugs threatened to overshadow the business of creating music and painting the world a more colourful place. Lennon and George Harrison – and later Paul McCartney – were all subjected to police raids and arrests which had repercussions for many years. Thankfully, however, with the notable exception of Epstein, the number of casualties in their circle was low. Drugs may have helped forge friendships, build and break relationships, change moods, open doors of creativity and eventually divide the Beatles, but each member left the 1960s with their critical faculties mercifully intact.

For many years they acted as what Mick Jagger memorably termed the 'four-headed monster': they moved as a quartet, discovering then conquering the world together with unified wit, sartorial looks and personality traits, and even in the depths of their post-split animosity would admit that their musicianship was bound by a shared vision which bordered on the telepathic. Yet they were no clones of one another. As the 1960s wore on, each Beatle pursued different interests, which emphasised their individuality despite often overlapping: Lennon gained a reputation as the dreamer and philosopher; McCartney the curious explorer; Harrison the scholar and disciple; and Starr the photographer, filmmaker and family man. These personality outlines, although crude and by no means comprehensive, were also manifest in each man's approach to drug taking – variously reckless, cautious, intrepid and intrigued.

Those hoping to find within these pages eulogies to the delights of acid or weed might care to look elsewhere. This book does not seek to glamorise drugs, and nothing written here should be seen as an endorsement. Although moral judgements have generally been avoided, it is at times necessary to address the negative effects of drug taking. Lack of condemnation, however, should never be mistaken for tacit approval.

The Beatles often spoke openly about their drug use, but never wanted their fans to mindlessly mimic their actions. 'I don't lead my life to affect other people,' John Lennon said in 1970. 'I do have a moral responsibility but only as much as any other individuals in society. I'm not tuning my behaviour to the fact that I'm famous, because I wouldn't be famous otherwise. To play that two-faced game you have to be in politics or a journalist.'[2] The following year he continued the theme: 'I don't ever feel responsible for turning [fans] on to acid. Because I don't think we did anything to kids; anything somebody does, they do to themselves.'[3]

It is necessary to mention that drugs have the power to ruin individuals, families and communities. Some people dabble and lose interest quickly; others develop lifelong bonds. Some drugs can be benign or beneficial; others are destructive and deadly. Reactions can vary wildly from one person to another, even for substances considered to be relatively low-risk. If you are tempted to take drugs please be well informed of the potential dangers.

At the back of this book is a section, titled Help!, which contains information for those seeking assistance and advice on drug abuse, whether for themselves or others. Be safe, be careful.

Finally, a short note about style. This book is written in British English, which has a number of differences from its US counterpart. These include realise instead of realize, colour rather than color, rumour not rumor and so on. This may be jarring to some non-UK readers, but it's what the Beatles themselves would recognise (not recognize).

Turn *on* your mind, relax and float downstream. The deeper you go, the higher you fly.

PART I

A TASTE OF HONEY

The bearded, tousle-haired, self-styled 'King of the Beatniks' cut a striking figure as he roamed the Liverpool streets looking for local musicians. This teenage poet was touring England giving readings, often backed by local jazz and rock 'n' roll musicians – a hybrid art form he termed 'Rocketry' – armed with just a typewriter and a few possessions crammed inside a duffel bag.

It was June 1960. Shortly after his arrival in the city, 19-year-old Royston Ellis called in at the Jacaranda coffee bar to see if any local musicians were available to play. The Jac was owned by Allan Williams, a Liverpool businessman and promoter who had recently booked a number of shows for a young local beat group, and considered himself to be their first manager. The band – known variously as the Beetles or Silver Beetles, and occasionally the Beatles – had just returned from Scotland, where they had supported singer Johnny Gentle for seven dates. It was their first spell on the road as professional touring musicians.

By chance Ellis bumped into the group's guitarist, George Harrison, at the Jac – 'a boy with a shock of long hair and a matelot-style striped t-shirt.'[4] Harrison evidently saw the poet as a kindred spirit, and grabbed an opportunity to get a booking for his band.

Harrison was just 17, and unemployed since his return from Scotland. He had recently left the family home and was dossing down in a flat at 3 Gambier Terrace, a space also shared by three students from Liverpool College of Art: John Lennon, Stuart Sutcliffe and Rod Murray. Lennon and Sutcliffe played with Harrison in the Beetles, along with guitarist Paul McCartney and a succession of temporary drummers.

Harrison took Ellis up the hill to the flat. 'And that's where I met John Lennon,' Ellis recalled, 'as one of the bodies lying on the floor of a room where the lights were draped in red gauze to give it an eerie glow and towels and clothes partitioned the room and the beds. John … was intrigued by the presence in his pad of a genuine beatnik poet who had been on television.'[5]

Ellis was writing *The Big Beat Scene* (1961), a contemporary account of the jazz, skiffle and burgeoning rock 'n' roll scenes centred on the coffee bars and clubs of Britain. He wrote about young people's sexual freedom and disdain for religion, was actively bisexual at a time when homosexuality was still illegal, and experimented with drugs. Unusual for straddling the worlds of pop and literature, he had appeared a number of times on stage and television, backed by musicians including the Shadows and Jimmy Page.

Ellis was booked to give a reading in a basement coffee bar at the Liverpool University Poetry Society on Friday 24 June 1960, as part of an event billed simply as An Afternoon of Poetry. The following day he took part in another session, A Reading of Beat Poetry, accompanied by gramophone records. The Gambier Terrace students were in the audience, and Rod Murray invited Ellis to stay for a few days. He slept on the floor, 'meeting John's friends and getting to know George better, as well as Paul and Stuart. John and I talked a lot. He badgered me with questions about the world of pop music and the life we led in London as though it were a different world. And it was.'[6]

The Beetles didn't perform at the Liverpool University events, and Ellis was poorly received by the undergraduate audience. Yet Lennon was particularly enthused by the idea of beat poetry set to live music, and later that month the band backed Ellis at an unadvertised 'poetry-to-rock' event at the Jacaranda. Afterwards, back at Gambier Terrace, Ellis's knowledge of a certain amphetamine truly opened the Liverpudlians' eyes.

'The big thing about Royston Ellis was that he discovered that if you opened a Vicks inhaler you find there was Benzedrine in it, impregnated into the cardboard inside,' said Harrison. 'We cracked open a Vicks inhaler, ate it and sat up all night until about nine o'clock the next morning, rapping and burping up the taste of the inhaler.'[7]

Ellis had learnt the Vicks trick from another band, the Crusaders, whose guitarist later found fame with the Yardbirds and Led Zeppelin: 'I was shown how to do that by a singer who later became Neil Christian and his guitarist, who used to accompany me in those days, Jimmy Page.'[8]

The chewed cardboard strip, known as a spitball, energised the users and had a euphoric effect. According to Lennon: 'Everybody thought, "Wow! What's this?" and talked their mouths off for a night.'[9]

But not everyone found the spitball to their taste. Paul McCartney found the experience fairly underwhelming, and was wary of experimentation, displaying a reticence which remained with him well into adulthood. 'You're supposed to stay up all night and talk,' he said. 'Well, we did that anyway. I don't remember, probably they didn't give me that much, probably they kept it for themselves. Also I was very frightened of drugs, having a nurse mother and thinking, I'm really hanging out with a slightly older crowd here, so I was always cautious.'[10]

Benzedrine was one of the first synthetic stimulants to be used for recreational purposes. Manufactured by Smith Kline and French, the Benzedrine nasal inhaler first went on sale in the USA in 1928, marketed as a bronchodilator to asthmatics and those suffering from hay fever. The inhalers contained paper wadding that had been soaked in amphetamine, which could be extracted and used in a way never anticipated by its manufacturers and the authorities.

Users typically cracked open the outer casing and swallowed the paper strip contained within. If dipped in alcohol, coffee or carbonated drinks, the wadding would become even more potent. B Bombs, as they became known, were used by Beat Generation writers including Jack Kerouac, Allen Ginsberg and William Burroughs, but the drug's influence stretched far further. In the mid-twentieth century Benzedrine pills were used by writers, artists, scientists, soldiers, mathematicians, musicians and many others. They often found that the drug enhanced their productivity and creative discipline while leaving their judgement and personalities largely unchanged, even if the physical toll could be high. By the time Benzedrine was made a prescription drug in the US in 1959, the fashion for recreational bennies among artists and intellectuals was being supplanted by a slower-paced substance: cannabis.

The brief Rocketry performance at the Jacaranda was Ellis's only one with the Beatles. The event might have faded from record but for a passing mention made by Lennon in a 1973 letter to the *International Times*. 'By the way,' he wrote, 'the first dope, from a Benzedrine inhaler, was given [to] The Beatles (John, George, Paul & Stuart) by an (in retrospect) obviously "English cover version" of Allen [Ginsberg] – one Royston Ellis, known as "beat poet" (he read poetry whilst we played 12/bar blues at the local in-place!).'[11]

The performance had even been forgotten by Ellis by then: 'It was only later when I read the letter in *International Times* from John Lennon about he and Paul, Stuart and George backing me, that I recalled it had happened.'[12]

UNTIL ROYSTON ELLIS's arrival in Liverpool, the Beatles' drug use went no further than nicotine, alcohol, and the world's most widely used psychoactive substance: caffeine. Illegal highs were scarce in suburban Liverpool, but curious and resourceful kids did a little experimentation regardless. 'We used to come back to our house and smoke tea in me dad's pipe,' said McCartney. 'Sometimes we'd bring a girl home or sit and draw each other. But most of the time we were playing guitars and writing songs.'[13]

For the most part, the Beatles were normal teenagers experimenting with whatever they could lay their hands on. They were certainly aware of drugs, but availability was limited. As an international seaport, Liverpool was often a destination for drug smugglers, and police and customs officers remained on alert. In August 1959 a shipment containing 155 kilos of hemp was stopped at the docks; the report in the *Liverpool Echo* placed the demand for the drug on 'coloured people' and 'women of immoral character'.

It was not only reefer madness that was cautioned against. George Harrison recalled watching, while a teenager, a biopic of trumpeter and heroin addict Chet Baker, 'and that and maybe something else made me aware that this thing [heroin] was just too much.'[14] The film, 1960's *All The Fine Young Cannibals*, did not deal with Baker's addiction or his 1957 trial for drug possession, and it is possible that Harrison was conflating it with another: *The Man With The Golden Arm*, starring Frank Sinatra as the heroin-addicted musician Frankie Machine, which was shown in September 1959 for one week at Liverpool's Palais de Luxe cinema. At 16 Harrison would have been just old enough to watch the X-certificate film.

It was illegal to buy tobacco products below that age, although this seldom prevented younger kids from smoking. Cigarettes, cigars and pipes were commonplace in 1950s

Britain, from bars and cinemas to offices and public transport. And although the full dangers were largely unknown, there were anecdotes, rumours and suspicions of the health implications.

The Beatles were all nicotine addicts by their teenage years. 'I wasn't born looking for drugs,' Lennon said in 1970, 'but I was damn well encouraged to smoke by society and I started to smoke at 15 although I hated the smell. And I started to drink at 15. And all I did later on was mix some stuff in the tobacco and add pills to the drink when I was on tour or working in Hamburg. It wasn't something I went looking for. The stuff was handed to me. It was everywhere.'[15]

Lennon's aunt Mimi and her sisters were all heavy smokers. Charles Powell, the father of Lennon's girlfriend Cynthia, died at the age of 56 when she was 17, having developed lung cancer after years of smoking unfiltered cigarettes. Others lived longer but still suffered lengthy bouts of ill-health. McCartney's father Jim died of bronchial pneumonia in 1976, while Harrison's father Harold succumbed to emphysema in 1978.

In 1997 Harrison was diagnosed with throat cancer, and blamed the disease on his lifelong smoking habit. He was a smoker by 1954, the year he turned eleven and enrolled at the all-boys Liverpool Institute. Behind the grammar school's old air-raid shelters was an area known as smokers' corner, which was where he bonded with fellow pupil Neil Aspinall, later to become the Beatles' road manager. 'This great mass of shaggy hair loomed up and in an out-of-breath voice requested a quick drag of my Woodbine,' Aspinall said. 'It was one of the first cigarettes either of us had smoked. We spluttered our way through it bravely and gleefully.'[16]

Another friend, Arthur Kelly, recalled Harrison's fingers being stained by the amount he smoked. 'I remember a teacher saying to George, "Smoking well, Harrison?" "What do you mean, sir?" "Look at your fingers, boy, they're like Belisha beacons!" And they were – they were bright orange.'[17]

Also at the Institute was Paul McCartney, one academic year

ahead of Harrison. McCartney began smoking shortly after Harrison, and the pair first encountered one another on the upper deck of the school bus, where smoking was permitted. McCartney became another fixture of smokers' corner; a few years later both gravitated towards the canteen at the art college next door, where they were allowed to smoke freely. John Lennon was a student at the college, and the schoolboys would occasionally visit him to make music and chat at lunchtime.

'It was unbelievably relaxed there,' said Harrison. 'Everybody was smoking, or eating egg and chips, while we still had school cabbage and boiled grasshoppers. And there'd be chicks and arty types, everything. It was probably very simple, but from where we came from it looked fun. We could go in there and smoke without anyone giving us a bollocking. John would be friendly to us – but at the same time you could tell that he was always a bit on edge because I looked a bit too young, and so did Paul. I must have only been 15 then.'[18]

Lennon was more than two years older than Harrison, a significant gap in adolescence. Although Lennon tended to accept anyone he liked regardless of their age or status, some of his fellow students reacted with amusement at his younger associates. The older students smoked Woodbines, cheap and strong cigarettes targeted at the working man, and occasionally other cheap brands including Park Drive and Embassy. Allan Williams remembered the Beatles at this time as 'just kids, starved rats, always hungry and puffing on the bedraggled remains of their ciggies.'[19]

Like Harrison, Ringo Starr had taken up the habit at around the age of 11, while a pupil at Dingle Vale secondary modern. Richy Starkey, as he was then known, would often skip school dinners to spend his lunch money on a bag of chips, a small loaf of bread and five Woodbines. He missed many lessons and fell behind academically, and the legacy of his childhood illnesses – pleurisy, peritonitis and tuberculosis – meant he lacked the strength and sporting ability of many of his peers.

The Dingle was a rough suburb of Liverpool, with dense rows of red brick terraced houses lining narrow streets. Although many residents were proud with a strong community spirit, the housing was of poor quality and quickly became sullied by damp and decay. Almost entirely a working class area, a high proportion of Dingle people were unemployed and broke, and violence, crime and alcoholism were never far away.

DRINKING, like smoking, was an everyday occurrence throughout the United Kingdom. The legal barrier for buying booze was 18, although once again this did little to prevent underage drinking at pubs and parties. And Liverpool's alcohol consumption was higher per person than anywhere else in England.

'I didn't realise I was from a dysfunctional family,' said Starr in 1989, after decades of hard-living had given way to sobriety. 'We had parties, everyone gets drunk and passes out, and that's part of life. My mother always told me that when I was nine, I was on my knees crawling drunk. A friend of mine's father had all the booze ready for Christmas, and we decided to try all of it. I don't remember too much. That was my first blackout.'[20]

In 1956, aged 15, Starr got a job working as a bar waiter on the steamboat St Tudno. The pleasure cruiser travelled from Liverpool to north Wales during the summer season, and alcohol was freely available. The bar on board never closed, allowing Liverpool's hardened drinkers to carry on boozing outside normal licensing hours.

Starr found that alcohol helped diminish his insecurities. He would gulp down ale when the opportunity arose, before hitting the pubs of Liverpool once the boat had returned to harbour. He developed a taste for Scotch and Coke while working at Butlin's holiday camp in 1960 with Rory Storm and the Hurricanes, where a heavy drinking culture prevailed. Beer was the *de facto* men's drink, and Ringo's request would often be greeted with bemusement and some questioning comments. But he was confident enough to stick to his guns, and in time Scotch and Coke came to be the Beatles' staple alcoholic drink.

McCartney recalled Lennon smelling of beer at their first encounter, at St Peter's Church hall on 6 July 1957: 'I also knocked around on the backstage piano and that would have been Whole Lotta Shakin' by Jerry Lee,' he said. 'That's when I remember John leaning over, contributing a deft right hand in the upper octaves and surprising me with his beery breath.'[21] At the time Lennon was 16, and McCartney had just turned 15.

Lennon had started drinking a year earlier. It was a time when his academic performance was in decline, just as his swearing, shoplifting and smoking were on the rise. He first got properly drunk at an open air party thrown by the aunt of Quarrymen drummer Colin Hanton in the summer of 1957. After their performance on the back of a lorry, Lennon wandered into the house with his closest friend, the band's washboard player Pete Shotton. The pair were delighted to find an abundance of free beer. After a few bottles each, while doubled up in drunken hysterics, Lennon grabbed the washboard and smashed it over Shotton's head. Lennon, who had been looking for a reason to eject the musically-challenged Shotton from the group, told him: 'Well, that takes care of that problem, doesn't it, Pete?' Their laughter continued long into the night, and their friendship endured for many more years.

When the Cavern Club opened in 1957, its owner Alan Sytner chose not to obtain a liquor licence. Tea, coffee and occasionally soup were sold from a small counter area, but alcohol was felt to cause unwanted problems. Those who wanted to drink were able to get a temporary pass-out to visit the nearby pubs on Mathew Street, the Grapes and the White Star, and the musicians who performed at the club would often be found there either side of showtime. As Ringo Starr later quipped: 'At the Cavern we'd get a pass-out, go to the pub – and then go back in and pass out!'[22]

By the time the Beatles became fixtures at the Cavern, new owner Ray McFall had chosen to keep the venue dry. The venue did not serve alcohol until 1970, three years before its first closure, although alcohol was often smuggled inside. The policy helped keep the venue friendly and welcoming, although violence did occasionally break out – most memorably in August 1962 when Harrison was given a black eye by a notorious local hard-nut, 19-year-old Denny Flynn.

Alcohol was not a requirement for many gig goers, for whom the music and socialising were excitement enough. Coffee bars were popular among 1950s teenagers – perhaps the most famous was London's 2i's Coffee Bar, which opened in 1956 and held skiffle and early rock 'n' roll shows. Stars including Cliff Richard, Tommy Steele, Adam Faith performed at the 2i's, often paid in coffee and Coca-Cola, and Larry Parnes and Jack Good were among the talent spotters on the hunt for future stars.

The success of the 2i's inspired others to open similar premises. Among them was Allan Williams, who had borrowed the money to rent a former watch repairer's shop on Liverpool's Slater Street. The Jacaranda opened in September 1958 and became the Beatles' social centre during their teenage years. The upstairs snack bar was popular during the daytime, but the building really came alive after dark.

The Jac's basement had a members-only private club with a tiny dance floor and space for bands to perform. 'The place was jam-packed every night, couples necking and dancing and drinking Coke,' said Williams. 'It was unlicensed, but people brought in liquor and spiked their soft drinks. For a while I didn't realise what was going on, but when I saw boys and girls staggering out of the place it dawned on me that they couldn't get that way on Coke alone.'[23]

Another venue, the Casbah Coffee Club, opened in Liverpool in August 1959. Lennon, McCartney, Harrison and Ken Brown performed as the Quarrymen on the opening night. The Casbah was the city's only coffee bar to have an espresso machine. Its owner, Mona Best, had wanted to make the club different from the competition, and its espresso was a big hit among the clientele. The basement club's reputation grew quickly: despite its capacity of just 200 and its out-of-town location, within weeks they had membership of more than a thousand.

As a student at Liverpool College of Art, Lennon mostly drank beer or black velvets – a mix of Guinness and cider that was popular among students. He and Cynthia were constantly close to going broke, living on just eight shillings a day. Still, with her support he managed to find enough for smokes, drinks and guitar strings. The pair would often make a single drink in a café or pub last for hours, and if they found themselves temporarily flush with cash might treat themselves to a cinema visit.

Their poverty may have been a blessing in disguise, for Lennon had a tendency to become aggressive and confrontational when drunk. This may have been a symptom of bereavement after the death of his mother Julia in July 1958 – John was 17 and struggled to find an outlet for his grief, and would sporadically lash out at undeserving targets. When drunk he often lost the witticisms which drew others to him, and his belligerent side came to the fore.

At one student party, blinded by jealousy and rage, he drunkenly launched himself at a sculpture student who had taken a fancy to Cynthia. This behaviour was not out of character while he was intoxicated, yet when sober he inflicted wounds with his acid tongue rather than his fists. Not always, though – the day after seeing Cynthia dance with Stuart Sutcliffe at another party, Lennon cornered her and hit her in the face. They split up for three months before he asked her to take him back. He also pledged never to be violent to her again; he kept his word, although his verbal mistreatment continued.

TWO MONTHS after they played as Royston Ellis's backing band, the Beatles departed Liverpool for Germany for the first time. They were without a permanent drummer, had rarely performed beyond Wirral and Wallasey, and were overshadowed by their more professional peers on the local live music circuit.

John, Paul, George, Stu and hastily-recruited sticksman Pete Best – the son of the Casbah's owner Mona – were booked to play at the Indra Club in Hamburg's St Pauli district, taking to the stage just a few hours after their arrival in the city on 17 August 1960. It was their first of five club residencies in the city.

The Indra was owned by Bruno Koschmider, a former circus performer who owned several strip clubs, adult cinemas and music venues. Needing authentic rock 'n' roll musicians for his clubs, he brought Tony Sheridan over from England, but, following Sheridan's defection to a rival club, Koschmider turned to Allan Williams. Two of Williams's acts, the Royal Caribbean Steel Band and Derry and the Seniors, had already played in Hamburg and spoke glowingly about the opportunities and attractions. This time Williams decided to send the Beatles – green about the gills and largely untested outside Liverpool, but eager and available to play.

Hamburg had once been the world's fourth largest seaport, but Allied bombing raids in the Second World War had reduced much of the city to rubble. By 1960 it was thriving once again, prosperous in comparison to Liverpool, with St Pauli a hub of vice, intemperance, criminality and fast living.

Although also a port city, Hamburg was nothing like Liverpool. This new underworld was a place of violence, of gangsters, scammers, beggars and thieves, where the clubs were staffed with waiters and bouncers quick to administer beatings to troublemakers, or even provoke a fight for the sheer love of brutality. McCartney placed the blame for the violence on visiting sailors. 'You could often tell what nationality they were by the smell of their cigarette smoke. You would smell English ciggies, Senior Service, in the club and you knew you might have trouble. The English guys would be very much on our side. "Ow yes, English! Orrrright, lads, play this! Play this!" The more drunk they got, the more they'd start to think they owned the club, but of course the Germans don't like that. Nobody likes that. And there would come a point when they would get into an altercation with a waiter. The waiters had a system, a little whistle that could be blown and there would be ten waiters where there was once one. And they were all big body-building guys. They weren't chosen for their waiting abilities.'[24]

The Indra, a former strip club, was situated at the top end of Grosse Freiheit ('Great Freedom'), a narrow cobbled side street off the main drag of the Reeperbahn. St Pauli was a warren of small streets strewn with clubs, bars and brothels, and an abundance of sex workers and pleasure seekers, with almost every imaginable desire catered for. The young musicians – all still teenagers with the exception of the older Sutcliffe – enthusiastically embraced the opportunities. As McCartney put it: 'There was a lot of it about and we were off the leash.'[25]

The Beatles were full-time professional musicians for the first time, but there was little glitz and glamour. They lived in squalid conditions at the nearby Bambi Kino, a run-down cinema also owned by Koschmider. The already damp, cold surroundings soon became a pit of filth. The Beatles stank, with few changes of clothes and the cinema toilets their only bathroom, and with cigarettes cheap in Hamburg they each smoked up to 40 a day.

Other drugs, though, had not yet entered the picture. The first Hamburg residency was fuelled by little more than alcohol, cigarettes, adrenaline, sex, and a grim determination to improve. Beer was their staple drink, supplemented occasionally with Scotch, schnapps or vodka. George Harrison described this period as 'really like our apprenticeship, learning how to play in front of people.'[26] Although their stage performances lasted up to six hours, they challenged themselves to never repeat a song during a set, which rapidly broadened their repertoire of cover versions. Allan Williams had a habit of telling the Beatles to 'Make a show, lads!' Koschmider, imitating Williams, would yell 'Mach schau!' at them, exhorting them to put on a show for the Indra patrons. The Beatles would leap around the stage, have mock fights, and jump from the stage into the audience mid-performance, to the delight of the crowds.

An elderly woman living above the club was less impressed with the noise, and repeatedly telephoned the police until Koschmider was threatened with its closure. The Indra reverted to being a strip club, and in October 1960 the Beatles relocated to another of his venues, the Kaiserkeller, at 36 Grosse Freiheit. This venue was larger, closer to the action, and with better facilities and bigger crowds.

Alternating hour-long sets with Rory Storm and the Hurricanes, the Beatles swiftly improved as musicians, although they had doubts over Best's competence as a drummer, and Sutcliffe remained uneasy on stage. 'We got better and better and other groups started coming to watch us,' McCartney said. 'The accolade of accolades was when Sheridan would come in from the Top Ten or when Rory Storm or Ringo would hang around to watch us.'[27]

Many, if not most, of those performances were drunken. Sometimes they'd be joined on stage by one of the local gangsters, dangerous men to get on the wrong side of, and many of whom would demand to be entertained. The Beatles wisely chose to keep them onside. 'We'd always be drunk because all these gangsters would come in, like the local Mafia,' said Lennon. 'They'd send a crate of champagne onstage, this imitation German champagne, and we had to drink it or they'd kill us, you know. They'd say, "Drink it," then do What'd I Say. So then they'd get us pissed, and we'd have to do this show for them. Whatever time of night they came in, if they came in at five in the morning and we'd been playing seven hours, they'd give us a crate of champagne and we were supposed to carry on. I used to be so pissed. I'd be lying on the stage floor behind the piano, drunk, while the rest of the group was playing. I'd just be on stage fast asleep.'[28]

It was at the Kaiserkeller that they met three art school students, Astrid Kirchherr, Klaus Voormann and Jürgen Vollmer. Voormann happened across a Beatles performance one night in 1960, and implored his friends to come and hear this exciting new music. All three fell under the Beatles' spell. Kirchherr, whose previously romantic relationship with Voormann was by now platonic, fell in love with Sutcliffe, and she and Vollmer took a series of photographs of the group around Hamburg which defined their image in this formative period.

The Beatles' first Hamburg trip ended in disaster. Their contract was terminated by a furious Koschmider after they agreed to play at a newly-opened rival venue, the Top Ten Club. Harrison, still just 17, was too young to be working in the clubs anyway, and was deported on 21 November 1960. Then McCartney and Best were arrested on suspicion of arson after lighting an object – different accounts mention rags, a wall tapestry, or a condom attached to a nail – in order to see while vacating the Bambi Kino. They spent a night at the St Pauli police station and were deported the next day. 'Hamburg totally wrecked us,' McCartney later recalled. 'I remember getting home to England and my dad thought I was half-dead; I looked like a skeleton. I hadn't noticed the change, I'd been having such a ball!'[29]

Sutcliffe chose to stay in Germany with Astrid until January, the break effectively ending his time with the Beatles. Lennon, too, remained for a while, but found it tough with no money for food. He returned to Liverpool ten days later, his amp on his back, despondent and wondering whether to continue as a musician.

When they played again in Liverpool, at the Casbah on 17 December, posters declared 'The Beatles, Direct From Hamburg, Germany'. The basement club was crammed with people expecting to see a German band perform, many of whom were disappointed when Lennon, McCartney and Harrison walked to the stage area. Once they began playing, however, the change was clear. The Beatles performed sensationally, the crowd went wild, and Beatlemania began to get underway in Britain.

They repeated the spectacle at their next major show, at Litherland Town Hall ten days later. 'Litherland was an explosion in the fortunes of the Beatles,' said Pete Best. 'We were playing for dancing in a hall that could accommodate some 1,500 on the floor at one time, but they stopped dancing when we played and surged forward in a crowd to be nearer to us, to watch every moment and above all to scream. People didn't go to a dance to scream: this was news!'[30]

The Beatles' name in Liverpool was made. They commanded a dedicated local following, with a number of fans attending every performance. Their reputation grew with their audiences, and they began to play new venues – including the soon-to-be-famous Cavern Club.

On 15 March 1961 Stuart Sutcliffe flew to Hamburg, where he and Astrid Kirchherr cleared some administrative paperwork to enable the Beatles to return to the city. At the end of the month the band arrived by train and boat, and on 1 April began their longest residency in Hamburg – 92 nights at the Top Ten Club. They were required to play from 7pm until 2am each weekday, 8pm to 4am on weekends, with a 15-minute break in each hour.

To get through the long nights they were given a new spur: Preludin, or 'Prellies' – German slimming pills which removed their appetites and gave them the energy to take their stage shows to new, often chaotic, levels.

THE DISCOVERY of Preludin came just ten months after Royston

Ellis had dropped the B Bomb. This time it was Tony Sheridan who opened the doors, helping the Beatles to boost their bodies and spirits as the long nights wore on. 'All the stomping and clowning on stage, plus our non-stop way of life, began to take its toll,' said Pete Best. 'There were nights when our spirits flagged and eyelids drooped and it was on one such night that Tony Sheridan held out a helping hand with the words: "Here's something to keep you awake."'[31]

Preludin was a branded stimulant with the main ingredient phenmetrazine. It was first patented in West Germany in 1952 as an appetite suppressant to aid slimming, without the dangerous side effects of amphetamines, and in 1955 became available with a doctor's prescription. Supplies of Preludin – small metal tubes of 20 pills – became widely available on the black market. At the Top Ten and other Hamburg clubs it seemed that almost everyone was on the pills, from the owners and door staff to the waiters and clientele.

Users found its welcome side effects to include euphoria and an energy boost, although its manufacturers were keen to downplay this. 'Preludin does not overstimulate,' claimed a 1958 advertisement. 'In clinical use the side effects of nervousness, hyperexcitability, euphoria, and insomnia are much less than with the amphetamine compounds and rarely cause difficulty.'

The Beatles' main supplier in 1961 was Rosa Hoffman, the sexagenarian *Toilettenfrau* who sat by the toilets downstairs at the Top Ten, exchanging paper towels for coins. Although she spoke barely any English, Hoffman was something of a matriarchal figure to the young musicians who found themselves in the city, and was variously known as Mama, Mutti, Röschen or Tante Rosa. Paul McCartney grew particularly close to her, and in turn she looked after the group. When she heard they were using stimulants she gained a supply of her own, which she kept in a large glass jar. If she ran out she was able to point people in the right direction. '"Vant some, lads?" she would ask temptingly in her fractured English,' recalled Pete Best. 'If this mysterious supply ever dried up she would only have to point a finger at one of the regulars in the audience and indicate that he or she had some.'[32]

Although Preludin normally required a doctor's prescription, in reality it was easy to find through the right connections. Kirchherr's mother Nielsa got hers from a local chemist who asked no questions, and this became a fallback when the Beatles couldn't get any in the clubs. 'They were fifty pfennigs each,' said Kirchherr. 'You had to have a prescription for them, but my mummy knew somebody at the chemist.'[33]

Their legal status helped legitimise pill-popping among the British musicians. 'You could buy them over the counter,' said Starr. 'We never thought we were doing anything wrong, but we'd get really wired and go on for days. So with beer and Preludin, that's how we survived.'[34] The drug's appetite-suppressing qualities were convenient too, because the Beatles had little money to spend on food. Already lean before their arrival in Hamburg, they became rake-thin and at times looked on the brink of malnourishment.

McCartney was reluctant to get involved with Prellies, just as he had been at Gambier Terrace. 'My dad was a very wise working-class guy, so he saw it all coming. As a lad going out to Hamburg on my own, I'd been forewarned: "Drugs and pills: watch out, right?" So in Hamburg, when the Preludin came around I was probably the last one to have it. It was: "Oh, I'll stick to the beer, thanks."

'They'd all get high, and I'd come up just on the buzz. I remember John turning to me, "Blah, blah, blah," saying, "What are you on?" and I said, "Nothing, blah, blah." I'd be talking just as fast as them; their high would do it for me.

'I really was frightened of that stuff, because you're taught when you're young to "watch out for those devil drugs". I actually saw the dangers and tried to keep away from it at first. Looking back, I realise it was only peer pressure: and to resist seems cooler now than it did at the time. It would have been rather wise and mature of me to say, "Hey guys, I don't have to do everything you do," but at the time it just felt like I was being a cissie. And that was the attitude that prevailed.'[35]

Although McCartney did eventually relent, he never took Preludin to the same degree as Lennon, Harrison and Sutcliffe. 'I'd maybe have one pill, while the guys, John particularly, would have four or five during the course of an evening and get totally wired. I always felt I could have one and get as wired as they got just on the conversation. So you'd find me up just as late as all of them, but without the aid of the Prellies.'[36]

The patrons of St Pauli would normally knock back one or two pills with a drink, which would keep them going through the night. Yet it took the Beatles a while to find their limits. 'We used to be up there foaming, stomping away,' Harrison remembered. 'We went berserk inasmuch as we got drunk a lot and we played wildly and then they gave us these pills. I remember lying in bed, sweating from Preludin, thinking, "Why aren't I sleeping?"'[37]

Pete Best was the only Beatle never to take pills, preferring instead to stick with alcohol. He was athletic and enjoyed staying fit, although he claimed he 'didn't deliberately try to avoid' Preludin. 'As long as a drink pepped me up sufficiently to carry on into the small hours I never thought of using drugs,' he said.[38]

For a time Best went out with a St Pauli stripper who worked till 4am. He would wait for her to finish, then they would stay up until he returned to the Beatles mid-morning. The rest of the band had stimulants to get through sleep deprivation, but Best's refusal to join them meant he sometimes faltered on stage. McCartney, in particular, often accused him of falling asleep for a split second on the drum stool, and a rift grew between them.

If Preludin wasn't available, the musicians of St Pauli would make do with whatever they could get their hands on. 'There was so much speed available that you couldn't move,' said Adrian Barber of the Big Three. 'You could buy little five-milligram amphetamine tablets in the stores. They weren't as strong as Preludin, but if you kept taking them, you got the desired result – you don't sleep and you can work and work and work. If you didn't like what they were selling in the shops, you could go to the bathroom in the Star-Club and buy what you wanted from the little ladies there. One gangster took me to some place in the country and his tractor trailer was full of amphetamines. He was feeling good that day and he gave me as much as I wanted so I could feel good too.'[39]

The pep pills made the Beatles thirsty, and the gangsters of St Pauli continued insisting on keeping them drunk. 'At times there were more bottles and glasses on stage than equipment,' said Best, 'and impelled by all the exertions of "making show," they would frequently roll off with a thump or a crash, leaving the waiters quickly to clear up the mess.'[40]

Harrison, who preferred the taste of English ale to fizzy German brews, switched to drinking Scotch and Coke. Lennon and McCartney began doing the same shortly afterwards, although neither was particularly fussy: they would happily drink heroic quantities of beer, given the opportunity.

The Beatles had a destructive streak which they unleashed in protest at their disenchantment with the long hours and hard work. 'We used to break the stage down,' recalled Lennon. 'That was long before the Who came out and broke things; we used to leave guitars playing on stage with no people there. We'd be so drunk, we used to smash the machinery. And this was all through frustration, not as an intellectual thought: "We will break the stage, we will wear a toilet seat round our neck, we will go on naked." We just did it, through being drunk.'[41]

Although friendships were strong at the core of the group, an undercurrent of tension and frustration would occasionally spill over. Lennon and McCartney would argue over who was the group's leader, McCartney would argue with Best and Sutcliffe over their performances, each could be cocky and headstrong, and fights took place on and off the stage. 'All the arguments became trivial, mainly because we were fucked and irritable with working so hard,' said Lennon. 'We were just kids. George threw some food at me once on stage. The row was over something stupid. I said I would smash his face in for him. We had a shouting match, but that was all; I never did anything.'[42]

Just as Lennon had been a belligerent drunk in Liverpool, so he was in Hamburg – with the effects amplified by pills and lack of sleep. 'The down, adverse effects of drink and Preludins, where you'd be up for days, were that you'd start hallucinating and getting a bit weird,' said Harrison, whose intake of pills was second only to Lennon's. 'John would sometimes get on the edge. He'd come in in the early hours of the morning and be ranting, and I'd be lying there pretending to be asleep, hoping he wouldn't notice me.

'One time Paul had a chick in bed and John came in and got a pair of scissors and cut all her clothes into pieces and then wrecked the wardrobe. He got like that occasionally; it was because of the pills and being up too long.'[43]

Lennon claimed that 'the only way to survive in Hamburg, to play eight hours a night, was to take pills. The waiters gave you the pills and drink. I was fuckin' drop-down drunk in art school. I was a pill addict until *Help!*, just before *Help!* where we were turned onto pot and we dropped drink. Simple as that. I've always needed a drug to survive. The others too, but I always had more, always took more pills and more of everything, 'cause I'm more crazy.'[44]

Others reported a softer side to Lennon, finding him less guarded and more open while under the influence. 'I was always close to John,' said Astrid Kirchherr, 'but he never allowed anyone to get inside him. Only when he took the pills did he open up about himself... It was from those pep pills that I had my best talks with John. He and I would take them and then go out of the club for a long talk. The pills would make a person feel more relaxed. When John took one, he lost all his inhibitions.

'He would talk about his feelings and the things he liked. He'd say: "Oh, I want to tell you so much how I feel. I love you and I love Stu." Without the pills, he could never have given me this honesty. He would have choked up at telling the truth. And so most nights John would say: "Come on, Astrid, let's take some beans and talk." But to say he was kept going by pills in Hamburg is really rubbish. He was kept going by something deep within himself.'[45]

During his time in Hamburg, Tony Sheridan had amassed a collection of Nazi memorabilia. One night the Beatles decided to wear it on stage, donning armbands, medals and other insignia to the shock and disgust of their audience. Lennon, covered in swastikas, goose-stepped across the stage giving a Nazi salute, holding a black comb below his nose like a Hitler moustache. 'We even thought they might have liked it,' recalled Sheridan, 'but actually a few people took offence and started getting nasty, so Peter Eckhorn told us to take it off.'[46] At other times Lennon would goad the locals in the clubs, calling them 'Nazi pigs' and other insults. These Second World War insults were not a rarity; Lennon often greeted audiences from the stage in Hamburg with a 'Heil Hitler' and a salute, more out of fascination with the war and eagerness to test boundaries than any genuine feeling for Nazism.

Sheridan was one of the few able to match Lennon's intake of pills. 'Once, Tony Sheridan unwrapped a packet of 20 Preludins and put them in a little tower in front of him,' said Ian Edwards, frontman of Ian and the Zodiacs. 'During the evening, he ate every one. He used to say, "I feel a headache coming on. Take a Prelly, headache's gone."'[47]

On at least one night at the Top Ten, Lennon's excessive consumption left him unable to perform on stage. 'John got more and more pissed,' said Cynthia Lennon, who visited the group during their second Hamburg residence. 'He fell about the stage in hysterical convulsions with so much booze and so many pills inside him that he was no way in control. He was still making sense with his guitar playing, which he could do in his sleep. That night ended with John sitting on the edge of the stage in a very unsteady manner with an ancient wooden toilet seat around his neck, his guitar in one hand, and a bottle of beer in the other completely out of his mind.'[48]

Cynthia and McCartney's girlfriend, Dot Rhone, travelled to Hamburg together in late May or early June 1961. They arrived early one morning, and were greeted at the railway station by Lennon and McCartney, who were still drunk and wide awake from the night before. 'As they got closer we saw that they looked even worse than we did,' said Cynthia. 'Exhausted and baggy-eyed, they reeked of alcohol and their clothes looked as though they hadn't been washed for a week.'[49]

Although Cynthia and Dot were new to stimulants, their initial bemusement soon gave way to intrigue: 'The pills and booze they had been stuffing into themselves had heightened their senses beyond our reason, and they overwhelmed us with their non-stop chat and frenzied excitement. Neither of us had seen them in this state before, but we were soon to get accustomed to the reasoning behind this need for artificial highs. Two weeks in Hamburg and we were all on them.'[50]

———

UNLIKE THEIR DEJECTED first return from Hamburg, in July 1961 the Beatles arrived back in Liverpool with fire and momentum. They were becoming a better band in every way, with a look, attitude and enough musical talent to position them as Liverpool's most compelling live act.

They brought back a stash of Preludin pills which they continued to use liberally. In later years Lennon spoke disparagingly of those who spiked people's drinks, but as a young man he had few such compunctions. One recipient was the Cavern Club DJ Bob Wooler, a *bon vivant* who enjoyed a drink but was unversed in other types of drug-taking. One afternoon he was taken by Lennon and Harrison to the White Rose Social Club, where alcohol could be drunk outside normal pub opening hours. As their drinking session wore on, Wooler noticed two white pills dissolving in his glass. The two Beatles eventually admitted what they were, but Wooler remained wary. Lennon, for whom caution was so often an alien concept, picked up the glass and downed the drink in one.

It wasn't long, however, before Wooler relented and began using Preludin. 'They all took them, even Brian,' he said. 'When I was introduced to the pills, they came in a tube. So when the Beatles would come in to the Cavern with glassy eyes, I'd say, "Been travelling by tube, have you?"'[51] Other Liverpool groups were also taking uppers in the city, and around this time Drinamyl started to become popular. This was the UK brand name of Dexamyl, a combination of amobarbital and dextroamphetamine which was intended variously as an antide-pressant, anti-anxiety and weight-loss drug. Known as purple hearts, the triangular tablets became an important part of the mod subculture in the early- to mid-Sixties.

The Beatles often smoked on stage in these pre-fame years, which only added to their everyday charm and normality. They were not out-of-reach stars, but people from Liverpool just like the bulk of their early fanbase, and they'd chat, smoke and eat in between songs, blurring the boundaries between performers and audience. This insouciance influenced other groups too. Tony Sanders, who drummed with Bootle group the Phantoms, recalled that when McCartney sang Elvis Presley's Wooden Heart, Pete Best would play his hi-hat with one hand and smoke with the other. 'We thought this was tremendous. We were all smoking the next time we went on stage, but it didn't go with our short haircuts and clean boy-next-door image.'[52]

One teenage fan was Freda Kelly, who in 1962 was asked by the Beatles' manager Brian Epstein to become his secretary and run the official fan club. 'Everyone smoked in those days, and the Beatles all used to be dragging on ciggies during their set,' she said. 'George would put one behind his ear for later, or wedge it in the head of his guitar. Paul smoked as much as the others, but we knew he used to buy his cigarettes at George Henry Lee, the department store, where they had a kiosk. That used to seem so much more sophisticated than going to an ordinary tobacconist's.'[53]

The Beatles signed their management contract with Epstein on 24 January 1962, and it came into force from 1 February. He immediately set about improving their image and reputation, booking them into better venues, lobbying broadcasters and record labels, and expanding their horizons beyond the northwest of England. He impressed upon them the need to be punctual and organised, and helped them prepare and shape their concert set lists. While he wasn't always wholly successful, their new professionalism helped them win the acceptance of producers, label bosses and, later, fans of all ages and backgrounds.

One of Epstein's first moves as manager was to ban the Beatles from swearing and smoking on stage, as well as devouring their lunch during midday shows at the Cavern Club. As Lennon recalled: 'Epstein said, "Look, if you really want to get into bigger places you have to stop eating on stage, stop swearing, stop smoking." It was a choice of making it or still eating chicken on stage.'[54]

Additionally, Epstein was adamant that the Beatles should steer clear of drugs, having become concerned by stories of jazz and pop stars falling foul of the law. Pete Best recalled: 'This was not for the Beatles, he said firmly. This was no way to the top and, in one of his impassioned pep talks, he implored us to steer clear.'[55] Yet despite his objections Epstein soon began using Preludin and other substances.

Just as Astrid Kirchherr had found Lennon more open and honest while on Preludin, Lennon saw the same in Epstein. 'I introduced him to pills … to make him talk – to find out what he's like. And I remember him saying, "Don't ever throw it back in me face, that I'm a fag." Which I didn't.'[56]

In Liverpool a local scally known as Judd the Pill supplied many of the Liverpool groups with not only Preludin, but also amphetamines including purple hearts and black bombers. Epstein found that the pills made him feel part of the in-crowd. 'I'm sure there was an element of being cool,' said Peter Brown, a friend and employee. 'He wanted to be part of the little group – I mean, part of the Beatles. I guess he wanted to show that he was cool and hip. I'm sure that was part of the whole idea initially, and also it did help when he was travelling so much.'[57]

Epstein was already a heavy drinker, and he combined alcohol with pills, just as the Beatles had done in Hamburg. Often he drank with the group in Liverpool pubs – the Beatles' usual drinks were black velvets or a 'brown mix' – mild and brown ale. Epstein preferred brandy, which earned him the nickname the Brandyman.

The Beatles, meanwhile, had a nose for lesser-known drinking dens. One such illegal establishment was the Colony Club, situated in the basement of a run-down Victorian terraced house with a brothel operating on the floors above. The club was run by Lord Woodbine, a friend of Allan Williams who had accompanied the Beatles on their first journey to Hamburg. In 1962 Lennon and McCartney would occasionally go to the Colony after a Cavern Club show.

A mutual friend, Bernie Boyle, recalled the scene: 'I was only 17 and here I was rubbing shoulders with all kinds of flotsam and jetsam: guys who'd just got out of jail and chicks who were on the game. The Colony was like John and Paul's little secret, showing how they knew their way around Liverpool. George was never there and Pete and Neil always went home, but John and Paul would buy a bottle of whisky and they'd have a couple of birds with them who they'd picked up in the Cavern, girls who had their own flat... We'd drink the bottle of whisky with Coke, and eventually get taxis home. Sometimes we were there so late I'd go back to Paul's and sleep on the sofa in the front room.'[58]

In April 1962 the Beatles returned to Hamburg for a third time. It was the first of three residencies that year at the Star-Club, another Grosse Freiheit venue almost opposite the Kaiserkeller. The club was bigger and better in every sense: a converted cinema with superior sound and lighting systems, a large stage with drums and a piano for the acts to use, and space for a thousand revellers to dance the night away. The Beatles shared the bill with other bands, playing in rotation and sometimes for just a couple of hours a night. Often their sound was augmented by Roy Young, who sang and played piano and keyboards with the house band.

On the day of their arrival, the Beatles learnt of the death of Stuart Sutcliffe. Their former bass guitarist was a promising painter who had quit the band to focus on his art, and had stayed in Hamburg to study and live with his fiancée Astrid Kirchherr. Sutcliffe had for some months been suffering from severe headaches and acute light sensitivity, although doctors were unable to determine the precise cause. He collapsed on 10 April and was taken to hospital by ambulance, accompanied by Kirchherr, but died in her arms during the journey. He was just 21 years old. The cause of death was cerebral haemorrhage caused by a blood clot on the brain.

But the show had to go on. The next night was the Beatles' first at the Star-Club, and they played with a febrile, frantic energy. 'John came on stage dressed like a cleaning woman,' said Klaus Voormann, 'doing his cripple act and carrying a long wooden plank. He walked across the stage and knocked over the microphones and some of the drum kit, then he went up and cleaned the microphones. He cleaned under Paul's armpit, and George's. The people in the club were laughing – they didn't know Stuart had died. They didn't know Stuart. It gave me shivers to watch it, but this is what clowns do, bring humour to tragedy. It was hilarious.'[59]

On that first night back in the city Lennon stayed up drinking with Epstein and the Star-Club's Horst Fascher. Epstein fell asleep and Lennon, once again wired on Preludin, poured a glass of beer over his manager's head. Epstein unsurprisingly took exception to the rude awakening, and a row ensued before he returned to his hotel, defeated.

This might be put down to youthful exuberance, but one incident from the first Star-Club period showed Lennon at his violent worst. A card game was taking place at the Beatles' apartment, and Lennon, probably drunk, on pills or both, poured water over a drummer sleeping in another room, said to have been Johnny Watson from Southampton group the Graduates. The bewildered Watson retaliated in kind, but Lennon, ever one to up the ante, smashed an empty beer bottle over Watson's head. Although the bottle shattered, the drummer was uninjured. The card players around the table slunk away before matters could escalate further, and the night was over. Lennon was left alone, ashamed but still some years from adopting the hippie mantra of peace and love.

The Beatles were virtually free to do as they pleased offstage, but were expected to behave with a degree of professionalism at the Star-Club. They never, however, forgot the 'Mach schau!' maxim of the Indra, and knew that audiences went for the wild spectacular antics as much as the music. Lennon in particular continued to find new ways to outrage and entertain. 'Some shows I went on in just me underpants,' he recalled in 1971. 'This was in later shows at the larger club, the Star-Club, when Gerry and the Pacemakers and the whole of Liverpool was over there. And we'd really get going then. I'd go on in me underpants, and with a toilet seat round me neck, and all sorts of gear on. And out of me fucking mind. And I'd do a drum solo, which I couldn't do, 'cause I couldn't play drums, while Gerry Marsden was playing.'[60]

The craziness wasn't actively discouraged by the club's management either. Owner Manfred Weissleder, a keen hunter, brought a selection of Arab clothes and, improbably, an entire orangutan fur and invited the Beatles to wear them. Lennon, unsurprisingly, went for the fur and played an entire set dressed as a great ape. Afterwards he donned the orangutan headpiece and leapt into the audience. Later that night Horst Fascher received a call from the police, saying Lennon was being held in a cell; he had been arrested after bursting into another St Pauli club, the Mambo Schänke, leaping on a table and scaring the patrons. Fascher had him released after paying a DM150 fine.

The first Star-Club residency drew to a close on 31 May 1962. Four days before they flew back to England, American rocker Gene Vincent arrived in Hamburg to top the bill at the venue. The Beatles had been Vincent fans for years, and had attempted their own versions of his songs including Be-Bop-A-Lula and Ain't She Sweet. 'We were almost paralysed with adoration,' said Lennon, although the group were less enamoured of Vincent's enthusiasm for violence, guns and knives.

The Beatles soon discovered that Vincent was a heavy drinker, with a particular liking for Scotch whisky drunk straight from the bottle. They wasted no time in joining in, discovering to their delight that the American was also a pill popper. A colour photograph shows Vincent, Lennon, Harrison and Best, all clad in black leather, looking deranged – Lennon and Best brandishing daggers which were pointed at Vincent's chest.

Another photograph from the same time is the only known one in which the Beatles are pictured with drugs. It shows Harrison and a wired-looking Lennon each holding a tube of Preludin. A smiling Pete Best is pointing to one of the tubes, and McCartney is hands-aloft, wild-eyed and gurning.

When the Beatles returned to Liverpool on 2 June, four days ahead of their first EMI recording session, John Lennon stuffed his luggage with as many Preludin tubes as he dared stow away. His use of any drug tended to correlate with its availability, but even at this early stage he showed signs of dependency, of not wanting to be without the pills which had kept him going for the past six weeks and more.

In November they were back in Hamburg for another fortnight, with little enthusiasm for being there. They were playing better venues back home, and had little left to gain from St Pauli, but Epstein insisted they honour the contract nonetheless. They also had Ringo Starr with them, the new drummer having joined in August.

Starr was another seasoned Hamburg performer, with almost as many performance hours under his belt as the other Beatles. Like them he was a drinker and fan of Prellies, and this was the first time all members of the group performed in the city under their influence. 'We were only 22 and we still loved the Preludins and we still liked to drink and we could get away with anything as long as we went on and played,' Starr said. 'The only thing that the Germans wouldn't tolerate was your not going on stage, and you could go on, and we did, in several states of mind.'[61]

They were no more thrilled at having to return to the Star-Club for the third and final time in December for another two-week booking. They soon reverted to their old habits, staying up late, drinking heavily, and guzzling pills to ward off the effects of sleep deprivation.

'Obviously, if you'd only had two hours sleep, and then you'd have to wake up and take a pill, and it would be going on and on and on,' said Lennon. 'And since you didn't get a day off, then you'd just begin to go out of your mind with tiredness. And then you'd think you'd be glad to get out of there. But then you'd go back to Liverpool, and you'd only remember the good fun you had in Hamburg, so you wouldn't mind going back. But after the last time, we really didn't want to go back, when Brian made us go back to fulfil the contract. If we'd had our way, we'd have just copped out on the engagement, because we didn't feel we owed them fuck all. I mean, we made all those clubs into international clubs.'[62]

THE BEATLES CONTINUED TAKING stimulants well beyond their Hamburg days. Pep pills kept them going through the long days of touring, recording, public appearances and interviews. The peaks of Beatlemania were fuelled by uppers, and their mood-changing properties did much to establish the exuberance that seduced and delighted so many fans around the world.

'I was the one that carried all the pills on tour,' Lennon said in 1980. 'Well, in the early days. Later on the roadies did it. We just kept them in our pockets loose. In case of trouble.'[63]

Pills were present in the studio too. During the recording of the Please Please Me single in November 1962, the Beatles were accompanied by Bobby Brown, their young fan club secretary who had travelled down from Liverpool. She was tired after the journey, and felt intimidated in the unfamiliar surroundings of the recording studio.

According to Brown, Lennon 'took out a pill and said "take that". I took it and didn't notice much difference. It could have been aspirin as far as I was concerned.'[64] The drug was Preludin, fresh from Hamburg, and Lennon had a ready supply in his pocket. It is unlikely that Lennon wasn't on the pills at the session too; restraint was never his strongest trait.

Preludin was soon supplanted by dexies, black bombers, purple hearts and other amphetamines. And Lennon still wasn't above administering pills to unwitting friends. A former school-friend, the comedian Jimmy Tarbuck, recalled how 'Lennon had a dreadful trick. When we were all in London and all made it, all had a crack at the big time, you'd go to a do with him – this is dreadful, what I'm going to tell you. I nod off quite easily. I mean, if I lose interest in a thing I just nod off. He would slip a drop of speed in your drink. You mightn't know what speed is, ladies and gentlemen, but it does liven you up. And he did that to me once. I never slept for three days – I thought I was [racing driver] Stirling Moss.'[65]

By this time Brian Epstein was taking great measures to sanitise the Beatles' public image, shutting down rumours and, in some cases, paying off particularly insistent claimants. Although he eventually came to realise that the Beatles' outlandish behaviour was irrepressible, and indeed was among their charms and strengths, he did make efforts to head off potential scandals.

Shortly after becoming the group's manager, Epstein sent Lennon to the offices of *Mersey Beat* newspaper. 'John rushed into the office and said, "Brian insists I've got to get them back – the pictures, everything you've got. I must take it all with me now",' recalled *Mersey Beat* editor Bill Harry. 'It wasn't enough to change their image; he was getting rid of the evidence as well.'[66]

There was nothing hugely scandalous in the images, which included stills of Lennon in his underpants and McCartney on the toilet, and Harry was unlikely to have published them anyway. But Epstein preferred to keep the evidence under his control. He made similar efforts with Star-Club owner Manfred Weissleder, imploring him not to put the daggers-and-Prellies photos of the group into wider circulation. Weissleder acquiesced, and the photographs remained largely unseen until the 1970s.

Yet there were some aspects that Epstein could not control. Lennon's drunken obnoxiousness reached a new low when he attacked Bob Wooler over suggestive comments made about a foreign holiday Lennon had taken with Epstein. 'I'll take it to the grave,' said Wooler of the words that so provoked Lennon. 'Let's just say it was the "emotional badlands" of my life, and to tell you the truth, I'd rather not relive it. All I'll say for the record is that it had something to do with an offhand comment about a "Spanish honeymoon".'[67]

The altercation took place on Paul McCartney's 21st birthday party in June 1963. 'He'd insinuated that me and Brian had had an affair in Spain,' Lennon later said. 'I was out of me mind with drink. You know, when you get down to the point where you want to drink out of all the empty glasses, that drunk. And he was saying, "Come on, John, tell me" – something like that – "Tell me about you and Brian, we all know." And obviously I must have been frightened of the fag in me to get so angry. You know, when you're 21, you want to be a man, and all that. If somebody said it now, I wouldn't give a shit. So I was beating the shit out of him, and hitting him with a big stick, too, and it was the first time I thought, "I can kill this guy." I just saw it, like on a screen – that if I hit him once more, that was going to be it.'[68]

Epstein drove Wooler to hospital, and the assault made the local press in Liverpool before being picked up by the national tabloid the *Daily Mirror*. A contrite and chastised Lennon vowed to give up violence – 'He swore he'd never do anything like it again and, to my knowledge, he didn't, certainly for as long as we were together,' Cynthia Lennon recalled.[69]

THE BEATLES MOVED to London in the summer of 1963. For three years Paul McCartney lived at the family home of his girlfriend Jane Asher.

To his amusement, while living there he was once again shown how to extract Benzedrine from an inhaler – the trick he had been taught years before by Royston Ellis. This time the demonstration came from Jane's father, Dr Richard Asher.

The doctor had prescribed McCartney an inhaler to treat a bad cold, and took the time to demonstrate how to get the best from the device. 'You take off the top and place it on your little finger,' he told McCartney. 'Then you take a sniff with each nostril as per normal; then, after you've finished with it, you can unscrew the bottom and eat the Benzedrine.' McCartney was delighted to have earned the confidence of his girlfriend's father, but was slightly wary of revealing how much he already knew. 'We learned about that stuff up in

Liverpool but hearing it coming from him was quite strange.'[70]

The Beatles also experimented while on tour. In August 1963 they played six consecutive dates in the English seaside town of Bournemouth. For a time George Harrison was unwell and stayed in his hotel room, where he wrote his first song, Don't Bother Me. Several years later, during the making of *Let It Be* at Twickenham Film Studios, Harrison recalled the song's genesis: 'I was in bed in Bournemouth when we were on a summer season, and the doctor gave me some tonic which must have amphetamine or something in it. Remember? And you all drank it to get high. And that's when I wrote that one.'

The memory sparked another, of a more recent incident. 'Oh, I met some fella at the traffic lights in a car,' Harrison continued. 'He said: "Hi man, remember me, Royston Ellis, Gambier Terrace? Gave you your first drugs!"'[71]

In many ways it might have been more surprising had the Beatles *not* regularly used stimulants during their ascent to fame. In the years 1962-64 they played over 750 concerts, often more than one a day; recorded and released 67 songs for EMI across eight UK singles, four albums and an EP (*Long Tall Sally*, the only one from that period to contain recordings unavailable elsewhere); appeared numerous times on television and radio; gave countless interviews and press conferences; starred in their first feature film; appeared in two Christmas pantomime shows; had their own US cartoon series; and conquered America. Their photographs were everywhere, their likenesses rendered on everything from toys and musical instruments to clothes and pillow cases, and their every word was devoured by their legions of fans.

Lesser groups would have crumbled under the pressure, but for many months the Beatles thrived, seemingly spurred on to ever greater creative heights. Their 1964 film *A Hard Day's Night* sums up the unrelenting pressures and mayhem which enveloped the group, depicted with only a small degree of artistic licence.

'I thought I was supposed to be getting a change of scenery and so far I've seen a train and a room, a car and a room and a room and a room,' said Wilfrid Brambell, playing McCartney's grandfather. 'Well, that's maybe all right for a bunch of powdered gee-gaws like you lot but I'm feeling decidedly strait-jacketed...'

Something had to give. The end of the year saw the release of *Beatles For Sale*, the weakest of their early albums. Unlike *A Hard Day's Night*, which wholly contained brand new compositions by Lennon and McCartney, *Beatles For Sale* found the group dredging their pre-Cavern songbook once again. The album was recorded between August and October 1964 amid British tour dates and media appearances, with opportunities snatched wherever there was a window in their hectic schedule. The cover photograph summed up their world-weary state: having been the world's property for two solid years, they looked emotionally, physically and mentally exhausted.

They continued to party hard, not least while on the road. 'The Beatles tours were like Fellini's *Satyricon*,' Lennon said in his landmark 1970 interview with *Rolling Stone*. 'We had that [wholesome] image, but man, our tours were like something else, if you could get on our tours you were in. Just think of *Satyricon*, with four musicians going through it. Wherever we went, there was always a whole scene going. We had our four bedrooms separate from – tried to keep 'em out of our room, and Derek and Neil's rooms were always full of junk and whores and fuck knows what. And policemen, everything. *Satyricon*, you know. We really ... well, we had to do something. And what do you do if the pill doesn't wear off – when it's time to go? You just go. I used to be up all night with Derek, whether there was anybody there or not. I just could never sleep. Such a heavy scene it was. They didn't call them groupies then, they called it something else. But if we couldn't have groupies we'd have whores and everything, whatever. Whatever was going.'[72]

Jimmie Nicol was the Beatles' stand-in drummer during their 1964 tour of Europe, Hong Kong and Australia, while Ringo Starr was suffering from tonsillitis. Although Nicol struggled to penetrate the Beatles' close-knit circle, he did accompany them to Amsterdam's red light district after a concert in the city.

'Paul is not the clean chap he wants the world to see,' he recalled in a 1987 interview. 'His love of blonde women and his general dislike of the crowds are not told. John, on the other hand, enjoyed the people, but used his sense of humour to ward off any that he didn't care for. He also drank in excess. In Denmark, for instance, his head was a balloon. He had drunk so much the night before that he was on stage sweating like a pig. George was not shy at all, as the press has tried to paint him. He was into sex as well as partying all night with the rest of us. I was not even close to them when it came to mischief and carrying on. I thought I could drink and lay women with the best of them until I caught up with these guys.'[73]

'When we hit town, we *hit* it,' Lennon confirmed. 'There's photographs of me crawling about in Amsterdam on me knees, coming out of whorehouses and things like that. And people saying "Good morning, John." The police escorting me to the places because they never wanted a big scandal, you see.'[74]

They were still using Prellies on the 1964 tour, as George Harrison admitted: 'The best flight I remember was that one to Hong Kong. It took several hours and I remember them saying, "Return to your seats, we are approaching Hong Kong." I thought, "We can't be there already." We'd been sitting on the floor, drinking and taking Preludins for about 30 hours and it seemed like a ten-minute flight. On all those flights we were still on uppers; that's what helped us get through, because we'd drink a whisky and Coke with anyone, even if he was the Devil – and charm the pants off him!'[75]

The Beatles kept their image intact with the complicity of

the media. Epstein reasoned that Beatles news could reach a far wider audience if it was syndicated across agencies and networks, and to that end kept a small number of regular reporters close at hand. The lucky few selected for the trip couldn't believe their good fortune, but it showed Epstein as a neophyte in music management: unfamiliar with journalistic conventions, he took a fresh approach to tour accreditation, inadvertently capturing for posterity the inside story of the tours.

US radio reporter Larry Kane was the only broadcast journalist to accompany the Beatles on every stop of their 1964 and 1965 American tours. A political reporter who was initially perplexed by the delirium surrounding the band, he quickly grew to love their music and personalities, and realised he was at the centre of a shift in popular culture. He also saw the darker side of the tours: encounters with underage groupies, scuffles with authorities and rabid fans, and plenty of womanising.

The Beatles could be surprisingly candid about their tour exploits. In his memoir *Ticket To Ride*, Kane wrote of his astonishment at seeing a line of 20 sex workers assembled at a party, from which Lennon invited the guests – including the reporters – to take their pick.

Kane knew, as did Lennon, that there was no way the Beatles' sexual exploits would reach the national press in 1964. They were international treasures, and any journalist who blew the lid on their peccadilloes would immediately be thrown off the tour. Losing access to the Beatles, and potentially incurring the wrath of millions of fans, would have outweighed any scoop.

Kane was present for the recording of the Beatles' fourth and final *Ed Sullivan Show* appearance in New York on 14 August 1965. 'Ed Sullivan came over to greet the party,' he said. 'That was about the time when I noticed a rare happening. John was fidgeting with his hair, he looked grim and nervous, beads of sweat were forming on his forehead, and his pace quickened towards the small dressing room in the back. Was something wrong? I'd been watching the Beatles arrive for shows for a while now. I had never seen the confident John Lennon look so unsure, so obviously perturbed.'

The Beatles often felt nervous before major events, but any apprehension normally dissipated once they took to the stage. But this seemed more serious. Kane spotted the Beatles' roadie Mal Evans emerge from the dressing room, and asked what was troubling Lennon. 'He answered, "He's sweating, shaking, looks like too many pills and shit." I said, "Pills?" He said, "Yeah, uppers, downers, pain stuff, I think, y'know."'

Kane knew of the Beatles' fondness for cannabis, but was unaware that they had ever used pills. Evans told the reporter to keep quiet about the incident and, when the group began their performance less than half an hour later, Lennon had recovered. 'Much to my surprise,' said Kane, 'he looked great, with colour in his face, a twinkle in his eyes and the boyish grin that made him so appealing.'[76]

In June 1966 the Beatles returned to Hamburg on tour, and were treated as returning heroes. During their stay they were reacquainted with a number of faces from their past. Lennon paid a visit to Astrid Kirchherr, who gave him a bundle of letters he had sent to Stuart Sutcliffe. They were also visited by Bert Kaempfert, who had produced My Bonnie and their other recordings with Tony Sheridan. And at the show was Bettina, the buxom blonde barmaid from the Star-Club to whom Lennon had been particularly close. 'She used to call out for her favourite numbers when we were on stage,' Lennon told the *New Musical Express*. 'She got me drinks when we had no money. And pills – print that!'[77] The words were notable for coming at a time when the Beatles were fairly guarded about their drug use, but clearly not all *that* guarded.

They had come unstuck once already. In October 1964, during the Beatles' autumn UK tour, the American writer and broadcaster Jean Shepherd interviewed them for *Playboy*. The feature ran in the February 1965 issue and began with a brief discussion of how Starr had joined the band.

'Ringo used to fill in sometimes if our drummer was ill,' Lennon told Shepherd. 'With his periodic illness.' It was followed up by an offhand comment from Starr: 'He took little pills to make him ill.'

The clean-living Best took exception to the baseless insinuation that he might have been a drug user. After the claim was picked up by other magazines and fanzines, he decided to take legal action to protect his reputation. He was already suing the Beatles for breach of contract following his 1962 firing, and while touring America in the summer of 1965 he instructed two US attorneys to file a defamation of character lawsuit against Starr. The two actions were settled out of court in January 1969 for an undisclosed sum, reportedly far less than the $18 million sought by Best.

'Money had not been my main concern when I sued for libel,' he said. 'I worried more about this attack on my character and derived most satisfaction from the fact that I had been cleared. However, accusations such as this have a habit of sticking.'[78]

As the 1960s progressed, bennies and other pep pills became more expensive and harder to find on the street. Other drugs including cannabis and LSD were changing behaviours and social norms, while the music, art and film that dominated 1960s popular culture were becoming more in tune with a slower, more meditative mindset.

2

WHAT'S THE NEW MARY JANE

Bob Dylan introduced the Beatles to cannabis in the summer of 1964. At least, that's the version in popular mythology. In truth, the Beatles were no strangers to the drug by then, and had come across it several times during their pre-fame period. Despite this, however, they were mostly content to stick to alcohol and pills until Dylan caused a sea-change in their lives.

One of the Beatles' first encounters with cannabis went back to the time of their failed audition for Decca Records, when the label's head of A&R Dick Rowe famously rejected them with the immortal words 'guitar groups are on the way out, Mr Epstein'. The audition took place at Decca's studios in West Hampstead, London, on New Year's Day 1962. John, Paul, George and Pete had set off from Liverpool the day before with driver and roadie Neil Aspinall. England was in the midst of a particularly cold spell, and the band, along with their equipment, were crammed in the back of a hired van. Beset by snow-storms and icy roads, Aspinall lost his bearings near Wolverhampton, but they eventually arrived in London at 10pm on 31 December.

They checked in at the Royal Hotel on Woburn Place, then drove a mile south to Charing Cross Road. Leaving Aspinall to search for a parking space, the others stopped at a pub for drinks and tried to get a bite to eat in a café, but were shocked by the high London prices. They were eventually thrown out by a disgruntled waiter after repeatedly complaining about the cost of soup.

Meanwhile, two men approached and asked Aspinall if they could use the van to smoke cannabis. Innocent of drugs and wary of the men's demeanour, he refused. 'We met two blokes in Shaftesbury Avenue who were stoned, though we didn't know it,' he later said. 'They had some pot, but I'd never seen that either. We were too green. When they heard we had a van they asked if they could smoke it there. We said, no, no, no! We were dead scared.'[79]

Pete Best recalled Aspinall excitedly relaying the tale to the group, and that he claimed the men were drug addicts, adding a further element of danger and confusion. 'Two fellows had approached him and asked if they could climb into the van for a few minutes,' Best said. 'It was some seconds before he realised they were junkies looking for somewhere to give themselves a fix, but once he had they were told to "bugger off".'[80]

Aspinall's innocence was genuine, but at least one of the Beatles had already tried cannabis. In a 1975 interview for French television, John Lennon claimed that he was given the drug around the time that Royston Ellis introduced them to Benzedrine: 'People were smoking marijuana in Liverpool when we were still kids, though I wasn't too aware of it at that period. All these black guys were from Jamaica, or their parents were, and there was a lot of marijuana around. The beatnik thing had just happened. Some guy was showing us pot in Liverpool in 1960, with twigs on it. And we smoked it and we didn't know what it was. We were drunk.'[81]

It isn't known whether 'we' refers to all of the Beatles, or perhaps to some of Lennon's art school friends. Either way,

Lennon's response indicates that the experience was some way short of life-changing.

With the disappointment of the failed Decca audition behind them, the Beatles returned to what they knew best – hard work performing in the clubs in and around Liverpool. On 20 February they had an evening booking at the Floral Hall in Southport, a seaside town 16 miles north of Liverpool. They headlined a 'Rock 'n' Trad Spectacular', with support from Gerry and the Pacemakers, Rory Storm and the Hurricanes, and the Chris Hamilton Jazzmen – providers of the 'trad' element of the night's entertainment.

'We first got marijuana from an older drummer with another group in Liverpool,' Harrison recalled in *Anthology*. 'We didn't actually try it until after we'd been to Hamburg. I remember we smoked it in the band room in a gig in Southport and we all learnt to do the Twist that night, which was popular at the time. We were all seeing if we could do it.'[82]

Harrison remembered being unimpressed with the weed. 'Everybody was saying, "This stuff isn't doing anything." It was like that old joke where a party is going on and two hippies are up floating on the ceiling, and one is saying to the other, "This stuff doesn't work, man."'[83] Lennon also later downplayed the event, saying: 'A guy brought us some grass but we didn't know anything about it and anyway we were already pissed.'[84]

Under Epstein's tutelage, the Beatles moved from playing clubs and coffee houses to ballrooms and dance halls. They also began to perform more often outside Liverpool, although the majority of their shows continued to be in the north-west of England. It wasn't until the summer of 1962 that Epstein began regularly booking Beatles shows further afield, in towns such as Stroud, Northwich, Rhyl, Doncaster, Swindon, Morecambe and Lydney.

Bob Wooler claimed that the Beatles became occasional cannabis users when they started to play outside the Merseyside area. 'We didn't have a strong drug scene by any means,' he said. 'Originally, it was just purple hearts, amphetamines, speed or whatever you want to call it. When the Beatles went down south, they sometimes brought back cannabis and gradually the drug scene developed in Liverpool.'[85]

CANNABIS IS a flowering herb which includes three species: *Cannabis sativa*; *Cannabis indica*; and *Cannabis ruderalis*. The plant has for centuries been used to make fibre, oils and medicine; Classical Greeks and Romans are known to have used the drug recreationally, and archaeological evidence suggests it was also part of prehistoric Euro-Asian and African societies. Its effects can include relaxation, heightened mood, increased appetite, dry mouth, and feelings of anxiety or paranoia.

The dried flowers, leaves and stems of the female cannabis plant are known as marijuana. The name comes from the Mexican Spanish words marihuana or mariguana; an Anglicised slang name for the drug is Mary Jane. Other synonyms include weed, reefer, ganja, tea, leaf or skunk. The slang term 'pot', first used in America in the late 1930s, derived from the Spanish words potiguaya or potaguaya – shortened versions of potación de guaya, a wine or brandy infused with marijuana buds whose name literally means 'the drink of grief'.

Hashish, or hash, is the compressed or purified resin from the plant. It is usually solid, and can be smoked in joints, cooked in food and eaten, or heated in a pipe, hookah, bong, vaporiser or other device.

Cannabis became a core component of the American jazz scene from the 1920s. Musicians found that the drug enhanced their senses and made them feel more imaginative, in contrast to the intoxicating and debilitating effects of alcohol, and gave them stamina to perform during long nights in the clubs.

The pre-war jazzmen called it gage, and it was legal – at least until the Marijuana Tax Act of 1937 effectively banned its sale and use across the US, nine years after it was criminalised in Britain. 'We always looked at pot as a sort of medicine, a cheap drunk and with much better thoughts than one that's full of liquor,' said Louis Armstrong. 'If we all get as old as Methuselah our memories will always be of lots of beauty and warmth from gage.'[86]

The Beat Generation writers of the 1950s were heavy users of cannabis, although their work was more often aided by copious amounts of speed. As they pushed the boundaries of modern literature, a new wave of jazz musicians were introducing a different tempo to the mainstream. Jack Kerouac's *On The Road* and Miles Davis's *Birth Of The Cool* both came out in 1957, but the two works could not be more different. Kerouac's great American road trip novel was completed in a three-week burst of creativity fuelled by coffee and Benzedrine. Davis, meanwhile, was kickstarting the cool jazz movement with slower tempos and a lighter tone, in contrast to the complex bebop styles that had previously dominated.

Cannabis was key to this new sound, and as the Fifties gave way to the Sixties it gradually replaced speed as the hipster drug of choice. 'We'd heard of Ellington and Basie and jazz guys smoking a bit of pot,' said Paul McCartney, 'and now it arrived on our music scene. It started to find its way into everything we did, really. It coloured our perceptions. I think we started to realise there weren't as many frontiers as we'd thought there were. And we realised we could break barriers.'[87]

Pot began to become widespread in postwar Britain following the arrival of immigrants from the West Indies. The drug had long been used in the Caribbean, and it began to assimilate into British society with the new arrivals. Around the same time, jazz musicians began to copy their American counterparts, and young people increasingly adopted the nonconformism of the Beats.

Members of the upper class, too, discovered its effects. Clouds of cannabis smoke spread from bohemian circles into the mainstream, partly due to its ubiquity among mid-Sixties musicians. 'It mightn't have affected creativity for other people,' said George Harrison. 'I know it did for us, and it did for me. The first thing that people who smoked marijuana and got into music [found] is that somehow it focuses your attention better on the music, and so you can hear it clearer. Or that's how it appeared to be. You could see things much different.'[88]

Convictions for cannabis possession increased nearly twofold in the UK between 1965 and 1966, and doubled again the following year. The demographics shifted too; at the start of the Sixties the majority of arrests involved West Indian immigrants, whereas by the Summer of Love in 1967 three-quarters were white and under the age of 25. The 1969 Wootton Report estimated that up to 300,000 people in Britain had used the drug.[89]

The illegal status proved scant deterrent for its consumers, many of whom preferred its calming effects to those of alcohol. 'A lot of young people were knocking booze on the head,' recalled McCartney. 'You'd go to a party and say: "God, whisky! How can you do that stuff, man? It kills you, you know?" So it was becoming very uncool. It was healthier to be involved in the pot scene. It seemed clearer, cleaner, more peaceful. It was pointed out that if you drink too much you can go kill someone quite easily on the road or murder someone in your family, whereas I'd never heard of anyone on pot doing anything like that. The worst the pot overdosers used to do was fall asleep a lot.'[90]

Many cannabis users believed it to be a more natural alternative to synthetic substances, which chimed with the hippie belief in purity of the mind and body. 'In 1967 it was thought that the best hashish came from the Muslim, Buddhist and Hindu areas, including Afghanistan and the Lebanon long before their trails were blasted into confusion, and the best marijuana available generally came from Mexico,' noted the Beatles' press officer Derek Taylor. 'It was made freely available by local street dealers, often friends or friends of friends. At the end of a long journey it would have changed hands many times, each dealer making just a little profit as well as taking as much as he needed for his own private use. These dealers didn't trade in other substances – *never* hard stuff – with the exception of LSD, also a consciousness-raiser and much loved by musicians and others who like to see the sights.'[91]

IN THE SUMMER OF 1964, at the height of Beatlemania, an American journalist from the *Saturday Evening Post* was sent to Liverpool to write a cover story on the Beatles. Al Aronowitz arrived with 'dexedrine spansules my doctor had given me as diet pills plus a prescription of Elavil, a mood elevator which I never bothered taking', but he was more interested in scoring some marijuana. 'The Liverpool kids were ready to trade me for any kind of pills I had in my pocket,' he said. 'All of England's youth seemed to be pillheads, hooked on uppers, mostly.'[92]

Aronowitz's interest in stimulants had been waning since his recent discovery of cannabis. 'To me, marijuana was a wonder drug. It was nourishment for the brain, the consummate head food. As Aldous Huxley had taught me, pot opened the Doors of Perception. But probably it was Jack Kerouac and Allen Ginsberg who most influenced me in my plunge into drug experimentation. When you first try it, marijuana immediately seems so enlightening and possesses such a liberating quality that those it liberates often turn into messianic Johnny Appleseeds. That happened to Neal Cassady, that happened to Allen Ginsberg, that happened to me and, in a much more cosmic way, that is what ultimately happened to the Beatles, who happened to have the power to spread psychedelia to all of contemporary culture.'[93]

He recommended cannabis to John Lennon, and was surprised to discover that the Beatles 'considered pot smokers to be the same as junkies. Like the DEA, they put grass into the same category as heroin.' Nevertheless, Lennon agreed to try the drug if the journalist was able to bring him some.

He also told Aronowitz that he would be interested in meeting Bob Dylan, whom the Beatles much admired. The journalist offered to broker an encounter, but Lennon – who was intimidated by Dylan's talents, and perhaps wary of an ego as large as his own – insisted it be on his terms and territory.

Brian Epstein had told Aronowitz to expect to hear from Lennon when the Beatles arrived in New York on 28 August. And so it was that he received a somewhat brusque call at his home in Berkeley Heights, New Jersey.

'Where is 'e?' barked Lennon.

'Who?'

'Dylan!'

'Oh, he's up in Woodstock, but I can get him to come down.'

'Do it!'[94]

Dylan had observed the Beatles' success as a pop act with a mix of curiosity and envy. Although he initially dismissed the band as makers of bubblegum pop, his growing admiration of their songwriting led him to agree to a meeting. He was driven from Woodstock by his road manager Victor Maymudes, picking up Aronowitz on the way.

The Beatles were staying at the Delmonico Hotel on Park Avenue, near Manhattan's Central Park. According to Derek Taylor, 200,000 incoming calls were received by the hotel switchboard during their two-day stay. Fans stood eight-deep outside, held back by barricades, and the lobby and corridors were patrolled by police officers. Nobody was able to visit the Beatles' sixth floor suite without full authorisation.

The band were relaxing after the first of two dates at the Forest Hills Stadium in Queens, and were enjoying room service dinner with Epstein and Neil Aspinall. In the hospitality suite next door, Taylor entertained reporters, photographers and celebrities including Peter, Paul and Mary, the Kingston Trio and radio DJ Murray the K, all of whom were hoping to meet and maybe party with the Beatles.

Police officers prevented Dylan, Maymudes and Aronowitz from entering the hotel elevators until Mal Evans arrived to usher them upstairs. The Beatles warmly greeted the American guests, and drinks were offered. Dylan expressed a preference for cheap wine. 'I'm afraid we only have champagne,' Epstein apologised, although there were other expensive French wines and Scotch and Coke. The Beatles began asking Evans to get some cheap wine, but Dylan got stuck in to what was available. They also offered him purple hearts, but Dylan and Aronowitz declined and suggested they smoke grass instead.

The band and Epstein were apprehensive. 'We've never smoked marijuana before,' Epstein finally admitted. Dylan was incredulous: 'But what about your song? The one about getting high?'

The confusion was mounting on both sides. 'Which song?' Lennon asked.

'You know,' Dylan replied. 'I get high, I get high…'

Dylan had misheard the lyrics of I Want To Hold Your Hand, considering it a drug ode rather than a simple pop song. But after the misunderstanding had been put right, the Beatles and their guests got down to business. Aronowitz was unskilled in rolling joints so asked Dylan to do the honours; Dylan wasn't much better, and much of the grass ended up in a fruit bowl on the room service table. 'Bob hovered unsteadily over the bowl as he stood at the table while he tried to lift the grass from the baggie with the fingertips of one hand so he could crush it into the leaf of rolling paper which he held in his other hand,' recalled Aronowitz. 'In addition to the fact that Bob was a sloppy roller to begin with, what Bob had started drinking had already gotten to him.'[95]

The Americans were rightly wary of the police presence outside the suite, and of the room service waiters who were streaming in and out. Dylan suggested they move to one of the bedrooms, so all ten crammed inside: Dylan, Aronowitz, Maymudes, Lennon, McCartney, Harrison, Starr, Epstein, Aspinall and Evans.

Dylan lit the first joint and passed it to Lennon. It was immediately given to Starr, whom Lennon dubbed 'my royal taster'. They didn't realise the etiquette was to pass the joint around, and Starr smoked as if it were a cigarette. Aronowitz asked Maymudes, a proficient roller, to make more joints, and soon everyone was smoking their own.

'We all had a puff and for about five minutes we went, "This isn't doing anything," so we kept having more,' said McCartney. '"Sssshhhh! This isn't doing anything. Are you feeling … ggggzzzzz!" and we started giggling uncontrollably.'[96]

The Beatles spent the next few hours in hilarity, looked upon with amusement by Dylan. The contagious laughter was kick-started by Starr. 'In no time at all, he was laughing hysterically,' said Aronowitz. 'His laughing looked so funny that the rest of us started laughing hysterically at the way Ringo was laughing hysterically. Soon, Ringo pointed at the way Brian Epstein was laughing, and we all started laughing hysterically at the way Brian was laughing.'[97]

Epstein kept telling anyone within earshot: 'I'm so high I'm on the ceiling. I'm up on the ceiling.' The usually refined manager also exhibited some self-deprecating humour. 'George and I were sitting on this bed and Brian was sort of lying there rather grandly as he would, very beautifully dressed and every-thing,' recalled McCartney. 'I have this image of him with a tiny little bit of a butt in his mouth like an old tramp, trying to be graceful with this terrible little fag end.

'We actually all got stoned and we were giggling. It was giggling time and we were uncontrollable. And Brian was looking at himself, saying, "Jew! Jew!" He saw the funny side of it. It was as if he was finally sort of talking about the fact. "Oh, I'm Jewish. I forgot." I don't think he smoked it a lot. I think the band smoked much more.'[98]

McCartney instructed Mal Evans to follow him around the hotel suite with a notebook, writing down everything he said. 'I suddenly felt like a reporter, on behalf of my local newspaper in Liverpool. I wanted to tell my people what it was. I was the great discoverer, on this sea of pot, in New York. I was sailing this sea and I had discovered it.'[99]

The marijuana had brought on something of an epiphany for McCartney. 'I'd been going through this thing of levels, during the evening. And at each level I'd meet all these people again. "Hahaha! It's you!" And then I'd metamorphose on to another level. Anyway, Mal gave me this little slip of paper in the morning, and written on it was, "There are seven levels!" Actually it wasn't bad. Not bad for an amateur. And we pissed ourselves laughing. I mean, "What the fuck's that? What the fuck are the seven levels?" But looking back, it's actually a pretty succinct comment; it ties in with a lot of major religions but I didn't know that then.'[100]

Dylan was in a mischievous mood, answering the telephone by saying 'This is Beatlemania here.' He also attempted to discuss music with John Lennon, but the two songwriters had differing priorities. 'He'd be saying, "Hey, John, listen to the lyrics, man",' said Lennon. 'Forget the lyrics! You know, we're all out of our minds, are we supposed to be listening to lyrics? No, we're just listening to the rhythm and how he does it.'[101]

Derek Taylor was still in the hospitality room. After several hours of being pressured for an audience with the Beatles, he called the suite to see whether some of the other guests might be admitted. 'A madman with the lowest of low Liverpool accents answered: "Ay, doanbingennywon inere kozweerorl oussu-varedz." It was impossible to identify the source, though it could only have been Neil, a Beatle or Mal – no one else in New York could do that accent except me.'[102]

Eventually Taylor left the hospitality suite, a bottle of Cour-voisier cognac in hand, only to encounter Epstein in the corri-dor. The manager's mood had darkened since the earlier hilarity, and he scowled at the press officer: 'You'll pay for that bottle, Derek. That is to go on your bill.' Taylor returned to fend off the celebrity guests and deal with the incessant phone calls, until a call came from the Beatles for him to come, alone.

'The room was quite dark,' he noted, 'lit only by a couple of lamps and some candles; the atmosphere was thick and fragrant with incense. Epstein, reeling around holding a flower, appeared to have gone mad. The visitors stood in a mystic threesome by a small table. The bearded and stout Aronowitz, my dear practical friend, was still recognisably sensible, though silent, immobile and beaming. The saturnine Maymudes was a romantic figure in exotic clothes; while between the two of them, thin and beaked, with the beady-eyed gaze of a little bird, stood Bob Dylan. Strange, thin cigarettes were being passed round and everyone looked very happy. Brian came over to me and said I *must* try it, this wonderful stuff that made everything seem to float upwards. Paul enveloped me in a bear-hug and told me he had been "up there"; up there, he repeated, pointing at the ceiling. George offered me a smoke. I refused: "Not for me, thanks. I'll stick to drink." I was fairly alarmed and saw it as my duty to "stay normal" – whatever *that* meant at this stage of my life. George said, "We've been turned on," and from then until I left, maybe 15 minutes later, it was a smoky, murky muddle of strange new expressions – "turned on, stoned, way out" – peppered with the more familiar "incredible, wow, fantastic, fab, gear, man".'[103]

Reporters and photographers were all strictly barred from the Beatles' suite that night. 'None of us travelling with the Beatles was even aware,' said Larry Kane, one of the travelling press pack.[104] The following day, and throughout the rest of the tour, no mention was made of their experimentation with cannabis. The Beatles would happily parade a line of sex workers before the American press, knowing that not a word would reach the newsstands, but a hint of drugs was still a risk too far.

The band knew the personal significance of the experience, and delighted in the fact that they felt no ill effects. George Harrison said: 'It was such an amazing night and I woke up the next day thinking, "What was that? Something happened last night!" I felt really good. That was a hell of a night.'[105]

McCartney was proud to have been turned on by Dylan. 'That was rather a coup,' he said. 'It was like being introduced to meditation and given your mantra by Maharishi. There was a certain status to it.'[106]

The meeting with Dylan was a game-changer, for the Beatles and for popular music at large. Although they would almost certainly have met at some point, the timing was perfect: in 1964 both acts were on the cusp of a major artistic break-through – the Beatles in their pursuit of more introspective songwriting and greater artistic credibility, and Dylan for his adoption of electric instrumentation and retreat from the purist expectations of the folk world. As their two worlds collided, the repercussions would be heard for many years.

IT DIDN'T TAKE LONG for cannabis to start influencing the Beatles' songwriting. Their first drugs reference appeared on She's A Woman, recorded in October 1964 and released the following month. 'Turn me on when I get lonely' was supposedly Lennon's line; he later said he was pleased it wasn't picked up by the censors. 'We put in the words "turns me on",' he said. 'We were so excited to say "turn me on" – you know, about mari-juana and all that, using it as an expression.'[107]

'Turn on', meaning to take drugs or introduce another person to drugs, had emerged from America in the 1950s, and became more prevalent in the following decade. Its later mean-ing, to stimulate or appeal to someone ('She really turns me on'), is now the more common interpretation.

Emboldened by the realisation that they could sneak coded

messages into their lyrics, and with lifestyles steadily enveloped in a cloud of marijuana smoke, the Beatles became audacious and carefree. Dylan may have misheard 'I get high' in I Want To Hold Your Hand but, less than a year after their meeting, that very phrase made its way into a Beatles song. It's Only Love, recorded in June 1965 for the *Help!* album, opens with the words 'I get high when I see you go by'. The Beatles' public image was still wholesome enough for the words to slip under the radar, but the meaning would have been clear to those who knew.

By the time the Beatles began working on *Help!* in February 1965 they were fully-fledged stoners. That album and its follow-up, *Rubber Soul*, complemented the folk-rock movement that was gaining ground in America, and the Beatles' songwriting became mellower and more introspective.

Lennon attributed this to the group's use of cannabis: 'I don't remember any changeover, other than when you take pot you're a little less aggressive than when you take alcohol.'[108] It should be remembered that the Beatles were far from alone; a great many Sixties groups were influenced by cannabis, and the drug became a facet of daily life – not just for those on *Top Of The Pops*, but for the general population too.

After the success of their first feature film, *A Hard Day's Night*, the Beatles were given the luxury of making the follow-up in colour and with a bigger budget of $1.5 million. Their popularity was at a peak, as was their cannabis use. They were often stoned on set, causing them to forget their lines. 'We were smoking marijuana for breakfast during that period,' Lennon recalled. 'Nobody could communicate with us because it was all glazed eyes and giggling all the time. In our own world.'[109]

The Beatles began filming *Help!* in February 1965. Eager to escape the cold and damp British climate, they lobbied the producers to set parts of the film in foreign locations: along with the Austrian Alps, it was decided to go on location in the Bahamas. There were three other reasons. They were burning out through the pressure of touring and many months in the public eye. Brian Epstein and NEMS's chief executive Geoffrey Ellis had also decided to divert most of the group's earnings from the film into a Nassau-based bank, and filming there would have let the UK tax authorities know they were spending time in the country where their earnings were being held. But perhaps chief among the Beatles' reasons was that the easy-going atmosphere on the Bahamas allowed them to smoke cannabis openly and regularly, without the fear of attracting police attention.

The band flew from London to the Bahamas on 22 February. They were carrying a big bag of marijuana, given to them by the American actor Brandon De Wilde. 'We smoked on the plane, all the way to the Bahamas,' said George Harrison. 'It was a charter flight, with all the film people – the actors and the crew – and we thought, "No, nobody will notice." We had Mal smoking cigars to drown out the smell.'[110] The plane stopped at New York to refuel, and a flight attendant informed the Beatles that they were required to pass through US Customs and Immigration. All four flatly refused to disembark, with Lennon being particularly vehement, and in the end the customs officials, reporters and fans were left without a glimpse of the stoned musicians.

The Beatles found filming deeply boring, and smoked cannabis to while away the time. 'A hell of a lot of pot was being smoked while we were making the film,' said Starr. 'It was great. That helped make it a lot of fun.' Soon enough they stopped caring whether anyone noticed. 'It became common knowledge on the film set that the boys were increasingly and openly smoking pot to relieve their stress and alleviate their irritation with the slow filmmaking process,' recalled press officer Tony Barrow.[111]

Cynthia Lennon concurred: 'They smoked it whenever they could – on the film sets of their second film *Help!*, in the recording studios, at home,' she said. 'It enabled them all to escape from the pressures and responsibilities of their position instead of seeing life in the raw. They enjoyed enormously the view that they had following a puff of a joint. It slowed them down and caused them to laugh at each other and the world. When they smoked the merry-go-round stopped for a while, the world looked brighter.'[112]

As well as enjoying the sun and sand in the Bahamas, the Beatles were required to film scenes on the Austrian ski slopes. Although none had skied before, they gamely gave it their best, fooling around with much of the slapstick vivacity of their first film. Cannabis was present too. 'In one of the scenes, Victor Spinetti and Roy Kinnear are playing curling; sliding along those big stones,' Starr recalled. 'One of the stones has a bomb in it and we find out that it's going to blow up, and have to run away. Well, Paul and I ran about seven miles, we ran and ran, just so we could stop and have a joint before we came back. We could have run all the way to Switzerland.'[113]

Ray Coleman, a journalist with the *Melody Maker*, visited the Austrian ski slopes in March 1965 to interview the band. He found Paul McCartney the most forthright of the four, adamant that, despite their positions as teen idols, they were under no obligation to moderate their behaviour. 'I can't be noble for the sake of it,' he said. 'The answer's no. I don't believe we have any responsibility, frankly, and it takes a bit of saying. It's insulting the intelligence of a lot of young people to say we have. We used to get requests from people, asking us if we'd go to a meeting and tell loads of people they shouldn't drink. What do they take us for? We'd get laughed at if we'd said the youth of Britain shouldn't drink. It'd be bloody impertinent. I haven't the right to interfere with anybody else's life. Do you think just because a Beatle said, "Don't go beating people up," the crime figures would go down? They wouldn't. And it's a cheek to expect us to do it.'[114]

The Beatles' colossal appetite for smoking dope inevitably caused problems for director Richard Lester and the rest of the production crew. Since the musicians were too famous to fire, and the film could scarcely be made without them, it was necessary to work around four lead actors who were almost perpetually stoned. The Beatles had trouble remembering their lines, particularly after midday, so most of their scenes were filmed in the morning. 'In the afternoon we very seldom got past the first line of the script,' said Starr. 'We had such hysterics that no one could do anything. Dick Lester would say, "No, boys, could we do it again?" It was just that we had a lot of fun – a lot of fun in those days.'[115]

Even the simplest of tasks could prove too much for the befuddled Beatles. Back in England they filmed the Buckingham Palace scenes at Cliveden House in Berkshire. 'We were all supposed to have our hands up,' remembered McCartney. 'It was after lunch, which was fatal because someone might have brought out a glass of wine as well. We were all a bit merry and all had our backs to the camera and the giggles set in. All we had to do was turn around and look amazed, or something. But every time we'd turn round to the camera there were tears streaming down our faces. It's OK to get the giggles anywhere else but in films, because the technicians get pissed off with you.'[116]

Lester eventually adopted a technique of feeding the script line by line to the Beatles, then filmed their performances before they had time to forget. This necessitated quick-fire edits between shots, and lacked the extended witty interplay seen in *A Hard Day's Night*. 'I think we pushed Dick Lester to the limit of his patience,' said Harrison. 'And he was very, very easygoing; a pleasure to work with.'[117]

The Beatles' love of getting high even made it into the script. After a performance of You're Going To Lose That Girl, a sound engineer notices interference on the tape. 'Boys, are any of you buzzing?' he asks, to which Lennon replies: 'No thanks, I've got the car' – meaning he was driving and unable to accept an offer of drugs. This was not an ad-lib; it was right there in the screenplay for *Beatles Two*, as the film was originally titled.

THE BEATLES WERE AWARDED MBEs in 1965. Their investiture took place in the Throne Room in Buckingham Palace on 26 October.

The band were happy to have been made members of the British Empire, although they observed the ceremony with a degree of detached curiosity and wry amusement. Towards the end of the Sixties, however, Lennon began to express doubts, and in November 1969 he returned his medal to the palace. The following year he was asked by French magazine *L'Express* whether he and the other Beatles had taken the investiture seriously. 'At first, we wanted to laugh,' he said. 'But when this happens to you, when someone decorates you, you don't laugh any more.' He went on to claim that the Beatles had smoked cannabis in a toilet in Buckingham Palace on the day they collected their MBEs. 'We giggled just the same, like fools, because we had just smoked a joint in the Buckingham Palace toilets. We were so nervous.'[118]

A spokesman for the palace attempted to play down the story, telling the press: 'Obviously when people come along to an investiture, toilet facilities are available.' Lennon's tale entered Beatles lore regardless, though George Harrison later said they had smoked nothing stronger than normal cigarettes. 'What happened was we were waiting to go through, standing in an enormous line with hundreds of people, and we were so nervous that we went to the toilet,' he said. 'And in there we smoked a cigarette – we were all smokers in those days. Years later, I'm sure John was thinking back and remembering, "Oh yes, we went in the toilet and smoked," and it turned into a reefer. Because what could be the worst thing you could do before you meet the Queen? Smoke a reefer! But we never did.'[119]

McCartney was less certain, saying: 'I might have smoked ciggies in the bog but I wasn't smoking anything stronger. That's not to say that someone might have. One of us might have had the nerve to do it. But not me.'[120] And Ringo Starr couldn't remember either way: 'I'm not sure if we had a joint or not. It's such a strange place to be, anyway, the palace.'[121] But Tony Barrow felt sure that nothing happened: 'I saw them very soon after the ceremony because they showed off their medals to the media at a press conference we organised at London's Saville Theatre, Shaftesbury Avenue, and although they were in particularly exuberant mood nothing about their eyes, their voices or their general attitudes suggested to me that they had been at the cannabis. I doubt if the group would have been foolhardy enough to take unlawful drugs with them into the palace, which was crawling with all levels of security forces.'[122]

Three decades after, the incident became fully enshrined in Beatles lore. The video for the 1996 single Real Love contained a brief still image of the palace, with overlaid MBE medals flying upwards... and a joint bringing up the rear. In the words of the newspaper editor in the 1962 film *The Man Who Shot Liberty Valance*: 'When the legend becomes fact, print the legend.'

DESPITE THEIR INCREASING indifference towards being moptop crowd-pleasers, the Beatles remained unready to go public on their smoking habits. Instead they opted for in-jokes and not-so-subtle allusions, such as the sharp inhalation of breath during the chorus of Girl, released on *Rubber Soul* in December 1965.

When at home in Kenwood, his mock-Tudor home in Weybridge, Surrey, Lennon kept his stash in an old Quality Street chocolate tin. Although the hours he kept were erratic, with late night parties or recording sessions leaving him tired during the daylight hours, his bedtime routine would include a 'nightcap' joint.

The Beatles may have been riding so high, but the good times weren't shared by all. Cynthia Lennon was becoming concerned at the legal risks and the company they had started to keep. 'The possession of drugs and the involvement with drug-pushers was a major worry in my life,' she said. 'At this time the boys took ridiculous risks, believing in many ways that they were immune and indestructible; so far from reality had they become they didn't give their reputations a second thought, so caught up in the frantic lifestyle were they. Pot smoking parties were the norm, and the acceptance of the situation and the consequences were all part of the way of life.'[123]

Among these consequences was a tragicomic dinner party hosted by the Lennons for comedian Peter Cook and his wife Wendy. John was late returning from the recording studio, leaving Cynthia to entertain the guests for two hours. Embarrassed by his absence, she gamely tried to keep the smalltalk going and glasses topped up.

'It was ten when John rolled in, full of apologies and a beatific smile on his face. He was clearly stoned. He was as nervous as I was about the evening, had smoked a couple of joints to fortify himself and lost track of the time. We had all drunk quite a lot, so when John produced a joint Peter and Wendy happily accepted. When I served the meal it was so late and they were so stoned that they wolfed it down, oblivious to its pre-packed origins and hideously overcooked state.'[124]

Although she had been happy to take Prellies with the Beatles in Hamburg, and was usually willing to try new drugs as they came available, Cynthia never had the same wide-ranging appetite as her husband. She found cannabis 'a total waste of time and money. It only made me sick and sleepy.'[125] Although she tolerated John's drug use, and had little leverage to prevent it anyway, her sobriety and his indulgence around this time set them on paths which diverged as the decade progressed.

Their housekeeper at Kenwood, Dot Jarlett, became aware of Lennon's cannabis use around 1966, the same time she noticed their marriage starting to falter. 'I began noticing drugs lying around in various parts of the house,' she wrote in a 1968 statement to Cynthia's divorce lawyers. 'It was quite clear to me that Mr Lennon was smoking pot, and we all hoped that it was a phase and that he would get over it. I have seen pot around the house since then.'

By 1966 the Beatles were thoroughly tired of touring. The frustrations were many: not being able to hear themselves perform; of audiences who came not to listen to the music but to worship in their presence; the hostile reactions to John Lennon's 'more popular than Jesus' remarks; and at their inability to fully appreciate the places they were visiting on the road.

Cannabis became a way of escape, to relax, and tune out the frenetic pace outside. 'There were good nights and bad nights on the tours,' Starr said. 'But they were really all the same. The only fun part was the hotels in the evening, smoking pot and that.'[126] Their assistant and roadie Mal Evans normally carried the drugs on tour, and would discreetly dispense joints on request.

They were still careful to preserve their wholesome image in front of Beatlemaniacs. The isolation of aeroplane travel and hotel accommodation sometimes left them frustrated at not being able to meet their fans, and occasionally a lucky few would be brought backstage for autographs, photographs and conversation. Junior press conferences and fan club meetings were other ways to get closer. During these meetings the Beatles – who were normally rarely seen without a cigarette – refrained from smoking and drinking.

Brian Epstein consistently urged them to keep their drug use hidden from the public, a demand which became more pressing as their consumption increased. At a party on the last night of their 1965 tour of North America, Larry Kane saw Epstein in action: 'It was a lively affair, with the Beatles upbeat about the tour's end, waiters roaming the room with finger food, and some glamorous young women setting their eyes on the boys. In a corner, John sat quietly and reached into his jacket for his cigarettes. He pulled out a thinner cigarette from his packet, a marijuana joint, and thumbed his lighter to start it. But before he was able to light the joint, Brian Epstein took a quick detour away from chatting with me and a few others, walked over to John, and glowered at him, shaking his head. John slipped the object of his desire back into his jacket pocket, pulled out a legal smoke from his pack and lit up.'[127]

The following day they flew back to England, but not before Harrison and McCartney dropped in on a Los Angeles recording session by the Byrds, whose publicist Derek Taylor had previously worked for Epstein. The presence of two Beatles in the studio control room proved distracting for the Byrds, who were struggling to record a cover of Bob Dylan's The Times They Are a-Changin'. As the session drew to a close Derek Taylor took a call from his wife Joan. An FBI agent had been at their house, asking some awkward questions about drugs, and was now on his way to the studio.

On a transatlantic flight earlier that year, the Byrds' Roger McGuinn had been carrying some hashish in an empty cigarette packet, which he had absent-mindedly left in Taylor's seat pocket. Now the authorities were looking for Taylor, and were closing in on Columbia Studios. Keen to avoid embroiling the Beatles or the Byrds in a potential drugs bust, he managed to lure the FBI man away from the building.

'Fortunately, the agent liked a drink, so to pursue our discussion further I took him to the La Brea Inn where he got surprisingly drunk while I remained astonishingly sober and, I would say, slippery. Yes, of course I had heard of hashish: "But, as you can see, Officer, I'm a gin man, man. That's my poison. And you, Officer? Another vodka, perhaps?" "Derek, if you could see the human wreckage I've seen with drugs." I couldn't but agree. Terrible!'[128]

Under the pretext of a bathroom time-out, Taylor ran back into the studio to tell the Byrds and the Beatles to leave right away, and to clear their houses of any drugs. Harrison and McCartney slipped out of a side door and went with the Byrds to Benedict Canyon, before flying back to London.

One of the most troubled chapters of the Beatles' final tour in 1966 was their three-day stop in the Philippines, which saw them give two concerts in the capital Manila. This culminated in an alleged snub to the first lady Imelda Marcos, and ended with a frenzied scramble to the airport, extortion from tax officials, and intimidation and violence from government thugs. But nerves were high from the moment of their arrival in the country.

As they left the airport 'the boys showed concern that Neil Aspinall had been left behind at the airport along with a load of baggage that included their supply of grass,' according to Tony Barrow. 'I said: "I'm sure he won't be far behind us." The penny hadn't dropped. I hadn't realised that their real fear was not for the wellbeing of Aspinall but that their baggage would be searched and illegal substances found.'[129]

In 1966 the Beatles carried personal attaché cases on their overseas trips. These were not government-issued diplomatic bags, as is sometimes claimed, and despite their great fame and popularity they remained vulnerable to the attention of law enforcers in more hardline countries. They could contain the risks to a degree – 'only on the tours we were protected, because everybody was paid off,' Lennon recalled[130] – and for the time being remained impervious to the legal risks. It wasn't until later on, when they were back for good in the United Kingdom, that their drug use made them a target of police attention.

IN EARLY 1966 BARRY MILES, co-founder of the Indica book-shop, asked McCartney about the songwriting process. 'He told me that he and John always gave themselves a three-hour limit, and that so far they had always come up with something. He said they never took drugs when they wrote the words and music, but afterwards, as a reward for writing the song, they would get stoned and decorate the words by colouring in all the letters and doing weird drawings in the margins. On *Rubber Soul* the words were mostly drawn on red paper or the backs of shirt packets, and they played from these at the recording sessions.'[131]

Any lyrical instance of the words 'grass' or 'high' was normally an intentional reference to cannabis. Sometimes it was unambiguous ('Jojo left his home in Tucson, Arizona, for some California grass'), although for the most part they attempted to be subtle ('Find me in my field of grass'; 'I don't know why she's riding so high'; 'Because the wind is high it blows my mind'). The Beatles often took clear delight in exploiting a double meaning, such as the 'roll up, roll up' refrain that runs through Magical Mystery Tour. However, to the straights and the older generation they still sounded like the wholesome Beatles of old.

Often people would look for meanings that simply weren't there. The chant at the close of I Am The Walrus – 'Every-body's got one, everybody's got one' – was misheard by some as 'Everybody smoke pot.' Challenged on this by *Playboy* journalist David Sheff, Lennon flatly denied that he would ever have been so blatant.

SHEFF: What about the chant at the end of Walrus: 'Smoke pot, smoke pot, everybody smoke pot'?

LENNON: No, no, no. I had this whole choir saying 'Everybody's got one, everybody's got one.' But when you get 30 people, male and female, on top of thirty cellos and on top of the Beatles' rock 'n' roll rhythm section, you can't hear what they're saying.

SHEFF: What *does* 'everybody got'?

LENNON: Anything. You name it. One penis, one vagina, one asshole – you name it.

SHEFF: Nothing about smoking pot?

LENNON: I wouldn't be so gross.[132]

Another codeword the Beatles used for marijuana was 'tea', a Harlem jive term which had also been adopted by the Beat writers of the 1950s. In *Anthology*, Harrison spoke of going to meet Elvis Presley in Los Angeles in 1965: 'We were in a Cadillac limousine, going round and round along Mulholland, and we'd had a couple of "cups of tea" in the back of the car. It didn't really matter where we were going: it's like the comedian Lord Buckley says, "We go into a native village and take a couple of peyote buds; we might not find out *where* we is, but we'll sure find out *who* we is."

'Anyway, we were just having fun, we were all in hysterics. We pulled up at some big gates and someone said, "Oh yeah, we're going to see Elvis," and we all fell out of the car laughing, trying to pretend we weren't silly: just like a Beatles cartoon.'[133]

Speaking of making tape loops for Tomorrow Never Knows, Ringo Starr recalled: 'I had my own little set-up to record them. As George says, we were "drinking a lot of tea" in those days, and on all my tapes you can hear, "Oh, I hope I've switched it on." I'd get so deranged from strong tea. I'd sit there for hours making those noises.'[134]

In early 1965 Starr had bought the lease for Flat 1, 34 Montagu Square, a Georgian maisonette in London's Marylebone district. He used it as a base in the capital and a bolthole for family and friends; its later tenants included Jimi Hendrix, the art collective the Fool, and John Lennon and Yoko Ono.

In 1966 McCartney used the apartment to work on compositions and make demo recordings, electronic audio experiments and films. 'Occasionally [William] Burroughs would be there,' he said. 'He was very interesting but we never really struck up a huge conversation. I actually felt you had to be a bit of a junkie, which was probably not true. He was fine, there never was a problem, it just never really developed into a huge conversation where we sat down for hours together. The sitting around for hours would be more with Ian Sommerville [electronic technician and Burroughs's lover and collaborator] and his friend Alan. I remember them telling me off for being a tea-head. "You're a tea-head, man!" "Well? So?"'[135]

The unrepentant tea-heads were also dedicated tea drinkers – of the legal kind – and 'tea' is also a British term for an early evening meal. In songs such as Good Morning Good Morning ('It's time for tea and *Meet The Wife*') and It's All Too Much ('Show me that I'm everywhere, and get me home for tea'), the words were most likely wholly innocent, but the Beatles took evident joy in the ambiguity – as McCartney explained in 1967 when discussing Lovely Rita: 'The song was imagining if somebody was there taking down my number and I suddenly fell for her, and the kind of person I'd be, to fall for a meter maid, would be a shy office clerk and I'd say, "May I inquire discreetly when are you free to take some tea with me?" Tea, not pot. It's like saying, "Come and cut the grass" and then realising that could be pot, or the old teapot could be something about pot. But I don't mind pot and I leave the words in. They're not consciously introduced just to say pot and be clever.'[136]

One song from 1966, however, was *entirely* about cannabis; the only such instance in the Beatles' canon. Got To Get You Into My Life was the second song to be recorded for *Revolver*. It was written by McCartney as a love song to the drug, but its true meaning eluded millions of listeners until he lifted the lid in the 1990s. 'I'd been a rather straight working-class lad but when we started to get into pot it seemed to me to be quite uplifting,' he said. 'It didn't seem to have too many side effects like alcohol or some of the other stuff, like pills, which I pretty much kept off. I kind of liked marijuana. I didn't have a hard time with it and to me it was mind-expanding, literally mind-expanding.

'So Got To Get You Into My Life is really a song about that, it's not to a person, it's actually about pot. It's saying, "I'm going to do this. This is not a bad idea." So it's actually an ode to pot, like someone else might write an ode to chocolate or a good claret. It wouldn't be the first time in history someone's done it, but in my case it was the first flush of pot. I haven't really changed my opinion too much except, if anyone asks me for real advice, it would be stay straight. That is actually the best way. But in a stressful world I still would say that pot was one of the best of the tranquillising drugs; I have drunk and smoked pot and of the two I think pot is less harmful. People tend to fall asleep on it rather than go and commit murder, so it's always seemed to me a rather benign one.'[137]

The song's lyrics feature personification, a literary device in which an object, phenomenon, idea or animal is given human traits. Outwardly, McCartney appears to recount a road trip, its destination unknown, 'where maybe I could see another kind of mind there'. In a revelatory moment an angelic figure appears, to whom McCartney pledges his everlasting devotion ('Say we'll be together every day'; 'If I'm true I'll never leave'; 'Did I tell you I need you every single day of my life?'). The quasi-religious imagery shows the full impact of that night with Dylan and the experiences that followed; to McCartney, cannabis is both his destiny ('You were meant to be near me') and his comforter ('When I'm with you I want to stay there'; 'You knew I wanted just to hold you').

McCartney's lyrics, composition and performance were maturing at a dizzying pace, and personification wasn't the only literary technique he was using. In another *Revolver* song, Here, There and Everywhere, he drew upon anadiplosis, a method of repetition whereby each verse begins with the last word from the previous line. He also began experimenting with third-person narratives. The Beatles had dabbled in storytelling before, most recently on the singles Ticket To Ride and Day Tripper, but had always brought their own perspective into the frame. That changed in 1966: Eleanor Rigby was exclusively written in the third-person, with the singer/narrator observing from a distance. For No One, meanwhile, adopts a second-person narrative for its detached meditation on a crumbled relationship, another first for a Beatles song.

Paperback Writer, the standalone single recorded during the *Revolver* sessions, features a persona-led story-within-a-story narrative, yet another lyrical leap forward from McCartney. In a period when Lennon was widely praised for his autobiographical or surrealist songwriting, his partner was pushing boundaries in different, equally innovative directions, yet receiving far less credit for doing so. From complex internal rhyming (Hey Jude; Maxwell's Silver Hammer) to deft use of assonance and consonance (Eleanor Rigby, Hello, Goodbye), his underrated wordplay experiments have often been unjustly overshadowed by his gift for melody.

Occasionally drug-induced accidents opened up new possibilities. Rain, the b-side of Paperback Writer, contained John Lennon's backwards vocals in its coda. 'We'd recorded the main part at EMI Studios, and the habit then was for us to take the tape of what we'd recorded back home with us and see what little extra gimmick or guitar bit we could add,' Lennon told *Rolling Stone* in 1968. 'So I got home, stoned out of me head, staggered up to me tape recorder, put my earphones on, and I just happened to put the tape in the wrong way round, and the song just came out *backwards*. I was in a trance in the earphones – *what is it? what is it?* – It was too much, you know, it just blew me mind, it was fantastic, it sounded like some kind of Indian music. And I just really wanted the whole song to be backwards. But instead we just tagged it onto the end.'[138]

The Beatles mostly avoided drugs while recording, although they made exceptions for cannabis and stimulants. During their often lengthy recording sessions, Mal Evans was invariably on hand to cater for their every need, whether fetching replacement drumsticks or guitar picks, bringing food or drinks, dealing with unwanted visitors or rolling joints. He did this out of sight behind the large sound screens which surrounded Starr's drum kit.

The band occasionally stole away for a smoke inside the room containing the studio complex's air conditioning plant, but more often would just get stoned in the studio. Sometimes they would light joss sticks to hide the smell, which was somewhat self-defeating since the burning incense was a clear indicator of what they were up to.

'Though we did take certain substances, we never did it to a great extent at the sessions,' said Starr. 'We were really hard workers. That's another thing about the Beatles – we worked like dogs to get it right.'[139] Out of respect for EMI Studios and its staff, the Beatles were careful not to parade their illegal activities. In turn their producer George Martin chose to look the other way. 'I knew that the boys smoked pot, and they equally knew that I disapproved,' he said. 'And they never did it in front of me. They would always have Mal roll them a joint and they'd nip out into the canteen and lock it, or else go into the loo and have a smoke and come back again, beaming all over their faces.'[140]

'We had a certain attitude towards EMI, that it was a workplace, that was always there underneath it all, although we would often party,' said McCartney. 'There was George Martin himself, who was fairly practical, and the engineers. You didn't want to mess around. Then there was our own controlling factor. We didn't want to be lying around unable to do anything. We knew why we were doing it: it was to enhance the whole thing. I think if we found something wasn't enhancing it, booze for instance, we gave it up. Once or twice we'd try a little wine when people were around, but generally you'd fuck up solos and you couldn't be bothered to think of a little complex musical thing that would have sounded great. You might have wanted to think of a harmony part to something and now it was a bit of a chore and tuning up is a bit of chore when you're stoned.'[141]

The majority of the Beatles' recordings were made in EMI's Studio Two. A long staircase ran along one side of the studio, leading to the control room on an upper floor where the producer, balance engineer and tape op were located. While the staff were positioned high above the studio floor, the Beatles were often high below them in quite a different sense.

Although the control room had a large window overlooking the studio, the physical separation meant the Beatles could go for several hours with just each other for company. 'Yet they isolated themselves further still,' recalled engineer Geoff Emerick, 'putting up screens, setting up a corner of the room as a private area. We never knew exactly what was going on in there a lot of the time; you'd just see a Beatle head pop round the screen and you'd smell the joss sticks and think: They're smoking dope again. I'm sure that they didn't suspect that we knew, which was silly: we were all aware of their drug use, although George Martin was perhaps a bit naive about it.'[142]

Sometimes this naivety had comical consequences. John Lennon's friend Pete Shotton was at a December 1966 session where a spliff was passed around: 'I had just taken the joint from Ringo when George Martin startled us by suddenly materialising from behind the screen to query the Beatles on some technical aspect of the recording. To make matters worse, I had also just lit up a regular cigarette, and thus found myself at this critical juncture clutching a biggie in each hand.'

Lennon introduced his friend to Martin, who extended his hand in greeting. 'Under the circumstances, I had little choice but to stuff the joint back in my mouth in order to shake Mr Martin's hand. Though it's unlikely that the schoolmasterly producer realised exactly what it was that I was smoking, he nonetheless fixed me with a very quizzical look as if to say, "What a strange fellow this is, smoking two cigarettes at once!" Such was my first meeting with George Martin.'[143]

The Beatles started work on *Sgt Pepper's Lonely Hearts Club Band* in the final weeks of 1966. Their status as the world's biggest-selling group gave them creative freedom to spend months ensconced in the studio, perfecting their music and creating sounds never before heard. 'There's no doubt that, if I too had been on dope, *Pepper* would never have been the album it was,' Martin said. 'Perhaps it was the combination of dope and no dope that worked, who knows? The fact remains that they often got very giggly, and it frequently interfered with our work.'[144]

'The main point was that George was the grown-up, not on drugs, and up behind the glass window, and we were the kids, on drugs, in the studio,' said McCartney. 'He was somebody completely different, an alien force really, performing his wartime role as the Fleet Air Arm observer from behind the glass window. When he was doing his TV programme on *Pepper*, he asked me, "Do you know what caused *Pepper*?" I said, "In one word, George, drugs. Pot." And George said, "No, no. But you weren't on it all the time." "Yes, we were." *Sgt Pepper* was a drug album.'[145]

Sgt Pepper was a work of art pop enclosed in a work of pop art. Peter Blake and Jann Haworth were the co-creators of the celebrated album artwork, which features the four Beatles in military-style uniforms flanking a bass drum, on which the fairground artist Joe Ephgrave painted the album title. They stand before 57 photographs of famous figures – musicians, actors, writers, comedians, sports stars, scientists and gurus among them – and surrounded by waxworks, medals, dolls, figurines, flowers and other assorted ephemera. A floral arrangement displays the group's name and the shape of a guitar; other plants nearby were thought by some to be cannabis. Not so, said Blake: 'Another myth is that the plants around the edge were marijuana plants, and for a time I thought someone had played a joke on me and put some in.'[146] Regardless, cannabis was never far away. 'Have a look at the cover and come to your own conclusion! There's a lot of red-eyed photos around,' noted Starr.[147]

The idea of the Beatles adopting the personas of another group was McCartney's; an attempt to distance themselves from their pop past and to be taken seriously as artists. Cannabis was a key catalyst in the transformation. 'We were fed up with being the Beatles. We really hated that fucking four little mop-top boys approach. We were not boys, we were men. It was all gone, all that boy shit, all that screaming, we didn't want any more, plus, we'd now got turned on to pot and thought of ourselves as artists rather than just performers.'[148]

The Beatles maintained that cannabis aided their creativity, and that they rarely overindulged. But sometimes their self-control would slip and fall – on one occasion quite literally. The final recording for *Sgt Pepper* was the assortment of gibberish sounds which filled the run-out groove of the vinyl record. The Beatles stood at the studio microphone and babbled nonsense on each track of a two-track tape, which was subsequently cut up and reassembled with some parts reversed.

The band were clearly relieved to put the finishing touches to their masterpiece, and an impromptu party was held in the studio. 'The Beatles stood around two microphones muttering, singing snatches of songs and yelling for what seemed like hours, with the rest of us standing round them, joining in,' Barry Miles recalled. 'Mal carried in cases of Coke and bottles of Scotch. Ringo was out of it. "I'm so stoned," he said, "I think I'm going to fall over!" As he slowly toppled, Mal caught him and popped him neatly in a chair without a murmur. In the control room no one seemed to notice.'[149]

ON 24 JULY 1967 a full-page advertisement appeared in *The Times* newspaper, signed by 64 prominent members of British society. It was headed 'The law against marijuana is immoral in principle and unworkable in practice,' and called for the legalisation of marijuana, the release of all people imprisoned due to cannabis possession, and further research into the drug's medical uses. Among the signatories were Brian Epstein, John Lennon MBE, Paul McCartney MBE, George Harrison MBE and Richard Starkey MBE.

It was sponsored by a drug research group named Soma, the Society of Mental Awareness, which had been formed by Stephen Abrams, a parapsychology researcher at Oxford University. The advert was in response to a conviction for possession handed to John 'Hoppy' Hopkins, a founder of *International Times*, the UFO Club and the 14 Hour Technicolour Dream event. The nine-month prison sentence was handed down on 1 June 1967, the day of *Sgt Pepper*'s release. An emergency meeting was held the day after at the Indica Bookshop, during which Abrams suggested bringing the issue into public debate by running a full-page advertisement. He agreed to organise the signatures, but the question of finance was more problematic.

None of the Beatles were present at Indica, but the co-owner Barry Miles telephoned McCartney and arranged a meeting at the Beatle's house the next day. 'Steve was well prepared and had the idea very thoroughly worked out in his head. He told Paul the names of some important people he thought would sign the advertisement. Paul said the Beatles would pay for the ad and that he would arrange for all of the Beatles and Brian Epstein to put their names to it.' As the visitors prepared to leave, McCartney gave them copies of *Sgt Pepper* from a large pile by the door. 'Listen to this through headphones on acid,' he told them.[150]

Brian Epstein sent *The Times* a personal cheque for £1,800, more than the average annual wage. Although McCartney had wanted to keep the funding a secret, fearing negative publicity, it proved impossible. The day after the advertisement appeared, the information appeared in the *Evening Stan-*

dard's Londoner's Diary column. Within a day questions were being asked in the House of Commons about the need for public awareness of the dangers of drugs.

In August Epstein gave a candid interview to the *Melody Maker* in which he held forth on drugs, homosexuality and the law. 'I really believe that pot, marijuana or hash – whatever you like to call it – is less harmful, without question, than, say, alcohol,' he said. 'I think there is a terrific misunderstanding about marijuana and its effects. So many people have said it must be bad that this verdict is accepted without question, and of course, there is the malicious association between drugs and pop music.'

The Sexual Offences Act 1967 had been passed by the UK parliament a month before, and decriminalised homosexual acts in private in England and Wales. Epstein saw a link between modern attitudes to sexuality and the shifting mood towards drugs.

'I think society's whole attitude to soft drugs must eventually change,' he said. 'There is a parallel with homosexuality when that was a cardinal sin. Isn't it silly that we have had to wait all this time for the reforming legislation to go through?'[151]

Drugs were a hot topic in the media. Pop stars were becoming fearful of being busted by an overzealous drug squad, following a handful of high profile arrests. Cannabis and other drugs had become widely available on the black market in the bigger British cities, and were no longer the preserve of small pockets of society. Musicians, actors and artists were among those openly discussing their use of drugs to aid creativity or reveal new ways of seeing, and much of London was lifted on a cloud of marijuana, patchouli oil and other exotic incenses.

Although they went through short spells of abstinence, cannabis was one substance from which the Beatles never fully moved on. Occasionally they visited the Baghdad House on Chelsea's Fulham Road, described by McCartney as 'the only place in London where you could smoke hash downstairs'.[152]

For a time, they seemed above the law, and continued smoking openly in the company of those they trusted.

Yet no band was as big as the Beatles, and they risked a faster and further fall than their fellow high fliers. 'I see now that most people were just living these really ordinary little lives while we were madmen riding this incredibly psychedelic whirlwind,' McCartney said. 'It seemed very normal to us to be smoking a lot of pot and flying around very late.'[153]

Aside from the advertisement in *The Times*, Ringo Starr kept his own counsel for much of the Summer of Love, preferring not to publicly advocate drug use. However, he did set forth his views in a *Melody Maker* interview conducted towards the end of 1967, in which he adopted a libertarian stance towards drugs: 'It used to be legal until a couple of fellas got round a table and said we'll make it illegal. Even in hospitals now they can't get into it as they're not allowed to have it for research, which is silly. You can't say to someone, "Don't take pot, it's no good," Or you can't say, "Take it 'cause it is good." It's up to the person. It's not a harmful thing. I don't see why the law suddenly says you can't have it.'[154]

3

THE INNER LIGHT

S tratheam Place, on the edge of Hyde Park in the north London district of Bayswater, is a grand thoroughfare of imposing late-Georgian period properties. Originally named Chester Place, the street has long been occupied by well-heeled residents. The pub on the corner, the Victoria, was where Charles Dickens worked on his final novel *Our Mutual Friend*, a tale of rebirth, renewal and defiance of social expectation.

Those same three elements were also present one evening at the midpoint of the Sixties, when the course of popular music was changed irrevocably.

The ground floor apartment of 2 Strathearn Place was the home of cosmetic dentist John Riley, the wealthy and charismatic 34-year-old son of a Metropolitan Police constable. Having completed his dental training in Chicago, Riley had set up a private practice on London's Harley Street. He attracted a range of high profile patients including the Beatles, of whom he was particularly friendly with George Harrison. Riley was often to be seen at the heart of Swinging London, and had even flown to the Bahamas to visit the set of *Help!* in February 1965.

Riley evidently had some unorthodox approaches to

dentistry. According to Pattie Boyd: 'No matter what he was going to do in our mouths, he would give us intravenous Valium. All of the Beatles went to him and we took it for granted that this was what happened – no one questioned it. We would go into a deep sleep and wake up not knowing what he had done. I watched him trying to revive George once by slapping his face. It was sinister – he could have been doing anything to us while we were out.'[155]

One evening in the spring of 1965, Harrison, Boyd, and John and Cynthia Lennon attended a dinner party at John Riley's apartment.[156] Riley's 21-year-old girlfriend Cyndy Bury, whom he later married, was also present. Following the meal the six adjourned from the dining room into the larger living room. Cups of coffee were served to the guests, into each of which was dropped a sugar cube impregnated with a dose of LSD.

The dentist had little knowledge of LSD's potency. While curious about its effects, he had never before taken the drug, and had no particular desire to be the first person to turn on the Beatles. He had presumed the guests would remain in the comfort of his apartment, in controlled and safe conditions, as the LSD took effect.

'It was nothing to do with getting "turned on,"' Cyndy Bury said. 'It wasn't really anything to do with "drugs" as such. It was totally innocent. I was a really straight girl who just liked my alcohol and cigarettes. My only "drug" was a little glass of champagne at the end of the day. We didn't have the idea that you can take this and it'll widen your horizons. Nobody knew what it would do. Nobody knew.'[157]

Harrison later suggested that Riley's LSD had been supplied by *Playboy* executive Victor Lownes: 'I had a dentist who invited me and John and our ex-wives to dinner, and he had this acid he'd got off the guy who ran *Playboy* in London,' he said in 1988. 'And the *Playboy* guy had gotten it off, you know, the people who had it in America. What's his name, Tim Leary.'[158]

This was incorrect on all counts. A friend of Riley in the

building trade knew of a chemist who was manufacturing LSD in a remote farmhouse in Wales. The friend arranged the purchase of a small amount for Riley, and had it delivered to Strathearn Place.

The guests had never meant to stay at the dinner party for long. They intended to visit the Pickwick Club to see the debut live performance by Paddy, Klaus & Gibson. Harrison, in particular, was keen to catch the band, but Bury persuaded them to stay a little longer. 'You haven't had any coffee yet,' she said, jumping to her feet. 'It's ready, I've made it – and it's delicious.'

After finishing their drinks the guests again made to leave. According to Boyd: 'We were really keen to get away and John Lennon said, "We must go now. These friends of ours are going to be on soon. It's their first night, we've got to go and see them."'

Riley's response stopped them in their tracks: 'You can't leave.'

'Why not?' asked Lennon.

'You've had LSD,' Riley told his guests. 'It was in the coffee.'

And so began what Harrison later termed 'the Dental Experience'.

WHILE HARRISON and Boyd claimed to have never before heard of LSD, Cynthia Lennon said it had been mentioned in general terms over dinner that evening. Her husband was certainly aware of it, having read A Visit To Inner Space, an article in the November 1963 edition of *Playboy* by novelist Alan Harrington. The piece recounted the author's first LSD experience, where he suffered the terrifying effects of a bad trip, including ego death, primal despair, panic and sobbing, as well as thrilling visions, uncontrollable laughter and a feeling of rebirth. It was heady stuff for the strait-laced early 1960s, and one can only wonder what Lennon made of it.

His response to Riley, meanwhile, was one of outrage. 'How dare you fucking do this to us?' Lennon angrily demanded. Harrison, who had never heard of LSD, shrugged it off. 'I just thought, "Well, what's that? So what? Let's go!"'

There was a suspicion among the guests that Riley was hoping to involve them in sex games. In the light of his tendency to administer intravenous Valium to his patients, this perhaps wasn't too fanciful. 'I'm sure he thought it [LSD] was an aphrodisiac,' said Harrison. 'I remember his girlfriend had enormous breasts and I think he thought that there was going to be a big gang-bang and that he was going to get to shag everybody. I really think that was his motive.'[159]

Lennon told *Rolling Stone* in 1970: 'He didn't know what it was, it was just, "It's all the thing," with the middle-class London swingers. They had all heard about it and didn't know it was different from pot or pills. And they gave it to us, and he was saying, "I advise you not to leave," and we thought he was trying to keep us for an orgy in his house and we didn't want to know.'[160]

Riley, mindful of the risks of having two world-famous Beatles and their partners wandering the streets of London under the influence of a powerful hallucinogenic, offered to drive them to the Pickwick Club and back to Strathearn Place after the show, but the idea was rejected. The four guests boarded Boyd's Mini Cooper and headed to the club, followed by Riley and Bury in their own car.

The LSD's effects were beginning to take hold. 'We were desperate to escape,' said Pattie Boyd. 'Riley said he would drive us but we ignored him and piled into my Mini, which seemed to be shrinking. All the way to the club the car felt smaller and smaller, and by the time we arrived we were completely out of it.'[161]

The Beatles were frequent visitors to the Pickwick. Situated in Newport House near Leicester Square, it had a recently-opened basement club called Downstairs at the Pickwick, where

Paddy, Klaus & Gibson were playing. The trio had formed in Hamburg, and featured Paddy Chambers on guitar and vocals, Gibson Kemp on drums, and the Beatles' friend Klaus Voormann – who later designed the Beatles' *Revolver* cover – on bass guitar (Kemp had replaced Ringo Starr in Rory Storm and the Hurricanes, and in 1967 married Astrid Kirchherr).

By the time the Lennons, Harrison and Boyd arrived at the Pickwick they were feeling increasingly disorientated. 'People kept recognising George and coming up to him,' said Boyd. 'They were moving in and out of focus, then looked like animals. We clung to each other, feeling surreal.'[162]

Riley and Bury had followed them into the venue but left after a short time. Unable to drive, they took a taxi back to Strathearn Place, and during the journey asked their incredulous driver to take them around Hyde Park several times while they lay on the floor looking up at the night sky.

The Pickwick was later described by Harrison as 'a little restaurant with a small stage'. 'I think we went to eat,' Lennon recalled in 1970, 'where the table went this long, just like I'd read somebody – who is it, Blake, is it? – somebody describing the effects of the opium in the old days. And I thought, "Fuck, it's happening."'[163]

Harrison remembered coping rather better. 'We'd just sat down and ordered our drinks when suddenly I feel the most incredible feeling come over me,' he said. 'It was something like a very concentrated version of the best feeling I'd ever had in my whole life.

'It was fantastic. I felt in love, not with anything or anybody in particular, but with everything. Everything was perfect, in a perfect light, and I had an overwhelming desire to go round the club telling everybody how much I loved them – people I'd never seen before.'[164]

Harrison's reverie was broken with the realisation that the Pickwick was closing for the night. 'Suddenly it felt as if a bomb had made a direct hit on the nightclub and the roof had been blown off: "What's going on here?" I pulled my senses together and I realised that the club had actually closed – all the people had gone, they'd put the lights on, and the waiters were going round bashing the tables and putting the chairs on top of them. We thought, "Oops, we'd better get out of here!"'[165] The group decided to move to the Ad Lib club, a short walk away in the heart of London's West End. Harrison described the walk as 'very Alice in Wonderland – many strange things. I remember Pattie, half playfully but also half crazy, trying to smash a shop window and I felt: "Come on now, don't be silly…" Then we got round the corner and saw just all lights and taxis. It looked as if there was a big film première going on, but it was probably just the usual doorway to the nightclub. It seemed very bright; with all the people in thick make-up, like masks. Very strange.'[166]

The Ad Lib was on the fourth floor of 7 Leicester Place. 'We finally got in the lift and we all thought there was a fire in the lift,' Lennon told *Rolling Stone*. 'It was just a little red light, and we were all screaming – it was hysterical. We all arrived on the floor, 'cause this was a discotheque that was up a building. The lift stops and the door opens and we're all going "Aaahhhh" [loud scream], and we just see that it's the club, and then we walk in, sit down, and the table's elongating. And then some singer came up to me and said, "Can I sit next to you?" And I was going, [loudly] "Only if you don't talk," 'cause I just couldn't think.'[167]

The club was the venue *du jour* for pop stars, actors, photographers and models. It was minimalist in design, with low tables and cushioned benches surrounding a central dance floor. The Beatles were treated like royalty there, with their own table; it was at the Ad Lib that Starr proposed to Maureen Cox in January 1965.

When the club closed in the early hours of the following morning, Harrison drove the others back to Kinfauns, the Esher bungalow he shared with Boyd. The journey was just 19 miles but took an inordinately long time. 'We were going about ten miles an hour,' said Lennon, 'but it seemed like a thousand. And Pattie was saying, "Let's jump out and play football, there's these big rugby poles" and things like that. I was getting all this sort of hysterical jokes coming out, like with speed, because I was always on that, too.'[168]

Harrison managed moments of lucidity during the journey, enabling him to drive safely. 'I seem to remember we were doing 18 miles an hour and I was really concentrating,' he said, 'because some of the time I just felt normal and then, before I knew where I was, it was all crazy again.'[169]

It was daylight by the time they arrived back at the bungalow. 'We went into Kinfauns and locked the gate so that the cleaner wouldn't come in and find us, put the cat into a room on her own and sat down,' said Boyd. 'The drug took about eight hours to wear off, but it was very frightening and we never spoke to the dentist again.'[170]

Of the four, Cynthia Lennon found the LSD experience the most distressing. 'John and I weren't capable of getting back to Kenwood from there, so the four of us sat up for the rest of the night as the walls moved, the plants talked, other people looked like ghouls and time stood still. It was horrific: I hated the lack of control and not knowing what was going on or what would happen next.'[171]

Her husband, however, described the trip as 'fantastic. I did some drawings at the time – I've got them somewhere – of four faces and "we all agree with you," things like that. I gave them to Ringo, I've lost the originals. I did a lot of drawing that night – just like that. And then George's house seemed to be just like a big submarine. I was driving it – they all went to bed and I was carrying on on me own – it seemed to float above his wall, which was 18 foot, and I was driving it.'[172]

Whereas Captain Lennon found the experience entertaining and enjoyable, for Harrison it gave a glimpse of enlightenment beyond his Western ways of thinking. 'That first time I had acid, a light-bulb went on in my head and I began to have realisations which were not simply, "I think I'll do this," or, "I think that must be because of that." The question and answer disappeared into each other. An illumination goes on inside: in ten minutes I lived a thousand years. My brain and my consciousness and my awareness were pushed so far out that the only way I could begin to describe it is like an astronaut on the moon, or in his spaceship, looking back at the Earth. I was looking back to the Earth from my awareness...'[173]

Harrison continued to maintain that his first experience with LSD had shown the path to a higher plane of consciousness. 'A big change happened in 1966 [sic], particularly to John and myself, because a dentist we were having dinner with put this LSD in our coffee,' he told Selina Scott in a 1987 interview. 'Now, people who have taken that will know what I'm talking about, and anyone who hasn't taken it won't have a clue because it transforms you. After that I didn't need it ever again. That's the thing about LSD: you don't need it twice.' A clearly incredulous Scott interjected, asking: 'You've only taken it once?' 'Oh no, I took it lots of times,' Harrison shot back, laughing. 'But I only needed it once.'[174]

LYSERGIC ACID DIETHYLAMIDE, or *lysergsäure-diathylämid*, was discovered by Swiss scientist Albert Hofmann in 1938. The chemist, who worked at the pharmaceutical-chemical department of Sandoz Laboratories in Basel, Switzerland, was experimenting with methods of extracting, purifying and synthesising chemicals derived from the fungus ergot, to be used as respiratory and circulatory stimulants.

Hofmann first synthesised LSD-25 on 16 November, but set it aside without fully investigating its properties. Five years later, he decided to test the substance once again. While re-synthesising it on 16 April 1943, he inadvertently absorbed small doses through his fingertips. He later described being 'affected by a remarkable restlessness, combined with a slight dizziness. At home I lay down and sank into a not unpleasant intoxicated-like condition, characterised by an extremely stimulated imagination. In a dreamlike state, with eyes closed (I found the daylight to be unpleasantly glaring), I perceived an uninterrupted stream of fantastic pictures, extraordinary shapes with intense, kaleidoscopic play of colours.'[175]

Intrigued by the experience, Hofmann decided to further investigate the properties of LSD. On 19 April he intentionally ingested 250 micrograms of the drug, which he judged to be the threshold dose − the lowest amount at which a measurable effect could be discerned. The actual threshold dose of LSD is 20 micrograms.

Within an hour Hofmann began to experience remarkable changes in perception. He asked his assistant to escort him home, but was unable to travel by car through the streets of Basel due to wartime restrictions. Instead the pair made the journey by bicycle. Hofmann's symptoms began to escalate, with feelings of anxiety, fear of insanity, and the belief that his neighbour was an evil witch. A doctor was called to the house, but was unable to find any physical conditions beyond abnormally dilated pupils. Reassured by the doctor's assessment, Hofmann's fear gave way to enjoyment. He later wrote: 'Little by little I could begin to enjoy the unprecedented colours and plays of shapes that persisted behind my closed eyes. Kaleidoscopic, fantastic images surged in on me, alternating, variegated, opening and then closing themselves in circles and spirals, exploding in coloured fountains, rearranging and hybridising themselves in constant flux.'[176]

19 April became known as Bicycle Day, and Hofmann's first intentional LSD trip came to be celebrated by others as an annual event. Hofmann remained interested in the psychological benefits of his discovery, describing it as 'medicine for the soul', and taking it on dozens of subsequent occasions. In a

speech at an international scientific symposium held in Basel on his hundredth birthday, he said: 'LSD wanted to tell me something. It gave me an inner joy, an open mindedness, a gratefulness, open eyes and an internal sensitivity for the miracles of creation ... I think that in human evolution it has never been as necessary to have this substance LSD. It is just a tool to turn us into what we are supposed to be.'[177]

Following a number of clinical tests on humans and animals, in 1947 Sandoz brought LSD to market under the brand name Delysid – pills containing 25 micrograms, or ampoules containing four times as much. To begin with, Delysid was supplied without charge to research institutions in exchange for the data from their experiments.

LSD is non-addictive and believed to be non-lethal. A typical dose of the drug, commonly known as acid, can range from around 100 to 300 micrograms; at the lower end, one gram of pure LSD is enough for 10,000 hits. In the 1960s, the biggest black market manufacturer in America, Owsley Stanley, was distributing acid with a standard concentration of 270 micrograms, although the average potency has fallen in successive decades.

The effects of the drug usually begin after 30 to 90 minutes. Physical symptoms can include dilated pupils, increased heart rate and wakefulness. Psychological effects – known as a trip – can vary widely between users, and can include altered time perception, hallucinations and synaesthesia. An acid trip normally lasts between six and 12 hours – longer depending on the strength of the dose – and visual effects can include heightened awareness of colour or shape, trails following movement, morphing patterns on surfaces, and objects changing shape. Thoughts can tumble and spiral, making it difficult for a person to put the experience into words. Some users report feeling closer to God – enhanced cosmic consciousness, a dissolution of the divide between themselves and the rest of the universe, and a temporary loss of their sense of identity (ego death). Uncontrollable laughter, glazed-eyed contemplation and a look of beatific contentment are common sights among LSD users, and many claim lasting benefits to their personality and outlook after taking the drug.

However, not all find the experience a positive one. The effects of LSD can be influenced by the user's state of mind and environment, and bad trips – the effects of which can include anxiety, anguish, panic and alarming hallucinations – can be extremely distressing. For this reason some recreational users choose to be accompanied by a 'trip sitter' who can help ensure their safety and guide them back to comfort if they are struggling to cope. High doses have been linked to long-term adverse psychological reactions including delusions, anxiety and psychosis, and the possibility that LSD can exacerbate underlying or dormant issues should not be ignored.

The product literature that accompanied LSD from Sandoz contained a stark warning which would have been unseen by legions of LSD users in the Sixties: 'Pathological mental conditions may be intensified by Delysid. Particular caution is necessary in subjects with a suicidal tendency and in those cases where a psychotic development appears imminent. The psycho-affective lability and the tendency to commit impulsive acts may occasionally last for some days. Delysid should only be administered under strict medical supervision. The supervision should not be discontinued until the effects of the drug have completely worn off.'

In 1951 Albert Hofmann wrote to German novelist Ernst Junger, who had conducted experiments with mescaline, and suggested they take LSD together. They each took 50 micrograms of pure LSD at Hofmann's house, while playing music by Mozart and burning Japanese incense. Hofmann later described the occasion as 'the first planned psychedelic test'.[178] However, for many years he remained opposed to LSD's use as a recreational drug. He blamed government prohibition and misuse among the 1960s counterculture for hindering research into the drug's beneficial properties, stating that 'It should be a controlled substance with the same status as morphine.'

Others disagreed. English writer Aldous Huxley was a high profile advocate of using psychedelic drugs for consciousness expansion. His experiences of taking mescaline were documented in *The Doors Of Perception* and *Heaven And Hell*. He was given LSD by Dr Humphrey Osmond, a British psychiatrist working in Canada, who encouraged doctors to take it to better understand schizophrenia.

Through Osmond, Huxley was introduced to Alfred Matthew Hubbard, an early proponent of LSD who spoke enthusiastically of the drug's visionary or transcendental potential. Hubbard is thought to have turned on more than six thousand people to LSD, including scientists, diplomats, politicians and religious figures.

Huxley took LSD for the first time in 1955, and continued to experiment with drugs until the end of his life. As he lay dying of laryngeal cancer in November 1963, he wrote a note to his wife Laura: 'LSD – Try it LSD 100 mmg [micrograms] intramuscular.' She administered two doses of the drug to him during the last hours of his life. Days later she wrote to Huxley's brother detailing the circumstances of his death. 'During the last two months I gave him almost daily an opportunity, an opening for speaking about death, but of course this opening was always one that could have been taken in two ways – either towards life or towards death, and he always took it towards life. We read the entire manual of Dr Leary extracted from the *Book Of The Dead*. He could have, even jokingly said – don't forget to remind me – his comment instead was only directed to the way Dr Leary conducted his LSD sessions, and how he would bring people, who were not dead, back here to this life after the session.'[179]

Dr Timothy Leary's book was published in August 1964 as *The Psychedelic Experience: A Manual Based On The Tibetan Book Of The Dead*. It was co-authored with Richard Alpert and Ralph Metzner, and dedicated to Huxley. The book was intended as an instruction manual for use during psychedelic drug use, and became a key influence on the Beatles' Tomorrow Never Knows.

Leary, a psychology lecturer at Harvard University, had been given LSD in 1961 by Michael Hollingshead, another psychedelic evangelist of the age. British-born Hollingshead, a friend of Huxley, had arrived in the US the previous year to work for the Institute for British-American Cultural Exchange. For the price of $285 Hollingshead bought a gram of pure LSD from Sandoz Laboratories for use in research experiments. He mixed the drug with powdered sugar and distilled water to make a thick paste which he stored in a mayonnaise jar.

Huxley suggested Hollingshead contact Leary, and the pair became friends. In the autumn of 1965 Hollingshead arrived in London, bringing with him 300 copies of *The Psychedelic Experience*; 200 issues of *The Psychedelic Review*; the same number of *The Psychedelic Reader* edited by Gunther Weil, Metzner and Leary; and half a gram of LSD. The drug was not yet illegal in Britain, and Hollingshead intended to introduce it to influential people in a short space of time.

Hollingshead opened the World Psychedelic Centre (WPC) in a large apartment in Pont Street in London's salubrious Belgravia district. Two Old Etonians, Desmond O'Brien and Joey Mellen, were the WPC's president and vice president respectively. Their high social status helped attract large numbers of aristocratic and upper class visitors, among them Viscount Gormanstone and Victoria and Julian Ormsby-Gore, and other Old Etonians including art gallery owner Robert Fraser and antiques dealer Christopher Gibbs. Other visitors included famous musicians, artists, film makers and writers.

Among those Hollingshead is said to have turned on to LSD were Keith Richards, Charles Mingus, William Burroughs, Roman Polanski, Donovan and Eric Clapton. The only Beatle known to have visited the WPC was Paul McCartney, who was taken there by John Dunbar, co-founder of the Indica gallery and bookshop.

The centre soon became littered with marijuana detritus, hypodermic syringes and pills. Hollingshead's intravenous methedrine and heroin habit had left him unstable and paranoid, and people had begun to keep their distance by the time the WPC was raided by police in January 1966, just three months after it opened. Hollingshead was imprisoned in Wormwood Scrubs for possession of hashish, grass, heroin and morphine.

An early street form of LSD was impregnated sugar cubes, although by the mid-Sixties microdot pills and blotter paper (acid tabs) were more commonly circulated. Blotter paper acid was made by dipping pre-printed perforated sheets – often with distinctive designs – into a solution of LSD, water and alcohol, which could then be torn into many individual hits. Towards the end of the decade 'clearlight' or 'windowpane' emerged: LSD inside thin machine-cut 6mm squares of clear, hard gelatine.

LSD was made illegal in Britain in September 1966, the same year Sandoz ceased supplying the drug. The following year the US federal government banned it, although by that time its worldwide popularity and creation in unlicensed laboratories were well established. Among Hollingshead's visitors in prison were Richard Alpert and Owsley Stanley, who brought with them supplies of marijuana and LSD. Stanley – Augustus Owsley Stanley III – had set up a private laboratory in California, and supplied the famous parties held by Ken Kesey and his Merry Pranksters. He became the first individual to mass produce the drug, and between 1965 and 1967 manufactured more than 1.25 million doses. Stanley, who also worked as a soundman for the Grateful Dead and other West Coast bands, did more than any other individual to turn on America.

LENNON SAID he was 'pretty stunned for a month or two' after the Dental Experience, and didn't take LSD again until five months later. He and Harrison both knew their first trip was significant, but were unsure of how to broach the subject with their bandmates. 'After that time,' Harrison recalled, 'John and I started thinking, "Hey, how the heck are we gonna tell the others?"' 'Cause, you know, there's no way back after that. It's like you can never return to being who you were before, thankfully. I think if you come out of it in one piece, then – well, it's individual reactions – but what I gained was certainly worth the hardship it put me through. It scrambled my brain for a year – it seems like years, but you know how it stretches time. It was actually a few months of trying to piece it back together: what do I do now, what do we do now, who am I, what is all this?

'Then we thought – since there's no way you can describe it – how are we ever gonna tell Paul and Ringo and the rest of our direct entourage? We've got to get some more and give it to 'em.'[180]

LSD arrived at a turning point in the Beatles' career. Whereas cannabis had insulated them from some of the pressures of life in the public eye, acid melted the bars altogether. It seemed to offer a route of total escape from their old lives, promising happiness, enlightenment and a glimpse of new creative avenues. 'Drugs probably helped the understanding of myself better, but not much,' Lennon told Beatles biographer Hunter Davies in 1967. 'Not pot. That just used to be a harmless giggle. LSD was the self knowledge which pointed the way in the first place. I was suddenly struck by great visions when I first took acid. But you've got to be looking for it, before you can possibly find it. Perhaps I was looking, without realising it, and would have found it anyway. It would just have taken longer.'[181]

In April 1965, just days after the Dental Experience, Lennon wrote Help!, the title track of the Beatles' fifth album and second film. In addition to the Huxleyan claim that 'I've opened up the doors,' the song lays bare the confusion and insecurity he was feeling at that time over fame, relationships, and the psychedelic journey he had just embarked upon.

Lennon stood at a crossroads in his life, looking back at his childhood and angry teenage years, contemplating the riches and fame he had achieved in his early twenties, and finding that it didn't necessarily bring the spiritual balm for which he yearned.

The period also marked a shift in the Beatles' working practices. Lennon and McCartney wrote together less often, normally only coming together to shape and complete ideas that the other had already begun. The whole group – McCartney and Harrison in particular – were becoming more accomplished musicians, stepping outside their previous roles to learn new musical forms, techniques and instruments.

While it is quite possible that this musical odyssey from beat group to studio pioneers might have been completed without LSD, it would inevitably have sounded quite different. Acid played a central role in unlocking the Beatles' willingness to experiment, write in new ways and pursue a multi-faceted creative vision, regardless of public expectation or the progress of their peers. And, crucially, many of the new sounds simply could not be reproduced outside the studio. The distance between their stage act and recordings became ever greater, and eventually contributed to their abandonment of live performance as they retreated inside the cocoon of the recording studio.

THE BEATLES' second encounter with LSD happened at an afternoon party in Los Angeles, during a five-day break from their 1965 North America tour. They were renting a large Spanish-style house owned by actress Zsa Zsa Gabor, secluded in the side of a mountain at 2850 Benedict Canyon, Beverly Hills.

Despite their efforts to remain incognito, the area soon

became besieged by fans. Some attempted to scale the canyon in an attempt to see their idols; others even rented helicopters to catch an aerial glimpse. The LAPD put a squad of officers on duty to guard the house and protect the Beatles, but the band found it impossible to leave. Instead they played host to a stream of visitors. On 24 August these included members of the Byrds, actor Peter Fonda and *Help!* actress Eleanor Bron.

'I had a concept of what had happened the first time I took LSD,' George Harrison said, 'but the concept is nowhere near as big as the reality, when it actually happens. So as it kicked in again, I thought, "Jesus, I remember!" I was trying to play the guitar, and then I got in the swimming pool and it was a great feeling; the water felt good.'[182]

Peter Fonda later described the scene to *Rolling Stone*: 'I finally made my way past the kids and the guards,' he said. 'Paul and George were on the back patio, and the helicopters were patrolling overhead. They were sitting at a table under an umbrella in a rather comical attempt at privacy. Soon afterwards we dropped acid and began tripping for what would prove to be all night and most of the next day; all of us, including the original Byrds, eventually ended up inside a huge, empty, sunken tub in the bathroom, babbling our minds away.

'I had the privilege of listening to the four of them sing, play around and scheme about what they would compose and achieve. They were so enthusiastic, so full of fun. John was the wittiest and most astute. I enjoyed just hearing him speak and there were no pretensions in his manner. He just sat around, laying out lines of poetry and thinking – an amazing mind. He talked a lot yet he still seemed so private.'[183]

Roger McGuinn of the Byrds, then known as Jim, also recalled the day: 'There were girls at the gates, police guards. We went in and David [Crosby], John Lennon, George Harrison and I took LSD to help get to know each other better. There was a large bathroom in the house and we were all sitting on the edge of a shower passing around a guitar, taking turns to play our favourite songs. John and I agreed Be-Bop-A-Lula was our favourite Fifties rock record.'[184]

Paul McCartney was the only Beatle not to take acid at the party. He remained wary of anything which might cause irreparable damage to his mental state, and preferred to stick to alcohol and marijuana. 'In LA Paul felt very out of it 'cause we were all a bit cruel,' said Lennon. 'It's like, "We're taking it and you're not."'[185]

McCartney later complained of the pressure he was under to conform. 'At the time, I felt bad about sayin' no,' he said in 1986. 'I thought, "Oh, here I go again, look at me, unadventurous, I'm always the one, they're gonna make such fun of me." I mean, I got such pressure when I wouldn't take acid the first time. I got a lot of pressure there … They were sayin', "What's wrong with him?" Now, looking back on it, I think, Jesus, I must have had some courage to actually resist that peer pressure. But at the time, I felt really goody-goody, you know: "Hey, Mr Clean, squeaky clean," you know? It was like "Aw, come on, fellas, I'm not really squeaky clean, but, you know, acid is maybe gonna do our heads in."'[186]

Ringo Starr, however, took his first trip in LA, as did Beatles roadie Neil Aspinall. The other key member of their entourage, Mal Evans, stayed straight to look after them all.

'I'd take anything,' Starr later said. 'John and George didn't give LSD to me. A couple of guys came to visit us in LA, and it was them that said, "Man, you've got to try this." They had it in a bottle with an eye-dropper, and they dropped it on sugar cubes and gave it to us. That was my first trip. It was with John and George and Neil and Mal. Neil had to deal with Don Short while I was swimming in jelly in the pool. It was a fabulous day. The night wasn't so great, because it felt like it was never going to wear off. Twelve hours later and it was: "Give us a break now, Lord".'[187]

Although Starr remembered visitors bringing LSD to the LA house, Harrison said the Beatles themselves had carried it from New York. 'John and I had decided that Paul and Ringo had to have acid, because we couldn't relate to them any more. Not just on the one level – we couldn't relate to them on any level, because acid had changed us so much. It was such a mammoth experience that it was unexplainable: it was something that had to be experienced, because you could spend the rest of your life trying to explain what it made you feel and think. It was all too important to John and me. So the plan was that when we got to Hollywood, on our day off we were going to get them to take acid. We got some in New York; it was on sugar cubes wrapped in tinfoil and we'd been carrying these around all through the tour until we got to LA.'[188]

The Beatles' likely supplier was David Schneiderman, a twenty-two-year-old Canadian in possession of a quantity of Sandoz LSD. Schneiderman was temporarily living in New York's Greenwich Village; the Beatles arrived in the city on the afternoon of 13 August, remaining for four days before flying to Toronto for the next stop on their tour.

One of Evans' and Aspinall's responsibilities at the LA party was to keep unwanted guests and hangers-on away from the Beatles. On this occasion they included Don Short, a journalist from UK newspaper the *Daily Mirror*. Short, according to Harrison, had been 'hounding us all through the tour, pretending in his phoney-baloney way to be friendly but, really, trying to nail us.'[189] Aspinall was charged with keeping the journalist away from the Beatles, a hard task when he himself was tripping.

'We still didn't know anything about doing it in a nice place and cool it and all that, we just took it,' Lennon said. 'And all of a sudden we saw the reporter and we're thinking, "How do we act normal?" Because we imagined we were acting extraordinary, which we weren't. We thought, "Surely somebody can see." We were terrified waiting for him to go, and he wondered why he couldn't come over, and Neil, who had never had it either, had taken it, and he still had to play road manager.

We said, "Go and get rid of Don Short," and he didn't know what to do, he just sort of sat with it.'[190]

'The thing about LSD is that it distorts your perception of things,' said Harrison. 'We were in one spot, John and me and Jim McGuinn, and Don Short was probably only about 20 yards away, talking. But it was as though we were looking through the wrong end of a telescope. He seemed to be in the very far distance, and we were saying, "Oh fuck, there's that guy over there." Neil had to take him to play pool, trying to keep him away. And you have to remember that on acid just a minute can seem like a thousand years. A thousand years can go down in that minute. It was definitely not the kind of drug which you'd want to be playing pool with Don Short on.'[191] Whether Short realised that Aspinall and three of the Beatles were tripping is not known, but certainly the group's use of LSD would remain outside public knowledge for almost two more years.

Of the guests at the afternoon party, Peter Fonda's presence possibly had the most far-reaching effects. The son of actor Henry Fonda and the younger brother of Jane, as a child he had accidentally shot himself in the stomach while playing with an antique pistol. He was rushed to hospital and nearly died; his heart stopped beating on three occasions, and he was fortunate to survive.

Fonda later claimed that he had attempted to comfort Harrison at the LA party. The guitarist was said to be frightened and struggling with the effects of LSD. 'I told him there was nothing to be afraid of and that all he needed to do was relax. I said that I knew what it was like to be dead because when I was ten years old I'd accidentally shot myself in the stomach and my heart stopped beating three times while I was on the operating table because I'd lost so much blood. John was passing at the time and heard me saying "I know what it's like to be dead." He looked at me and said, "You're making me feel like I've never been born. Who put all that shit in your head?"'[192]

Lennon recalled the scene in 1980: 'He was describing an

acid trip he'd been on. We didn't want to hear about that! We were on an acid trip and the sun was shining and the girls were dancing and the whole thing was beautiful and Sixties, and this guy – who I really didn't know; he hadn't made *Easy Rider* or anything – kept coming over, wearing shades, saying, "I know what it's like to be dead," and we kept leaving him because he was so boring! And I used it for the song, but I changed it to "she" instead of "he". It was scary. You know, a guy... when you're flying high and [whispers] "I know what it's like to be dead, man." I remembered the incident. Don't tell me about it! I don't want to know what it's like to be dead!'[193]

The song Lennon wrote about the encounter was She Said She Said, from 1966's *Revolver*. With neat symmetry, it features each of the Beatles apart from McCartney.

The LA acid experience ended with a viewing of *Cat Ballou*, a 1965 comedy western starring Lee Marvin and Jane Fonda. It was a copy from a drive-in cinema, as George Harrison recalled: 'The drive-in print has the audience response already dubbed onto it, because you're all sitting in your cars and don't hear everybody laugh. Instead, they tell you when to laugh and when not to. It was bizarre, watching this on acid. I've always hated Lee Marvin, and listening on acid to that other little dwarf bloke with a bowler hat on [Stubby Kaye], I thought it was the biggest load of baloney shite I'd ever seen in my life; it was too much to stand.'[194]

Harrison claimed that he established some telepathy with John Lennon during the evening. 'I noticed that I'd go "out there"; I'd be gone somewhere, and then – bang! – I'd land back in my body. I'd look around and see that John had just done the same thing. You go in tandem, you're out there for a while and then – boing! whoa! – "What happened? Oh, it's still *Cat Ballou*." That is another thing: when two people take it at the same time; words become redundant. One can see what the other is thinking. You look at each other and know.'[195]

Don Short may have narrowly missed out on a world exclusive in Los Angeles, but the Beatles were increasingly unguarded about their drug consumption. One week earlier, on 18 August 1965, the Beatles had met Art Unger, editor of teen magazine *Datebook*, backstage at an Atlanta Stadium concert. The Beatles were featured regularly in the publication, which the following year would cause a storm by reprinting Lennon's 'We're more popular than Jesus' remarks.

While Unger was interviewing McCartney in a dressing room at the stadium, Lennon passed and said to his bandmate: 'Watch him. He'll try to sell you LSD.' Unger's brother Sanford had been introduced to the drug at Harvard by Timothy Leary, and later conducted clinical trials into its effects. Lennon's words were duly reported in *Datebook*, becoming the first time any of the Beatles had mentioned LSD in print.

DUE TO McCARTNEY'S natural reticence, it wasn't until the end of 1965 that he decided to take LSD. 'I'm conservative,' he told Hunter Davies. 'I feel I need to check things. I was last to try pot and LSD and floral clothes. I'm slower than John, the least likely to succeed in class.' He did, however, acknowledge that the Beatles' lives were far from conventional. 'I'm just the conservative of the four of us. Not compared with outside people. Compared to my family I'm a freak-out.'[196]

When McCartney did use LSD for the first time, it was not in the company of his bandmates, but with Tara Browne, a young socialite whose death in December 1966 inspired the opening lines of A Day In The Life. Browne was the heir to a £1 million Guinness fortune. He lived on Eaton Row, a secluded mews in London's Belgravia district, with his wife Noreen (known as Nicky). McCartney's decision not to take his first trip with the other Beatles was indicative of a gap that was opening up between him and the rest of the group, which would widen further towards the end of the decade.

It took place the night after the Beatles' final British tour date.[197] After performing in Cardiff on 12 December 1965 they were driven to London, where they celebrated the end of the tour at the Scotch of St James nightclub. The following night Lennon and McCartney returned to the club, where they met the Who's John Entwistle and the Pretty Things' former drummer Viv Prince. Nicky Browne was also there, and she invited them all back to Eaton Row. Lennon declined and returned to Weybridge, but McCartney and Prince accepted the offer, as did several girls, and a dancer, Patrick Kerr, from the television show *Ready Steady Go!*

At the house, Tara Browne suggested they all take LSD. McCartney and Prince were unsure, having never tried the drug. 'I was more ready for the drink or a little bit of pot or something,' recalled McCartney. 'I'd not wanted to do it, I'd held off like a lot of people were trying to, but there was massive peer pressure. And within a band, it's more than peer pressure, it's fear pressure. It becomes trebled, more than just your mates, it's, "Hey, man, this whole band's had acid, why are you holding out? What's the reason, what is it about you?" So I knew I would have to out of peer pressure alone. And that night I thought, well, this is as good a time as any, so I said, "Go on then, fine." So we all did it.'[198]

Nicky Browne served the guests tea, also offering them sugar lumps impregnated with liquid LSD. Unlike the Dental Experience, however, nobody had their drinks spiked, and all stayed in the house through the night. 'It was such a mind-expanding thing,' McCartney remembered. 'I saw paisley shapes and weird things, and for a guy who wasn't that keen on getting that weird, there was a disturbing element to it. I remember looking at my shirtsleeves and seeing they were dirty and not being too pleased with that, whereas normally you wouldn't even notice. But you noticed and you heard. Everything was supersensitive.

'We sat around all evening. Viv Prince was great fun. Someone said, "Do you want a drink?" And everyone would say,

"No thanks, don't need drink, this is plenty." If anything, we might smoke a joint. But Viv demolished the drinks tray: "Oh yeah, a drink!" Cockney drummer with the Pretty Things. "Orrright, yeah! Nah, does anyone want a drink? I fink I'll 'ave one of them." And he had the whisky and he had everything. He was having a trip but his was somehow a more wired version than anyone else's. In the morning we ended up sending him out for ciggies.

'Then one of the serious secretaries from our office rang about an engagement I had; she had traced me to here. "Um, can't talk now. Important business" or something. I just got out of it. "But you're supposed to be at the office." "No. I've got 'flu." Anything I could think. I got out of that one because there was no way I could go to the office after that.'[199]

McCartney took LSD several more times, although he didn't embrace it with the fervour of Lennon and Harrison. 'I had it on a few occasions after that and I always found it amazing,' he said. 'Sometimes it was a very very deeply emotional experience, making you want to cry, sometimes seeing God or sensing all the majesty and emotional depth of everything. And sometimes you were just plain knackered, because it would be like sitting up all night in a train station, and by the morning you've grown very stiff and it's not a party any more. It's like the end of an all-nighter but you haven't danced. You just sat. So your bum might be sore, just from sitting. I was often quite wiped out by it all but I always thought, Well, you know, everybody's doing it.'[200]

Indeed, it was McCartney's lack of stamina which largely put him off LSD. 'The thing I didn't like about acid was it lasted too long. It always wore me out. But they were great people to be around, a wacky crowd. My main problem was just the stamina you had to have. I never attempted to work on acid, I couldn't. What's the point of trying, love?'[201]

THE BEATLES' final single of 1965, Day Tripper/We Can Work It Out, was released on 3 December 1965, the same day as *Rubber Soul* and ten days before McCartney's first trip. Day Tripper was 'a drug song,' according to Lennon.[202] In one of his final interviews he explained that the song was about those who dabbled but failed to fully commit to an alternative lifestyle. 'Day trippers are people who go on a day trip, right? Usually on a ferryboat or something. But it was kind of – you know, you're just a weekend hippie. Get it?'[203]

Rubber Soul was the Beatles' first major musical step forward, and marked the beginning of the boundary-pushing studio experimentation that peaked in 1967. Folk, American R&B, Fifties rock 'n' roll and Indian influences could all be heard in the songs, and it was clear that the Beatles were reaching for new ways to express themselves. This magpie-like appropriation continued during 1966's *Revolver* sessions, and it wasn't until the following year's *Sgt Pepper* that they fully left behind the rock 'n' roll music that had underpinned their earlier work. For now, only the proselytisation of The Word gave any direct indication of the acid revolution taking place within the band.

Childhood nostalgia was a key feature of the psychedelic era, and the Beatles were enthusiastic flag bearers. As they moved beyond their early monochrome pop phase into the mid-Sixties technicolour wonderland, various threads came together in the music: remembrance of things past, irreverent surrealism, sonic experimentation, and drugs.

A key song on *Rubber Soul* was In My Life, in which Lennon reminisced about places and memories from his Liverpool past. 'In My Life started out as a bus journey from my house on 250 [*sic*] Menlove Avenue to town, mentioning every place I could remember. And it was ridiculous. This is before even Penny Lane was written and I had Penny Lane, Strawberry Fields, Tram Sheds – Tram Sheds are the depot just outside of Penny Lane – and it was the most boring sort of "What I Did On My Holidays Bus Trip" song and it wasn't working at all.'[204]

Lennon's childhood may have been far from perfect, but his mid-Sixties recollections were of an idyllic time. Just as Help! had recalled his youth as carefree and independent, Revolver's She Said She Said recast his younger years as unsullied by worry: 'When I was a boy, everything was right.'

Lennon was – whether by luck, accident or perceptive foresight – at the forefront of the psychedelic era's passion for rose-tinted introspection, which channelled the likes of children's literature, Victorian fairgrounds and circuses, and an innocent sense of wonder. McCartney, too, moved with the times when writing his children's singalong Yellow Submarine. Among the hippie era's other moments of nostalgia were Pink Floyd's Bike and The Gnome from their debut album Piper At The Gates Of Dawn, recorded at EMI Studios as the Beatles worked on Sgt Pepper's Lonely Hearts Club Band; Jefferson Airplane's White Rabbit, laid down in 1966 but released in the same month as Sgt Pepper, and which drew from Lewis Carroll's Alice stories just as Lennon did; and many more, from Tiny Tim's Tiptoe Through The Tulips to Traffic's psychedelic fantasy Hole In My Shoe.

The Beatles continued writing songs evoking childhood to the end of their days. Sgt Pepper – itself a loose concept album harking back to earlier, more innocent times – referenced Lewis Carroll (Lucy In The Sky With Diamonds), youthful anticipation of old age (When I'm Sixty-Four), a stroll down memory lane (Good Morning Good Morning), and the sensory barrage of a circus big top extravaganza (Being For The Benefit Of Mr Kite!). It was followed by Magical Mystery Tour and Yellow Submarine, two films firmly pitched at the widest possible audience. A splendid time was, indeed, guaranteed for all.

And therein lies a curious paradox at the heart of the Beatles' late-1960s output: while their personal and professional lives became tumultuous and troubled, including drug experimentation, affairs and break-ups, a range of personal crises and loss of group cohesion, their songwriting leaned the opposite way, with family friendly songs of innocence that often seemed aimed at their very youngest fans. Even in their darkest moments, such as the fractious sessions for the *White Album*, they could turn out such breezy songs as Wild Honey Pie, Piggies and Ob-La-Di, Ob-La-Da just as readily as the experimental Revolution 9 or rockers like Helter Skelter. Not one of the Beatles was immune to the fashion for childlike whimsy.

George Harrison said he couldn't see 'too much difference between *Rubber Soul* and *Revolver*. To me, they could be Volume One and Volume Two.'[205] But by April 1966, when the *Revolver* sessions began, it was almost as though the Beatles were a completely different band. Gone were the folk-rock leanings of *Rubber Soul*, and in their place was a harder, edgier sound, with biting guitars, rasping horns, and unearthly, experimental sounds which had never before been pressed to vinyl. Having all but discarded the notion of playing the songs live, they focused on creating soundscapes and textures that could only be created in the studio. From the doleful count-in of Taxman to the squalling sound effects of Tomorrow Never Knows, *Revolver* was awash with new recording techniques, instrumentation and lyrical ideas.

The Beatles' drug use had been subtly referred to in previous songs and interviews, but with *Revolver* they went all-out. Three of the first four songs recorded for the album – Tomorrow Never Knows, Got To Get You Into My Life and Doctor Robert – were written about LSD, cannabis and pills respectively, while She Said She Said was directly inspired by the Peter Fonda encounter in Los Angeles. I'm Only Sleeping and Rain, the b-side recorded during the *Revolver* sessions, occupied the distracted, dreamy mindspace that Lennon preferred to inhabit throughout much of 1966, and saw the Beatles experimenting with tape speeds, altering the texture of recorded sound, and adding backwards vocals and guitars.

But the clearest sign that the Beatles were a changed group came with *Revolver*'s final song, Tomorrow Never Knows. Paul McCartney believed it to be their only recording about the LSD experience. Speaking to *Playboy* in 1984, he said: 'It was a kind of Bible for all the psychedelic freaks. That was an LSD song. Probably the only one.'[206]

One afternoon in late March 1966, McCartney brought Lennon to the Indica bookshop for the first time. Lennon was looking for a book by someone he thought was called 'Nitz Ga'. It took the perplexed owner Barry Miles some moments before he realised Lennon was referring to the German philosopher Nietzsche. Embarrassed by his mispronunciation, Lennon began ranting defensively about university-educated snobs. McCartney calmed him down by pointing out that Miles, like Lennon, had had an art school education. In the meantime, Miles found a copy of *The Portable Nietzsche*, which he gave to Lennon.

Lennon's mood improved in an instant. As he glanced over the shelves in the bookshop his eyes alighted on *The Psychedelic Experience*, the reworking of the *Tibetan Book Of The Dead* by Leary, Alpert and Metzner which Michael Hollingshead had brought to London the previous year. Lennon curled up on a sofa in the shop and began reading. In Leary's introduction he found words which would be paraphrased in the opening line of Tomorrow Never Knows: 'Trust your divinity, trust your brain, trust your companions. Whenever in doubt, turn off your mind, relax, float downstream.'[207]

Lennon bought a copy of *The Psychedelic Experience*, taking it back to Kenwood. The book recommends that people record themselves reading aloud sections of the text, personalised for their own needs, to listen to while tripping. If Lennon recorded the First Bardo Instructions, in the section titled Instructions for Use during a Psychedelic Session, he would have read aloud more sentiments which found their way into his song:

> *O John,*
> *Try to reach and keep the experience of the Clear Light.*
> *Remember:*
> *The light is the life energy.*

The endless flame of life.
An ever-changing surging turmoil of colour may engulf
your vision.
This is the ceaseless transformation of energy.
The life process.
Do not fear it.
Surrender to it.
Join it.
It is part of you.
You are part of it.
Remember also:
Beyond the restless flowing electricity of life is the ultimate
reality –
The Void.[208]

From the mid-Sixties to the end of his life, Lennon took seriously the requests and commands of those he revered, until their influence waned. If he followed the book's instructions to the letter he would have made great efforts to destroy his ego, and to experience the death, rebirth and clear living that Leary and his cohorts believed could be attained through psychedelic drugs.

George Harrison later questioned whether Lennon fully comprehended the book's meaning. 'The whole point is that we are the song,' he said. 'The self is coming from a state of pure awareness, from the state of being. All the rest that comes about in the outward manifestation of the physical world, including all the fluctuations which end up as thoughts and actions, is just clutter. The true nature of each soul is pure consciousness. So the song is really about transcending and about the quality of the transcendent.

'I am not too sure if John actually fully understood what he was saying. He knew he was onto something when he saw those words and turned them into a song. But to have experienced what the lyrics in that song are actually about? I don't know if he fully understood it.'[209]

A few days after Lennon purchased *The Psychedelic Experience*, the Beatles and George Martin met at Brian Epstein's London home to discuss ideas for what would become *Revolver*. 'John got his guitar out and started doing Tomorrow Never Knows and it was all on one chord,' McCartney recalled. 'This was because of our interest in Indian music. We would be sitting around and at the end of an Indian album we'd go, "Did anyone realise they didn't change chords?" It would be like "Shit, it was all in E! Wow, man, that is pretty far out." So we began to sponge up a few of these nice ideas.

'This is one thing I always gave George Martin great credit for. He was a slightly older man and we were pretty far out, but he didn't flinch at all when John played it to him, he just said, "Hmmm, I see, yes. Hmm hmm." He could have said, "Bloody hell, it's terrible!" I think George was always intrigued to see what direction we'd gone in, probably in his mind thinking, How can I make this into a record? But by that point he was starting to trust that we must know vaguely what we were doing, but the material was really outside of his realm.'[210]

It wasn't just outside Martin's realm. Tomorrow Never Knows was, to 1966 audiences, so far beyond the boundaries of conventional pop music that it may as well have come from another dimension. The song – the first to be recorded for *Revolver* – was initially known as The Void, although it was never recorded as such; early studio takes had the working title Mark I. Lennon sensed that The Void might be too bizarre for the majority of Beatles fans, and so settled on the appropriately ambiguous Tomorrow Never Knows.

———————

THROUGHOUT MUCH OF the 1960s Lennon, Harrison and Starr lived in secluded houses in the rarefied stockbroker belt in

Surrey, a short drive to London but removed from the bustle of the city. They often shied away from public life for fear of being mobbed, and instead spent time at each other's homes, ferried from one to another in their Rolls-Royces and Ferraris with blacked out windows. Occasionally they attended clubs or events, often as a group, occasionally accompanied by their partners.

On 26 May 1966 Bob Dylan played at London's Royal Albert Hall, after which he visited the Lennons at Kenwood. The following day the two musicians were driven to Dylan's London hotel. Present in the limousine were director DA Pennebaker, who was making a documentary on Dylan's UK tour, and sound operator Bobby Neuwirth. The film, *Eat The Document*, was later shelved after it was deemed unpalatable for a mainstream audience.

Two ten-minute film reels were filled during the journey to London. Lennon and Dylan both wore sunglasses and smoked cigarettes, and were evidently coming down from drugs. 'He just wanted me to be in the film,' Lennon recalled in 1970. 'I thought, "Why? What? He's going to put me down!" I went through this terrible thing. So in the film, I'm just blabbing off, I'm commenting all the time, like you do when you're very high and stoned… It was his movie and I was on his territory. That's why I was so nervous. I was on his session.'[211]

For a man of his fame and status, during the mid-Sixties Lennon appeared to live a remarkably isolated life. Although far from living as a recluse, he would be chauffeured to and from recording sessions at EMI Studios, and his social life tended to involve visits to exclusive nightclubs such as the Bag O'Nails, the Pickwick and the Scotch of St James, after which he would often bring an entourage of fellow clubbers back to Kenwood. After years of touring and late night recording sessions, the languorous Lennon had become accustomed to keeping irregular hours. He ate and slept whenever he needed to, thought nothing of setting off at two o'clock in the morning to go clubbing, and spent hours at his home reflecting inwardly in drug induced reveries.

In January 1966, Lennon gave an interview to Maureen Cleave of London's *Evening Standard* newspaper. It became infamous for Lennon's comments on religion: 'Christianity will go,' he told her. 'It will vanish and shrink. I needn't argue about that; I'm right and I will be proved right. We're more popular than Jesus now; I don't know which will go first – rock 'n' roll or Christianity. Jesus was all right but his disciples were thick and ordinary. It's them twisting it that ruins it for me.'

Just as revealing as Lennon's thoughts on Christianity, though far less inflammatory, were Cleave's depictions of his domestic life. 'Ringo and his wife, Maureen, may drop in on John and Cyn; John may drop in on Ringo; George and Pattie may drop in on John and Cyn and they might all go round to Ringo's, by car of course. Outdoors is for holidays.

'They watch films, they play rowdy games of Buccaneer; they watch television till it goes off, often playing records at the same time. They while away the small hours of the morning making mad tapes. Bedtimes and mealtimes have no meaning as such. "We've never had time before to do anything but just be Beatles," John Lennon said.'[212]

Off the record, Lennon told Cleave about his recent experiences with LSD. Although it gave acid no mention, her article did, however, dwell on the inaction which dominated Lennon's life. The impression was of a daydreaming millionaire who was curious and optimistic in the face of a directionless existence. 'There's something else I'm going to do,' he told her, 'something I must do – only I don't know what it is. That's why I go round painting and taping and drawing and writing and that, because it may be one of them. All I know is, this isn't it for me.'

Lennon's quest for meaning, and his ready willingness to embrace new discoveries, was a dominant feature of his adult life. In the beginning it was rock 'n' roll that captured his heart, from the day he first heard Heartbreak Hotel: 'It was Elvis who really got me out of Liverpool,' he said. 'Once I heard it and got into it, that was life, there was no other thing. I thought of nothing else but rock 'n' roll; apart from sex and food and money – but that's all the same thing, really.'[213]

As the Beatles' fame grew, sex and money became addictive, as did drugs and adulation: 'I just found meself in a party! I was an emperor, and I had millions of chicks, drugs, drink, fuckin' power! And everybody sayin' how great I was. How could I get out of there, it was like being in a fucking coach! I couldn't get out, I couldn't create either! I created a little, it came out, but I was in the party, man! You don't get out of a thing like that! It was fantastic! … I came out [of] the fucking sticks to take over the fucking world, it seemed like to me! I was enjoying it, and I was in it and I was trapped in it too. I couldn't do anything about it. I was just going along for the ride, I was hooked. Hooked, just like on junk.'[214]

Yet Lennon soon tired of the pleasures of fame. He pored over books on religion and psychology, and even at one point considered subjecting himself to trepanning – the drilling of a hole into the skull to relieve pressure. 'I'll fucking do it if it works,' he told his close confidant Pete Shotton.[215]

Lennon's eagerness to surrender himself to a drug, guru or social movement became a hallmark of his restless quest for contentment. It extended to music, too. In 1999 David Bowie explained how Lennon would immerse himself in the lives and work of others. 'I remember talking with John at the time,' he said, 'about people we admired, and he said to me, "Y'know, when I've discovered someone new, I tend to become that person. I want to soak myself in their stuff to such an extent that I have to be them." So when he first found Dylan, he said, he would dress like Dylan and only play his kind of music, till he kind of understood how it worked.'[216] Meditation, heroin, primal therapy, radical politics, astrology and numerology would come later, but for a three-year period in the mid-Sixties Lennon was content to remain in thrall to the fantasy wonderland LSD appeared to reveal.

'It went on for years,' he recalled in 1970. 'I must have had a thousand trips. I used to just eat it all the time.'[217] His intake was confirmed by Pete Shotton: 'He saw acid as a godsend – a magical key to uncharted regions of his own imagination, and a potential cure for most of his psychological problems. It gave almost tangible form to his lifelong perception of the world as a surrealistic carnival, and it enabled him – instantaneously, effort-lessly, and without leaving his chair – to experience the semblance of mystical visions and even communion with God. By the time the Beatles started work on *Revolver*, in the spring of 1966, both John and George were taking the drug on an almost daily basis. They quite literally used to eat it like candy.'[218]

Shotton had known Lennon since childhood, and was used to the violent and cruel streak which was rarely far from the surface. However, he noticed a softening in Lennon's personality after he began taking LSD. Out went the 'cripple' imperson-ations, bravado and acid-tongued mockery, and in came a more tolerant, enthusiastic Lennon who forswore alcohol and meat and, for a time, rose each morning with the sun. He would open the gates of Kenwood and allow fans to wander the grounds, occasionally even inviting them inside for a cup of tea.

Shotton moved in to Kenwood in 1967 to keep Lennon company. The Beatle persuaded his friend to join him on a first trip, which took place in April 1967 at Julian Lennon's fourth birthday party. 'From that point onwards, John and I tripped together almost constantly,' said Shotton. 'During his early-bird phase, in fact, he used to appear in my bedroom every morning with a breakfast tray containing a cup of tea and a tab of acid.'[219]

PAUL MCCARTNEY's lifestyle was markedly different. Between

November 1963 and March 1966 he lived in an attic room in 57 Wimpole Street, the central London house owned by the parents of his girlfriend Jane Asher. The arrangement, while not ideal for a young couple, positioned McCartney in the heart of the city, and allowed him a prime opportunity to absorb the cultural delights of the capital. In April 1965 he bought 7 Cavendish Avenue in St John's Wood, but remained with the Ashers while his new house was substantially remodelled inside.

McCartney appears to have had little enthusiasm for secluded countryside living. Even during the heights of Beatlemania he had made efforts to retain a normal existence, meeting fans and wandering around towns and cities, despite being one of the most recognisable people in the world. His *modus operandi* during the mid-Sixties was to actively seek out and devour contemporary, underground and alternative art, film, literature, theatre and music; he roamed London with his 'antennae out',[220] absorbing new forms of creative expression, many of which he adopted and incorporated into his own work. 'I don't want to sound like Jonathan Miller going on,' he said in 1966, 'but I'm trying to cram everything in, all the things that I've missed. People are saying things and painting things and writing things and composing things that are great, and I must know what people are doing. I vaguely mind people knowing anything I don't know.'[221]

Jane Asher's brother Peter was one half of the musical duo Peter and Gordon; their first single, A World Without Love, written by McCartney, had been a transatlantic number one hit. Peter's best friend at the time was John Dunbar, former art critic for *The Scotsman* newspaper, who was married to the singer Marianne Faithfull. Dunbar was in the process of setting up the Indica bookshop and gallery with Barry Miles. They rented premises at 6 Masons Yard, in the courtyard where the Scotch of St James nightclub was also located. Miles ran the bookshop on the ground floor of the building; the basement housed the gallery run by Dunbar.

Peter Asher had agreed to co-fund Indica – named after the *Cannabis indica* plant – by lending Miles and Dunbar £700 each, and putting in the same amount himself as a silent partner. For a time the book stock was held in the Wimpole Street basement, where two years earlier Lennon and McCartney had written I Want To Hold Your Hand. McCartney got in the habit of browsing through the stock and taking titles that piqued his interest, in the process becoming Indica's first customer. On one such occasion they included *And It's A Song* by Finnish poet Anselm Hollo; *Drugs And The Mind* by biochemist Robert S de Ropp; and *Gandhi On Non-Violence*.

McCartney and Miles first met in August 1965 at the Ashers' house, and quickly became good friends. Miles's wife Sue mentioned to McCartney that she had just made a batch of hash brownies using the recipe for 'Haschich Fudge (which anyone could whip up on a rainy day)', from *The Alice B Toklas Cookbook*. A few days later Miles returned to his flat in Hanson Street, and was astonished to find McCartney sitting on the kitchen worktop, eating hash brownies and chatting to Sue. He regularly visited the flat from then on, smoking cannabis and listening to their record collection.

McCartney proved himself a down-to-earth friend to the Indica set, unpretentious and eager to learn about their lives and passions. He helped prepare the bookshop and gallery for launch, hammering nails, sawing wood and filling holes, much to the surprise of passers-by who spotted him through the windows. He also arranged to have wrapping paper printed for the bookshop, and gave monetary assistance when the gallery moved to 102 Southampton Row in the summer of 1966. He also provided financial support to *International Times*, the underground newspaper co-founded by Miles which frequently fell foul of the authorities due to its items on drug taking and police raids, LSD-inspired cartoons, and similar countercultural features.

John Dunbar, meanwhile, struck up a friendship with Robert

Fraser, whose eponymous gallery at 69 Duke Street in London's Mayfair gave early exposure to the works of Peter Blake, Richard Hamilton, Bridget Riley, Andy Warhol, Claes Oldenburg and other stars of the visual arts. The Beatles, too, entered Fraser's world – he was the art director for *Sgt Pepper's Lonely Hearts Club Band* – as did members of the Rolling Stones and other musical luminaries.

Indica and the Robert Fraser Gallery provided the gateway to much of Lennon's and McCartney's expanding social circle in the mid-Sixties. Class boundaries were falling, and the innovators in music, art and literature were establishing a new, young cultural aristocracy pioneering new forms and techniques, with the Beatles at the forefront.

The mercurial Fraser was one of the lynchpins of Swinging London, the momentous period of hedonism, optimism and cultural revolution that flourished in the English capital in the 1960s. His easy charm and ability to transcend class boundaries ensured his popularity among artists, customers and friends of all backgrounds, despite a chaotic personal life which often overshadowed his pioneering work in the art world. Fraser's apartment on Mount Street became a hub for the young and beautiful stars of the Sixties, where musicians, models and artists congregated day and night for conversation, culture and illicit pleasures.

'I think Robert saw the Beatles as a hustle,' said Mick Jagger. 'Everyone did. They were the richest people in that age group. Very silly with their money, they didn't seem to care. They did very good things, like *Sgt Pepper*, and did attract good people. But people did target them as a hustle.'[222]

Fraser was gay at a time when such practices were illegal. He was a gambler who ran up huge debts, and at one stage owed notorious gangsters the Kray brothers £20,000. He often failed to pay his artists, enraging many and testing their loyalty, although few ever fully disowned him. 'Robert wasn't very good with money,' said McCartney. 'I lent him bits of money that I didn't see back. The way I looked at it, he'd actually made me so much money with some of the paintings he'd helped me get that it didn't matter. We didn't have to dot the Is and cross the Ts. I figured I'd won financially. Not that it was a competition, but he certainly made me a lot more money than he lost me. But he did have a bad reputation with money.'[223]

Fraser was also a heavy drug user, at a time when many in his field were dabbling recreationally. Although he later turned to harder substances including heroin, Fraser was one of the first high profile figures in the London counterculture to take LSD, which he was given at a party in Rome. On returning to England, Fraser began using acid regularly; he gave Brian Jones and Anita Pallenberg their first trips, which brought it into the Rolling Stones' circle.

McCartney and Jane Asher moved into 7 Cavendish Avenue in March 1966. They owned no furniture, so quickly filled it with new acquisitions and hired architects John and Marina Adams – she was the sister of John Dunbar – to design the interior to McCartney's specifications. The three-storey Regency townhouse was situated a few streets away from EMI Studios at Abbey Road, which allowed McCartney to begin recording before the other Beatles arrived from their homes in Surrey. The house also functioned as a social hub for his London friends. He had been largely unable to entertain guests in private at Wimpole Street, so he seized the opportunity to host afternoon tea, dinner parties and all-night sessions. Visitors would regularly drop by unannounced: 'It was a bit more of a salon really,' he said. 'Everyone just came round, anyone stuck for somewhere to stay.'[224]

McCartney dabbled with cocaine in 1966-67, but preferred the social and relaxing qualities of marijuana. He also hosted long nights on LSD. 'We'd occasionally have some acid trips out at my house in Cavendish Avenue. That was the secure place to do it.'[225] He claimed to have given Mick Jagger his first taste of cannabis. 'I believe I turned Mick Jagger on to pot in my little music room at Cavendish Avenue, which is funny because everyone would have thought it would have been the other way round.'[226] (Jagger denied this, saying he first smoked cannabis in California during the Stones' first US tour in 1964.)

By the time they moved in together, McCartney and Asher were growing apart. She was committed to her acting career, and from October 1965 spent much of her time working at the Bristol Old Vic theatre or touring with the company, while McCartney worked long days and nights in the studio and on the road. The distances allowed McCartney to carry on living like a young bachelor; he continued to sleep with other women throughout their relationship, considering it permissible as they weren't married. They announced their engagement on Christmas Day 1967, but the relationship ended in 1968 when Asher returned from Bristol to find McCartney in bed with another woman, Francie Schwartz.

In addition to his infidelities, Asher felt that McCartney's character had changed since he had started taking LSD. She did not use drugs, and had little in common with his friends who did. 'When I came back [from America] after five months,' she said, 'Paul had changed so much. He was on LSD, which I hadn't shared. I was jealous of all the spiritual experiences he'd had with John. There were 15 people dropping in all day long. The house had changed and was full of stuff I didn't know about.'[227]

In early April 1967, as the Beatles put the finishing touches to *Sgt Pepper*, McCartney and Mal Evans flew to the west coast of America. The main purpose of the trip was to surprise Asher on her 21st birthday – she was touring a production of Shakespeare's *Romeo And Juliet*. McCartney and Evans landed in San Francisco and visited the Fillmore, where Jefferson Airplane were rehearsing. Afterwards they went back to the band's Oak Street apartment where McCartney played them an acetate of early *Sgt Pepper* mixes. McCartney smoked cannabis with

Jefferson Airplane, but declined an offer of DMT – another hallucinogenic similar to LSD.

After reuniting with Asher in Denver, McCartney flew with Evans to Los Angeles, staying for two nights at the home of Derek and Joan Taylor. Derek had resigned his position as the Beatles' press officer at the end of their 1964 US tour, and was now working as the PR man for groups including the Beach Boys, the Byrds and the Mamas and the Papas. He remained good friends with the Beatles, and saw them on their US tours of 1965 and 1966; George and Pattie had also visited during a short stay in California. Despite the company he kept, Taylor was an acid greenhorn, and looked on in wonder at the change he saw in his friends.

'Paul and Mal, this time, were full of tales of this here LSD and what it could do,' Taylor wrote in his memoir *Fifty Years Adrift*. 'Unrecognisable psyches on familiar heads and shoulders: the voice was Paul's but the tone was… God's? Paul said he and John had had "this fantastic *thing*"; which really wasn't very informative, so I pressed him to flesh it out. "Incredible, really, just locked into each other's eyes… Like, just *staring* and then saying, 'I *know*, man' and then laughing… And it was great, you know." It wasn't easy to explain to me, whose idea of a great experience was still two Drinamyl, a large brandy and a crab cocktail.'[228]

JOHN LENNON'S marriage to Cynthia was also in a slow terminal decline. Lennon's acid use peaked in 1966 and '67. He obtained a supply which he described as 'the best stuff it's possible to get in the world',[229] and to his wife's distress surrounded himself with various hangers-on who were all too happy to accompany a Beatle on some far-out trips.

'Soon he was bringing home a ragged assortment of people he'd met through drugs,' Cynthia said. 'After a clubbing session he'd pile in with anyone he'd picked up during the evening, whether he knew them or not. They were all high and littered our house for hours, sometimes days on end. They'd wander around glassy-eyed, crash out on the sofas, beds and floors, then eat whatever they could find in the kitchen. John was an essentially private man, but under the influence of drugs he was vulnerable to anyone and everyone who wanted to take advantage of him.'[230]

Cynthia, burnt by the horrors of the Dental Experience, was reluctant to join them, and felt her husband's infatuation with LSD was broadening the emotional rift between them. 'When John was tripping I felt as if I was living with a stranger,' she said. 'He would be distant, so spaced-out that he couldn't talk to me coherently. I hated that, and I hated the fact that LSD was pulling him away from me. I wouldn't take it with him so he found others who would. Within weeks of his first trip, John was taking LSD daily and I became more and more worried. I couldn't reach him when he was tripping, but when the effects wore off he would be normal until he took it again.'[231]

According to Cynthia, Lennon would take acid after studio sessions and concerts, and particularly when the Beatles were between recording projects. When he returned to Earth he would be the old John she knew, but this was soon replaced by vacant stares and incoherent communication as he fell back into a hallucinatory state.

Lennon's solution was to persuade his wife to join him on another trip. He hoped that LSD would bring them closer together, and promised to look after her if the trip went awry. Eventually she succumbed to his persuasion, and 'Mission Cynthia' was put into action. They set a weekend date and their son Julian was dispatched to stay with their housekeeper Dot Jarlett, while trusted friends were invited over to Kenwood. Lennon, whom Cynthia described as 'ecstatic' at her agreement to take LSD again, went to great lengths to reassure her that it would work out.

Terry Doran, a Liverpudlian employee at Brian Epstein's company NEMS, was the first to arrive, followed by George and Pattie Harrison, and Pattie's friend and fellow model Marie Lise. Several other friends of Lennon, barely known to Cynthia, were also present. Candles were lit and music played, and Scotch and Coke was shared among the guests. Cynthia wondered how the LSD would be taken, before realising she had already been given it without her knowledge.

As the acid took hold she left the room for the nearest bathroom. There, she looked in a mirror and saw her own skeleton staring back at her. 'The vision kept moving, changing from a blurred prism of me to a grinning skeleton. I was transfixed. The next thing I remember was hearing John's voice: "Cyn, are you okay? Come on, Cyn, you'll be fine, nothing will hurt you. Terry and I are here. You're safe."'

Cynthia was guided back into the main room where her friends attempted to make her feel safe, but she hallucinated Doran as a snake, then an alligator. 'His voice emanated from a monster that kept moving toward me, every scale on its body shining, glistening and changing colour. I thought I was in hell. I couldn't look at anything without it changing its form and colour – even the carpet seemed to be breathing.'

As the LSD wore off she saw those around her hugging and kissing in a loving communion. 'I was aware of periods of lucidity when I was spoken to gently and my cheeks were kissed. Slowly I came back to earth. All the others were coming down, too, and they were hugging and kissing, telling each other how wonderful it all was and how much they loved each other.'[232]

To Cynthia, the chemically-assisted intimacy felt false and phoney. She decided not to dabble any further, telling her husband that she wanted nothing more to do with LSD. He reluctantly accepted her decision, although it did little to temper his own use.

In addition to his emotional detachment, Lennon was often unpredictable and obnoxious to her while in his drug stupors.

Cynthia decided to resume painting, which she had put on hold since their 1962 wedding, and while the Beatles were working long hours in the studio she painted an elaborate floral design on the surround of the family's television. 'The following morning I was up with Julian, about to give him his breakfast, when I glanced at my artwork. I could hardly believe what I saw. It was completely covered with circular stickers that read, "Milk Is Good For You." John had come in during the early hours, high on drugs, and destroyed my efforts. I was shaken and hurt. Did he not want me to have anything for myself? Was he so determined to have my total attention focused on him? Or was he simply so stoned that he hadn't realised what he was doing?'[233] The couple's dislike of confrontation meant the situation was left unresolved, and mutual resentment continued to build.

Lennon had given little regard to fidelity during the Beatles' touring days. He also struggled to relate to his young son Julian. The domestic pressures were compounded by his feelings for Japanese artist Yoko Ono, to whom he grew closer in the months before their relationship began in May 1968. Lennon and Ono first met at the Indica Gallery, where she had persuaded John Dunbar to put on an exhibition of her conceptual art. Unfinished Paintings and Objects opened on 8 November 1966,[234] two days after Lennon had arrived back in England from Spain, where he had been acting in Richard Lester's film *How I Won The War*. Lennon immediately embarked on a three-day LSD binge.

In the middle of the prolonged acid trip, presumably during a period of relative lucidity, he was chauffeured to London and called in at Indica to see Dunbar. The pair were good friends – a 'relationship cemented by drugs', as Miles described it. A joint was being passed around when Lennon arrived in the downstairs gallery, where Ono was putting the finishing touches to her exhibition. The Beatle, who by this point had been awake for more than 24 hours, had heard about the exhibition and was curious. 'There was going to be something about black bags, and I thought it was all gonna be sex: artsy-fartsy orgies. Great! Well, it was far out, but it was not the way I thought it was going to be.'[235] Eventually Dunbar brought Ono over to meet Lennon, and the pair linked arms as they wandered through the gallery.

Lennon was initially cynical, but eventually became intrigued by her artworks. One piece was titled Painting to Hammer a Nail In. Visitors to the exhibition were to drive a nail into a white piece of wood. Lennon asked if he might be the first; Ono objected, but Dunbar insisted he should be allowed. Ono relented, but only if he paid five shillings. Lennon, who rarely carried money, retorted: 'Well, I'll give you an imaginary five shillings and hammer an imaginary nail in.' That, he later said, was the moment when they 'really met. That's when we locked eyes and she got it and I got it and that was it.'[236] Lennon had found his new guru.

They met again at the end of November 1966 at the opening of a Claes Oldenburg exhibition at the Robert Fraser Gallery. She sent Lennon a copy of her book *Grapefruit* shortly afterwards and, although his reactions to the book were mixed, he was intrigued enough to invite her over to Kenwood for a platonic meeting. They remained in semi-regular contact throughout 1967, and on 25 September were photographed in conversation during the recording of The Fool On The Hill at EMI Studios.

Although he had an art school background and was a keen illustrator, Lennon felt insecure in the company of the more established Ono. He may have sat at the apex of the pop world, but she inhabited a domain populated by painters, sculptors, writers and theatrical performers which he was yet to penetrate. By the autumn of 1967 Lennon was feeling mentally punished by a year spent tripping, had lost much of the fight that characterised his early adulthood, and was steadily acceding leadership of the Beatles to the ambitious McCartney. The self-assured

Ono became the latest in a line of teachers and leaders at the feet of whom Lennon prostrated himself in search of guidance.

———

POP MUSIC'S nostalgia for childlike wonderment reached its apotheosis in Lucy In The Sky With Diamonds. Although never banned by the BBC, it became notorious for its title, which many believed was a reference to LSD. It sparked a craze for searching for hidden meanings in the group's work.

'I first became aware of the depth of the lyrics to the Beatles' songs when I went to a party in 1967 during the *Sgt Pepper* era,' wrote the artist Alan Aldridge in the 1969 book *The Beatles Illustrated Lyrics*. 'Someone whispered in my ear that Lucy In The Sky With Diamonds was a song about an LSD trip. Although ambiguity in the lyrics to popular music was no new thing, the scale of the various interpretations of the songs on the *Sgt Pepper* album so intrigued me that I began reading all the lyrics of Beatles songs and finding, or imagining, all kinds of hidden meanings.'[237]

The Beatles and their close associates always vociferously denied that the title was anything other than coincidental. 'The idea that Lucy In The Sky With Diamonds stands for LSD is rubbish,' George Martin insisted. 'John wasn't like that and people credit him with too much subtlety. He liked to shock people, and if he'd really wanted to write about drugs he would have done it straight out. You'd never have been in any doubt as to what he was singing about.'[238]

In his 1970 interview for *Rolling Stone*, Lennon suggested he didn't make the connection until *Sgt Pepper* was released. 'Only after I heard it [did I realise] – or somebody told me, like you coming up. I didn't even see it on the label, I didn't look at the initials. I never play things backwards, I just listened to it as I made it… Every time after, I would look at titles, see what it said, but it never said anything.'[239]

Cynthia Lennon, Ringo Starr, Pete Shotton and NEMS's Alistair Taylor all claimed to have been present at the song's genesis, when the four-year-old Julian Lennon brought home a drawing of Lucy O'Donnell, a friend from Heath House, a private nursery in Weybridge. 'I was actually with John when Julian came in with this little kid's painting, a crazy little painting,' Starr later said. 'And John said, "Oh, what's that?" and Julian said, "It's Lucy in the sky with diamonds." And then John got busy.'[240]

Shortly afterwards McCartney arrived at Kenwood. 'I went up to John's house in Weybridge,' he recalled in 1997. 'We were having a cup of tea, and he said, "Look at this great drawing Julian's done. Look at the title!" He showed me a drawing on school paper, a five-by-seven-inch piece of paper, of a little girl with lots of stars, and right across the top there was written, in very neat child handwriting, I think in pencil, "Lucy in the sky with diamonds". So I said, "What's that mean?" thinking Wow, fantastic title! John said, "It's Lucy, a friend of his from school. And she's in the sky." … And we loved it and she was in the sky and it was very trippy to us. So we went upstairs and started writing it. People later thought Lucy In The Sky With Diamonds was LSD. I swear we didn't notice that when it came out.'[241]

There is little doubt, though, that LSD informed and influenced the imagery in the lyrics, and it is all but inconceivable that Lennon and McCartney would have written such a song before their discovery of the drug. According to McCartney: 'In songs like Lucy In The Sky With Diamonds, when we were talking about "cellophane flowers" and "kaleidoscope eyes" and "grow so incredibly high!", we were talking about drug experiences, no doubt about it.'[242]

Lennon had loved Lewis Carroll since childhood, and Wonderland gave him the ideal setting for some nostalgic psychedelia. The song's themes were loosely drawn from the Wool And Water chapter of *Through The Looking-Glass*, and from its languid closing acrostic poem Carroll wrote for Alice Liddell. 'John had the title and he had the first verse,' said McCartney. 'It started off very Alice in Wonderland: "Picture yourself in a boat, on a river…" It's very Alice. Both of us had read the Alice books and always referred to them, we were always talking about Jabberwocky and we knew those more than any other books really. And when psychedelics came in, the heady quality of them was perfect. So we just went along with it. I sat there and wrote it with him: I offered "cellophane flowers" and "newspaper taxis" and John replied with "kaleidoscope eyes". I remember which was which because we traded words off each other, as we always did … And in our mind it was an Alice thing, which both of us loved.'[243]

Eyewitness reports aside, there will probably always be obstinate believers who maintain that the Beatles left coded messages in their songs. Yet there are reasons why the Beatles would never have been so brazen as to knowingly write, record and release a song with a title directly referencing LSD. Firstly, they were mindful of their status as teen idols, and their drug use remained largely discreet until the release of *Sgt Pepper*.

Furthermore, by late 1966 Lennon was using a loose song-writing formula which he deployed for much of the remainder of his life. He absorbed television, radio, newspapers, books and other media, playing with words and phrases from them until a song emerged. Lennon often wrote lyrics before music, developing melodies around combinations of words that struck him as special.

Each of the four *Sgt Pepper* songs that Lennon initiated or largely wrote alone – Lucy In The Sky With Diamonds, Being For The Benefit Of Mr Kite!, Good Morning Good Morning and A Day In The Life – was inspired by words or phrases which Lennon happened to notice as he composed at Kenwood. Mr Kite! was taken almost verbatim from a Victorian circus poster; Good Morning Good Morning combined advertising jingles and references to television shows ('a Kellogg's Corn

Flakes ad at the time – that's how desperate I was for a song'[244]);
while A Day In The Life combined two *Daily Mail* news reports
with an opaque reference to *How I Won The War*.

In each song Lennon was exploring a direct, simple form of
writing that would later develop into instant, swiftly executed
'postcard' songs such as The Ballad Of John And Yoko and
those on the album *Some Time In New York City*. He was always
most comfortable writing about himself or his immediate
surroundings, and the *Sgt Pepper* songs were Lennon conveying
the here-and-now to his listeners. It was partly necessity, too:
Lennon knew that McCartney was the more prolific writer, and
he had to come up with enough songs to make his mark on the
album. 'He'd work something out for a song or an album and
then suddenly call me and say, "It's time to go into the studio.
Write some songs." He'd have all *his* prepared, ready with ideas
and arrangements, while I would be starting from scratch. On
Sgt Pepper, which was his idea, too, I managed to come up with
Lucy In The Sky and A Day In The Life under the pressure of
only ten days.'[245] With the remarkable consistency of the eyewitness reports of its creation, and knowledge of Lennon's songwriting methods of the time, it becomes entirely plausible that
the title of a painting by his infant son could be appropriated for
a song.

Lucy In The Sky With Diamonds was not the Beatles' only
1967 song to be inspired by Lewis Carroll. Among the myriad
literary references and surrealist thoughts which came together
in I Am The Walrus was The Walrus And The Carpenter, a
poem from *Through The Looking Glass*, although Lennon later
realised with dismay that he'd identified with the villain of the
piece. 'It never dawned on me that Lewis Carroll was
commenting on the capitalist system,' he said. 'I never went into
that bit about what he really meant, like people are doing with
the Beatles' work. Later, I went back and looked at it and
realised that the walrus was the bad guy in the story and the
carpenter was the good guy. I thought, Oh, shit, I picked the

wrong guy. I should have said, "I am the carpenter." But that wouldn't have been the same, would it?'[246]

———

PETER BLAKE, who designed the *Sgt Pepper* cover with his then-wife Jann Haworth, recalled a night when McCartney and Fraser called at his studio while tripping on LSD: 'They were seeing things that weren't there – seeing colours and seeing things that simply weren't there and persuading me that I had to do it! You know, saying, "Look, you've got to, you're not living a full life unless you experience these things." I don't know how I ever insisted on not doing it, because the pressure to participate was enormous, but I just never did, you know. Which I am not particularly proud of. I mean, I am glad I didn't, but it would have been a great deal easier to. The idea of that amount of responsibility being taken away from you. I never mind getting drunk and I never mind losing that sense, but LSD did frighten me. That was probably a good thing.'[247]

Blake and Haworth were invited to EMI Studios at Abbey Road to hear the work in progress on the album. They found a world very much removed from their usual domain. 'A very strange scene met us the first time we went over to the studio,' said Haworth. 'The Beatles were recording, and their "court" of Marianne Faithfull and all these weird spaced-out people sat around the walls. Peter and I were probably the only people who were stone-cold sober. It was really funny, two very upright people doing this psychedelia … I don't think the final *Sgt Pepper* cover is at all psychedelic. Neither Peter nor I had anything to do with drugs and it was very much a continuum of both his work and mine.'[248]

The cover of *Sgt Pepper* was shot by photographer Michael Cooper, who also took the portrait of the Beatles used for the inside gatefold. 'One of the things we were very much into in those days was eye messages,' said McCartney. 'I had seen a

thing on TV about eye contact in apes, and I'd become fascinated by this whole idea that you don't look at each other. I'd
thought this was a way to get a breakthrough here on acid and
this became a sort of party game we used to play then. I used to
play it all the time with Mal and John, you get a feedback. Quite
trippy… So with Michael Cooper's inside photo, we all said,
"Now look into the camera and really say 'I love you!' Really try
and feel love, really give love through this! It'll come out, it'll
show, it's an attitude." And that's what that is, if you look at it
you'll see the big effort from the eyes.'[249] Lennon, meanwhile,
intimated that LSD was in use during the *Sgt Pepper* cover shoot:
'If you look closely at the album cover, you'll see two people
who are flying, and two who aren't.'[250]

The Beatles had a policy of no LSD, alcohol, or any other
drug which blurred their senses while recording. However, their
use of pep pills, which had continued since the Hamburg days,
led to one of their most infamous studio incidents. It happened
on the evening of 21 March 1967.

As George Martin sat in the control room with balance engineer Geoff Emerick, the Beatles were on the studio floor
working on Getting Better. Over the course of the session they
were joined by music publisher Dick James, NEMS employee
Peter Brown, and Ivan Vaughan, the man who had introduced
Lennon to McCartney back in 1957. Also present was Hunter
Davies, who had recently been commissioned to write the Beatles' authorised biography. Starr was the only absent band
member.

Lennon, McCartney and Harrison positioned themselves
around a single microphone to record their vocals, with the
song's backing track playing in their headphones. Yet as work
continued into the small hours of the morning, Emerick and
Martin realised something was wrong. 'We were looking down
into the studio and I think George Harrison and Paul went over
to John and put their hands on his shoulders,' recalled Emerick.
'I think they brought him up to the control room and said to

George Martin: "We don't think John's very well." John Lennon suddenly looked up and said: "Cor, look at the stars, George." This was inside the control room. George Martin's looking around for these stars.'[251]

Lennon often carried with him a small silver art nouveau pill box which he had bought from Liberty of London. He kept a range of stimulants inside the box, and was in the habit of taking it out and selecting different drugs to get him through the night. On this occasion he had inadvertently ingested a tab of LSD, and was alarmed to start feeling its effects.

'I thought I was taking some uppers, and I was not in a state of handling it,' he later recalled. 'I took it and then [*whispers*] I just noticed all of a sudden I got so scared on the mic. I said, "What was it?" I thought I felt ill. I thought I was going cracked.'[252]

Martin went down into the studio, and could tell that Lennon was struggling to cope. He decided that some fresh air was called for, and offered to take Lennon outside. 'The problem was where to go,' said Martin. 'There were the usual five hundred or so kids waiting for us at the front, keeping vigil like guard-dogs, and if we had dared to appear at the entrance there would have been uproar and they would probably have broken the gates down.'[253]

The back door of the studio was opened up. 'There was the sound of loud banging and cheering on the other side,' recalled Hunter Davies. 'The door began to move slightly inwards, under the strain of a gang of fans who'd somehow managed to get inside the building.'[254] George Martin, a man used to finding creative solutions to practical problems, decided that the roof of the building would be a better destination. He was still unaware that Lennon was tripping.

'I remember it was a lovely night, with very bright stars,' said Martin. 'Then I suddenly realised that the only protection around the edge of the roof was a parapet about six inches high, with a sheer drop of some ninety feet to the ground below, and I had to tell him, "Don't go too near the edge, there's no rail there, John." We walked around the roof for a while.'[255]

McCartney and Harrison continued work on Getting Better until Martin returned. McCartney asked how Lennon was, and was told: 'He's on the roof, looking at the stars.' 'You mean Vince Hill?' McCartney joked, referring to the singer, then he and Harrison burst into an impromptu version of Edelweiss, the *Sound Of Music* song with which Hill was enjoying chart success. But then realisation dawned of the potential danger Lennon was in, and the Beatles rushed to the top of the studio to help their friend down before he came to serious harm.

'He was just stuck there on the roof, and George left him there,' said Emerick. 'And of course when he came back down and told Paul and Ringo [*sic*] and George what he had done they flew up the stairs to retrieve John.'[256]

That effectively marked the end of the session, although Martin remained behind to add a piano solo to another *Sgt Pepper* song, Lovely Rita. 'It wasn't until much later that I learned what had happened,' he said. 'But Paul knew, and went home with him and turned on as well, to keep him company. It seems they had a real trip. I knew they smoked pot, and I knew they took pills, but in my innocence I had no idea they were also into LSD.'[257]

McCartney and Mal Evans drove Lennon to 7 Cavendish Avenue, where McCartney decided to drop acid to keep his bandmate company. It was McCartney's second trip, and his first with Lennon.

'I thought, maybe this is the moment where I should take a trip with him. It's been coming for a long time. It's often the best way, without thinking about it too much, just slip into it. John's on it already, so I'll sort of catch up. It was my first trip with John, or with any of the guys. We stayed up all night, sat around and hallucinated a lot.'[258]

McCartney's decision to take LSD to help his friend get through a bad trip shows the tenderness and depth of their friendship. Watched over by a sober Evans, McCartney managed to keep Lennon on an even keel, although their reactions offer an illuminating insight into their different attitudes towards the drug. Whereas McCartney was happy to dabble but quickly grew weary, Lennon remained absorbed in every moment.

'It was very tiring, walking made me very tired, wasted me, always wasted me,' said McCartney. 'But "I've got to do it, for my well-being." In the meantime John had been sitting around very enigmatically and I had a big vision of him as a king, the absolute Emperor of Eternity. It was a good trip. It was great but I wanted to go to bed after a while.

'I'd just had enough after about four or five hours. John was quite amazed that it had struck me in that way. John said, "Go to bed? You won't sleep!" "I know that, I've still got to go to bed." I thought, now that's enough fun and partying, now... But of course you don't just sleep off an acid trip so I went to bed and hallucinated a lot in bed. I remember Mal coming up and checking that I was all right. "Yeah, I think so." I mean, I could feel every inch of the house, and John seemed like some sort of emperor in control of it all. It was quite strange. Of course he was just sitting there, very inscrutably.'[259]

ON SUNDAY 28 MAY 1967, Brian Epstein threw a party at Kingsley Hill, his country home in Warbleton near Heathfield in Sussex. It was both Epstein's house-warming and an opportunity to bring together the beautiful people he counted as close friends. All the Beatles were present apart from Paul McCartney, who chose to stay with Jane Asher after her return from the United States.

Also invited, with just two days' notice, were Derek and Joan Taylor. He was in the process of setting up the three-day Monterey International Pop Music Festival, but the couple flew six thousand miles back to England to attend the party. Joan was seven months pregnant. They were hoping for a weekend of alcohol, pills and cannabis, and were wholly unprepared for the rich sensory assault that awaited.

At the airport the Taylors were met by Lennon, Harrison, Starr, Terry Doran, and Barry Finch of design collective the Fool. They had been up all night on what Harrison described as 'an all-night (or all-week) bells-on-the-knees and perms-in-the-hair LSD trip.' All were dressed in full psychedelic finery: silk and satin clothes, embellished with scarves and bells and other ornaments. 'Their brains seemed somewhat apart from their bodies,' Taylor said, 'and yet they were not drunk or reeling or grinding their teeth. The other passengers stood and stared, and so did we.' To his dismay, the three Beatles greeted them with hugs and kisses. 'This is the new thing!' Lennon told him. 'You hug your friends when you meet them and show them you're glad to see them. Don't stand there shaking hands as if every-one's got some disease! Get *close* to people!'[260]

The Taylors were ushered into Lennon's Rolls-Royce, painted in gypsy psychedelic livery and guaranteed to turn heads. As they set off for Weybridge, Harrison snatched a cigarette from Taylor's mouth and threw it out of the window. 'You don't need them; they'll poison you,' he admonished Taylor, who was used to smoking three packets a day. 'Acid for breakfast,' Lennon said gnomically, as they listened to Procol Harum's A Whiter Shade Of Pale. 'It gets you like that.'[261]

Lennon took the guests to Kenwood, while Harrison returned to Kinfauns. Taylor was still dressed in a blazer, grey flannel slacks and a black tie: a man out of time. 'When we got to George's house, we saw for the first time what young psychedelic women were wearing for parties. Pattie and her sister Jenny and Marijke of the Fool were in glittering flowing robes of beautiful colours, with velvet here and there and all absolutely original. These were the fairest of flower children and as they walked through the Claremont Estate of suburban

Esher, they made an indelible impression. Already it was Wonderland, and no one had put anything in our tea yet.'[262]

They left in three cars. Harrison drove while on LSD with Pattie in his Mini. 'We were moving along the road at about 85mph in a little psychedelic box with tantric symbols, Shiva radio aerials and "hello Pisces" on the door, yantra, tantra, mantras and all that,' he recalled. 'Suddenly, the big gypsy caravan, the $40,000 Phantom Five Rolls bearing the Romany gypsies going to Brian's, was coming the opposite way. Now were they going the right way and we going back the way we came, or were we heading towards the party and they'd missed it? It didn't matter, just hah… great; let's get out.'[263]

Inside the Rolls-Royce, spirits were high. 'It had all the feeling of a school outing,' Cynthia Lennon said. 'Every time the car passed through town or villages it stopped the traffic. Crowds of jeering, waving people pressed up against the tinted windows trying to get a better look at the occupants of this crazy car. It was like travelling in a time machine. The boys were smoking pot and, even if you don't smoke it yourself, breathing in the fumes can affect you in much the same way. A pill was passed around and everyone giggled stupidly and had a nibble. It was very hard for me to explain what the atmosphere was like in that car at the time. I can only describe it as insane, freaky, self-destructive, irresponsible. A contagious mood that spread like wildfire in the dark, squashed confines of that crazy vehicle.'[264]

Remarkably, all three cars and their passengers arrived unscathed at the Epstein party. Taylor found the Beatles' manager free of the stress and anxiety that had overshadowed many of the group's US tours; instead Epstein was relaxed, in joyous mood and full of love for his guests, among whom were maverick radio DJ Kenny Everett, musicals composer Lionel Bart, the Beatles' Hamburg friend Klaus Voormann, and many other glittering showbusiness figures.

The Taylors were offered Indian tea in china cups. 'John,

who had been sitting with us on the lawn, said he'd just given Joan some "acid" in her tea,' Derek recalled. 'Would I like some in mine? Sure, why not? He snapped a tablet in two, gave me a portion about two thirds of the total. "That'll do to start with," he said cheerfully, dropping the tiny jagged pink pill into my cup. "Stir it up well, there's a good lad." George came by and said: "What are you giving them?" "What do you think?" said John. "Oh," said George. "Derek's..." But I had already drained it, and George's tea, too. "Derek's already had... well, it's too late now." He laughed. "Derek's got a double dose inside him."'[265]

Taylor had already unwittingly ingested 500 micrograms of Owsley Stanley-sourced LSD. Coupled with Lennon's offering, he was in for an unusually strong first trip. Fortunately he was in trusted company in a safe space, allowing him to enjoy the experience without too much turbulence or fear. The Beatles and their wives retreated to a room with a log fire burning. A joint was passed around and more tea poured. Taylor, not knowing what to expect from the acid, took a Desbutal tablet – amphetamine combined with barbiturate – 'just in case there wasn't enough stimulation'.

He needn't have worried. 'Before long I found myself swimming like a parcel of Escher lizards through the lines of a purple jigsaw of increasing and then decreasing size. "What the hell's going on?" I asked, crying with laughter. "You're tripping," said Joan, with a new vocabulary already. Tripping? Me? ... "Are you tripping?" I asked Joan. She nodded lovingly. "We all are," George said. "Everyone is."'

As the effects of the double dose peaked, it proved too much for Taylor, who was assailed by disturbing visions and dark thoughts. Harrison, with enough experience to spot the warning signs, and the calmness – despite tripping himself – to provide reassurance, talked Taylor back from his descent into misery. 'Derek, create and preserve the image of your choice,' Harrison told him. 'It's up to you. The thing is to see what you want to see. Do you want to create something nice? Then look into the fire and see something nice.'

The intervention worked, and much of the remainder of Taylor's trip was filled with talking, laughter and visions. He and Joan bonded over the shared experience, and led a singalong on Epstein's grand piano.

Late into the night Taylor was cornered by Harrison, who reiterated his words of wisdom: 'Derek, I love ya. I just want you to know that. I love ya and it's going to be OK. Create and preserve the image of your choice. Don't forget, Derek. Gandhi said that. Pick your own trips.'

Coping less well was Cynthia Lennon, who was on her third and final trip. Once again it was a bad experience, though unlike Taylor she had nobody to comfort and guide her. Her husband was hardly faring better. 'When John moved away from me I followed hoping that he could in some way comfort and support me. But John was not happy; he was not enjoying the experience as he had before. He ignored me and glared as though I were an intruding stranger.'[266]

Distraught at the rejection from her husband, tongue-tied and paranoid, Cynthia retreated into a bedroom where she contemplated suicide. 'I felt desolate. I sat on the windowsill of an upstairs room contemplating the long drop to the paving-stones below, musing to myself that it wasn't really that far down and that I could even jump. I was drifting off into a very deep depression when someone called my name and I was snapped out of my apathetic reverie. Even though I was under the influence of the drug I knew that all hope for John and I carrying on with our marriage in the same vein flew out of that upstairs window with my thoughts.'[267]

UPON ITS RELEASE in June 1967, the Beatles' eighth album was instantly recognised as a major leap forward for modern music.

It united critics and fans alike in admiration of its variety-show concept, elaborate arrangements and songwriting, and innovative cover artwork. Even more so than its predecessors, *Sgt Pepper's Lonely Hearts Club Band* found the Beatles pushing boundaries within the studio, creating sounds never before heard. Recorded in over 400 hours during a 129-day period, combining a variety of musical styles including rock, music hall, psychedelia, traditional Indian and Western classical, *Sgt Pepper* was the perfect sound for the Summer of Love, managing the dual feat of possessing a timeless quality and capturing the zeitgeist.

Although its appeal was international, at the core of *Sgt Pepper* was the sound of the Beatles' English background, with tales of runaway girls, circus attractions, holiday cottages, domestic violence, home improvements, *Daily Mail* news items, memories of school days and favourite childhood literature – a remembrance of times past and wonder at what the future might hold. *Sgt Pepper* reaffirmed the Beatles' place at the peak of popular music after a lengthy absence, and silenced media rumours that had predicted their demise. They had become flag bearers for a new psychedelic age, with a popularity which transcended generation, class and culture.

Yet not everyone fell under *Sgt Pepper*'s spell. The 6 May edition of *Disc and Music Echo* carried the front page headline 'Beatles "drug" song is BANNED!' The paper revealed that a number of Los Angeles radio stations had blocked A Day In The Life from the airwaves, after concerns that the line 'I'd love to turn you on' was a reference to drug taking.

The British Broadcasting Corporation, for decades the nation's moral barometer, requested an advance copy from Northern Songs. On 12 May Mark White, the BBC's assistant head of gramophone programmes, wrote to Richard D'Arcy Marriott, the assistant head of sound broadcasting, asking for guidance on the matter: 'It is thought by the experts to be one of the best on the album, and other programmes may well want to play it later. HGP [head of gramophone productions, Anna Instone] and I have listened to the tape, and neither of us is sure about the content, nor about whether or not it should be broadcast. We would welcome a ruling from you at the earliest opportunity.

'Whilst on the subject, we would like to have your advice also on the use of the word "Psychedelic". In our opinion, which I believe is shared by CLP [controller of the Light Programme, Robin Scott], this word derives exclusively from the use of the drug LSD, and it might be wise if we were to instruct all DJs not to use it. On the other hand this is only our opinion, and other people claim that the word is not connected exclusively with drugs at all.'[268] The memo went on to express concern that the BBC might be out of step if it banned the song, particularly if pirate stations continued to enjoy greater freedom. Additionally, it was noted that enacting a ban would attract press scrutiny.

Seven days later Roland Fox, the BBC's assistant head of publicity, informed the corporation's press officers that A Day In The Life had indeed been banned. 'The BBC takes a pretty liberal attitude towards the products of the gramophone industry,' he wrote. 'However, we have listened to this particular song over and over again and we have decided that as far as we are concerned it goes a little too far and can encourage a permissive attitude to drug-taking. Therefore we have exercised our editorial discretion in deciding not to broadcast this particular song.'[269]

Fox told his colleagues that the decision was not to be publicised, but to be prepared in case the story broke. And it did, that very evening, at the launch party for *Sgt Pepper* at Brian Epstein's London home. The BBC received a stream of calls from reporters throughout the weekend.

A week before the album's release, the BBC's director of sound broadcasting, Frank Gillard, wrote to EMI head Sir Joseph Lockwood with news of the ban – which remained in place until March 1972. Gillard's letter, dated 23 May 1967, read: 'I never thought the day would come when we would have to put a ban on an EMI record, but sadly, that is what has happened over this track. We have listened to it over and over again with great care, and we cannot avoid coming to the conclusion that the words "I'd love to turn you on", followed by that mounting montage of sound, could have a rather sinister meaning.

'The recording may have been made in innocence and good faith, but we must take account of the interpretation that many young people would inevitably put upon it. "Turned on" is a phrase which can be used in many different circumstances, but it is currently much in vogue in the jargon of the drug-addicts. We do not feel that we can take the responsibility of appearing to favour or encourage those unfortunate habits, and that is why we shall not be playing the recording in any of our programmes, radio or television.

'I expect we shall meet with some embarrassment over this decision, which has already been noted by the press. We will do our best not to appear to be criticising your people, but as you will realise, we do find ourselves in a very difficult position. I thought you would like to know why we have, most reluctantly, taken this decision.'[270]

The Beatles hit back, with McCartney telling reporters: 'The BBC have misinterpreted the song. It has nothing to do with drug taking. It's only about a dream.' Lennon added: 'The laugh is that Paul and I wrote this song from a headline in a newspaper. It's about a crash and its victim. How can anyone read drugs into it is beyond me. Everyone seems to be falling overboard to see the word drug in the most innocent of phrases.'[271]

A Day In The Life was one of three songs left off *Sgt Pepper* when it was released in south Asia, Malaysia and Hong Kong, due to supposed drugs references. The others were With A Little Help From My Friends and Lucy In The Sky With Diamonds. McCartney confirmed to the press that the reference to cannabis in With A Little Help From My Friends had been intentional, although it was not the primary message of the song.

Lennon concurred, saying: 'It's really about a little help from my friends, it's a sincere message.'[272] He saw the fashion for extracting hidden meanings from Beatles records, however fanciful, as both amusing and mildly infuriating. It inspired him to write Glass Onion, which he purposefully filled with hidden meanings, red herrings and bogus clues to encourage more determined and delusional fans to join the dots.

Hunter Davies was present on the day in March 1967 when With A Little Help From My Friends was written. He claims that the double meanings in the song were fully intended. 'They were well aware at the time of the sexual connotation of "I know it's mine" and also of the double meaning of the phrase "I get high with a little help from my friends". The drug reference was deliberate, to amuse their friends, and most fans. It was a song about pot, something all four of them looked upon as a friend – but only if you wanted to read it that way.'[273]

Sgt Pepper was released two weeks before the Monterey Pop Festival took place in California. It was the first major showcase for a new wave of acid rock bands, and became the template for many subsequent large-scale outdoor events. Although the Beatles chose not to appear, they sent a piece of artwork to be included in the festival programme. The illustration was drawn in February 1967 with coloured pencils and pens, and had text by McCartney which read: 'Peace to Monterey from Sgt Peppers Lonely Hearts Club Band. Loving You. It happened in Monterey a long time ago. Sincerely John, Paul, George and Harold. I Love You.' At the festival, rumours circulated that the Beatles were to appear, although by then their performing days were well over. McCartney did suggest that Derek Taylor enlist the Who and the Jimi Hendrix Experience, both of whom performed on the final night.

Another Monterey legend, first floated by NEMS's Peter

Brown, was that the Beatles had sent a consignment of film equipment to the festival, despite knowing that the rights had already been sold. When permission was inevitably denied to the Beatles, the airtight film canisters were transported back to England containing liquid LSD (some accounts have the LSD in purple tab form). Although the story has remained part of Beatles lore ever since, the notion of them going to such extravagant lengths is somewhat fanciful, and was never confirmed by any of the band. Nor was Brown's assertion that 'several pint-size vials of this Owsley LSD now graced the bookshelves in the sunroom at Kenwood, while others had been converted to more convenient little pink pills, which made their way through the Beatles' inner circle.'[274]

PAISLEY PATTERNS, mandalas and other psychedelic imagery may have brightened popular culture before optimism faded and flower power became passé, but the era also had its share of bandwagoneers – musicians and fans alike – who were content to put on a paisley shirt and some beads and affect to be hippies without fully embracing the lifestyle – the 'day trippers' that Lennon decried in late '65. Groups including the Bee Gees, the Move, Status Quo and the Troggs all surfed the psychedelic wave, discovering their inner dandies and ditching the suits in favour of bright colours, beads and bells. Their music changed too, with elaborate rococo arrangements and florid, seemingly acid-drenched lyrics, often based on some far-out concept or hinting at an enlightened mindset. But it was all too often merely for show, ersatz versions of the psych-pop pioneers.

There were many other people who, lacking the luxury of fortune, fame and freedom, had to conform in order to keep their jobs or status in society. More still simply had no interest in dropping out or experimenting with alternative consciousness. Britain was still socially conservative, and the majority passed through the Sixties without encountering anything stronger than spirits and painkillers. As parts of London continued to swing, the space between the old establishment and young aspirants grew wider. The bemused attitude towards the colourful clothes and wayward music was best summed up by the Queen in August 1967. At an event held at Buckingham Palace she asked one of the guests, EMI's Sir Joseph Lockwood: 'The Beatles are turning awfully *funny*, aren't they?'[275]

Earlier in the year, Lennon and his friend Alexis Mardas – known to the band as Magic Alex – hatched a plan to buy a set of Greek islands where the Beatles could live and work alongside family and friends. All the band except Starr were keen to explore the idea further; he was reluctant to leave England, and suggested they live in a hundred-acre site in Devon instead.

'It was a drug-induced ambition,' said McCartney. 'We'd just be sitting around: "Wouldn't it be great? The lapping water, sunshine, we'd be playing. We'd get a studio there. Well, it's possible these days with mobiles and…" We had lots of ideas like that. The whole Apple enterprise was the result of those ideas.'[276]

According to Peter Brown, Mardas struck a deal with the Greek authorities ahead of an exploratory trip to the islands. If the Beatles were given VIP treatment at the airport and exempted from bag searches, they would pose for publicity photographs for the Greek ministry of tourism. This deal, effectively giving the group diplomatic immunity and allowing them to bring drugs into the country, was agreed without their knowledge. Unfortunately it also often meant that their destinations were broadcast on Athens Radio, causing hordes of fans and journalists to follow them around. As Alistair Taylor noted: 'Once on a trip to a hill village, we came round a corner of the peaceful road only to find hundreds of photographers clicking away at us.'[277]

Shortly after arriving in Athens, Lennon realised he had left his LSD in England. Mardas had no drug contacts in Greece, but the desperate Lennon, for whom it was by now unthinkable to go away without a supply, demanded he fix the problem. Mardas was worried that his phone line was being monitored, and cautiously spoke to Mal Evans in London. 'John isn't well, Mal. You've got to come to Greece and bring his medicine.' When Evans failed to pick up on the cryptic message, Mardas made it slightly more explicit: 'You know, the medicine for his acidity…'[278] The next day Evans boarded a plane for Greece, and Lennon was reunited with his beloved LSD.

On 26 July Lennon, McCartney and Harrison were taken to the main island they were thinking of buying – often referred to as Leslo, although no island of that name appears to exist. 'We rented a boat and sailed it up and down the coast from Athens, looking at islands,' Harrison recalled. 'Somebody had said we should invest some money, so we thought: "Well, let's buy an island. We'll just go there and drop out". It was a great trip. John and I were on acid all the time, sitting on the front of the ship playing ukuleles. Greece was on the left; a big island on the right. The sun was shining and we sang Hare Krishna for hours and hours.'[279]

The Beatles spent the early part of the day island-hopping, swimming, sunbathing and taking drugs. 'We went on the boat and sat around and took acid,' said McCartney. 'We went out there and thought, We've done it now. That was it for a couple of weeks. Great, wasn't it? Now we don't need it. Having been out there, I don't think we needed to go back. Probably the best way to not buy a Greek island is to go out there for a bit.'[280]

His pragmatic approach overruled Lennon's more impulsive nature. 'It's a good job we didn't do it,' McCartney concluded, 'because anyone who tried those ideas realised eventually there would always be arguments, there would always be who has to do the washing-up and whose turn it is to clean out the latrines. I don't think any of us were thinking of that.'[281]

Three months earlier, a *coup d'état* had taken place in which the Greek military junta seized power, established a dictatorship and immediately curtailed press freedom and an array of civil liberties. Political parties and demonstrations were banned, surveillance was widespread, and police brutality became commonplace. More than six thousand suspected communists and political activists were imprisoned or exiled, and torture was routinely used against opponents of the state. Oddly, however, the junta continued to allow its citizens access to Western films and music. Tourism was encouraged, a vibrant holiday destination nightlife developed, and a hippie colony on the island of Crete was left undisturbed. The Beatles either chose to overlook the actions of the police state they were thinking of entering, or were naive about the suffering of the Greek people.

While much of the West bathed in sunshine during the Summer of Love, peace and love were in short supply in other parts of the world. The Six-Day War broke out in the Middle East just days after *Sgt Pepper*'s release, and there were bloody conflicts in Vietnam, Aden, Guatemala, Oman, Mozambique, North Yemen and Rhodesia. Anti-establishment riots in Hong Kong grew into full-scale demonstrations against British colonial rule, and the summer of 1967 saw 159 race riots across the United States, the most serious of which took place in July in Newark and Detroit. Revolution was in the air, although it took several more months for the Beatles to recalibrate. For some months they were content to protest using more abstract, indirect methods.

'We felt obviously that Vietnam was wrong,' said George Harrison. 'I think any war is wrong, for that matter – and in some of our lyrics we expressed those feelings and tried to *be* the counterculture, to try and wake up as many people as we could to the fact that you don't have to fight. You can call a halt to war and you can have a laugh and dress up silly and that's what that period was all about: get your hair long, and grow a moustache, and paint your house psychedelic, and write songs. It was all part of our retaliation against the evil that was taking place and still is taking place.'[282]

THE BEATLES only openly acknowledged their drug use after the release of *Sgt Pepper*. The 16 June 1967 issue of *Life* magazine carried a feature by Thomas Thompson headlined 'The New Far-Out Beatles'. The article was intended to reveal the band's current attitudes to fame, philosophy and music to a public that had seen relatively little of them during the long sessions for *Sgt Pepper*, and to shine a light on their changed lives.

'Sure, we're going to lose some fans,' McCartney told Thompson. 'We lost them in Liverpool when we took off our leather jackets and put on suits. But there's no point in standing still… We've reached the point now where there are no barriers. Musically, now, this moment, tonight, this is where we are.'[283]

Thompson described McCartney as being 'deeply committed to the possibilities of LSD as a universal cure-all.'

'After I took it, it opened my eyes,' he said. 'We only use one tenth of our brain. Just think what we could accomplish if we could only tap that hidden part! It would mean a whole new world. If the politicians would take LSD, there wouldn't be any more war, or poverty or famine.'

It was but a small part of the *Life* interview. The effect, however, was explosive. Although McCartney didn't directly say that the Beatles had taken LSD, the implication was clear. Controversy engulfed the group once the article reached the newsstands, and his words were rebroadcast and analysed around the world.

On 19 June, the day after his 25th birthday, McCartney was doorstepped by a television crew from Independent Television News. He agreed to be interviewed in his garden at 7 Cavendish Avenue.

'I remember a couple of men from ITN showed up, and then the newscaster arrived: "Is it true you've had drugs?" They were at my door – I couldn't tell them to go away – so I thought, "Well, I'm either going to try to bluff this, or I'm going to tell him the truth." I made a lightning decision: "Sod it. I'll give them the truth."

'I spoke to the reporter beforehand, and said, "You know what's going to happen here: I'm going to get the blame for telling everyone I take drugs. But you're the people who are going to distribute the news." I said, "I'll tell you. But if you've got any worries about the news having an effect on kids, then don't show it. I'll tell you the truth, but if you disseminate the whole thing to the public then it won't be my responsibility. I'm not sure I want to preach this but, seeing as you're asking – yeah, I've taken LSD." I'd had it about four times at that stage, and I told him so. I felt it was reasonable, but it became a big news item.'[284]

The interview, broadcast later that evening, showed McCartney defiant and unrepentant:

> *ITN: Have you taken LSD?*
> *McCARTNEY: About four times.*
> *ITN: And where did you get it from?*
> *McCARTNEY: Well, you know, I mean, if I was to say*
> *where I got it from, you know, it's illegal and*
> *everything. It's silly to say that.*
> *ITN: Don't you believe that this is a matter which you*
> *should have kept private?*
> *McCARTNEY: Well the thing is, I was asked a question*
> *by a newspaper, and the decision was whether to tell a*
> *lie or to tell him the truth. I decided to tell him the*
> *truth, but I really didn't want to say anything,*
> *because if I had my decision, if I had my way I*
> *wouldn't have told anyone 'cause I'm not trying to*
> *spread the word about this. But the man from the*
> *newspaper is the man from the mass medium. I'll*
> *keep it a personal thing if he does too, if he keeps it*
> *quiet. But he wanted to spread it so it's his*
> *responsibility for spreading it, not mine.*

> *ITN: But you're a public figure and you said it in the first place, and you must have known it would have made the newspapers.*
>
> *McCARTNEY: Yeah, but to say it is only to tell the truth. I'm telling the truth, you know? I don't know what everyone's so angry about.*
>
> *ITN: Do you think that you have now encouraged your fans to take drugs?*
>
> *McCARTNEY: I don't think it'll make any difference. I don't think my fans are going to take drugs just 'cause I did. But the thing is, that's not the point anyway. I was asked whether I had or not, and then from then on, the whole bit about how far it's gonna go and how many people it's going to encourage is up to the newspapers, and up to you on television. I mean you're spreading this now, at this moment. This is going into all the homes in Britain, and I'd rather it didn't. But you're asking me the question. You want me to be honest; I'll be honest.*
>
> *ITN: But as a public figure, surely you've got the responsibility to not* −
>
> *McCARTNEY: No, it's you who've got the responsibility. You've got the responsibility not to spread this now. I'm quite prepared to keep it as a very personal thing if you will too. If you'll shut up about it, I will.*

McCartney's protestations, though undoubtedly well intended, were at best disingenuous. As one of the most famous men on the planet, whose words and actions had been pored over for the past four years, he would have been only too aware of the weight his comments would carry. Inviting a reporter and camera onto his property and going on the record about his drug use, then accusing them of spreading his words, betrays at the very least a wilful ignorance of journalism. If McCartney had truly wished 'to keep it as a very personal thing' he had the means to do so, and to blame reporters for its dissemination was a weak excuse.

The Beatles formed a united front. 'I never felt any responsibility, being a so-called idol,' Lennon told Hunter Davies. 'It's wrong of people to expect it. What they are doing is putting their responsibilities on us, as Paul said to the newspapers when he admitted taking LSD. If they were worried about him being responsible, they should have been responsible enough and not printed it, if they were genuinely worried about people copying.'[285]

McCartney called Brian Epstein to warn him about the ITN interview, and the manager – for whom anxiety was a near-constant companion – endured a sleepless night before concluding that honesty was the best strategy and that he, too, should publicly admit to taking LSD. 'There were several reasons for this,' he told the *Melody Maker*. 'One was certainly to make things easier for Paul. People don't particularly enjoy being lone wolves; and I didn't feel like being dishonest and covering up, especially as I believe that an awful lot of good has come from hallucinatory drugs.' Epstein told the paper he had used acid 'about five times in the last 14 months', and that he was unsure whether he would take it again.

Epstein also spoke of how LSD had lessened his anger and tempered his ego. 'The feeling is too impressive and personal to convey in words. I know that I have sometimes had too much to drink and felt awful and unpleasant the day after. But I have never had a hangover from smoking pot or taking LSD. I think LSD helped me to know myself better, and I think it helped me to become less bad tempered.'[286]

Lennon and Harrison showed solidarity by admitting that they too had used the drug, although they gave no indication of the extent. Harrison, however, later expressed doubt over the way the message was conveyed. 'I thought Paul should have been quiet about it,' he said. 'I wish he hadn't said anything, because it made everything messy. People were bugging us about it for ages. Somebody must have heard a rumour and then gone to ask him about it. It seemed strange to me, because we'd been trying to get him to take LSD for about eight months – and then one day he's on the television talking about it.'[287]

Lennon also suggested that McCartney, the most infrequent user of LSD in the band, had made the announcement to bolster his underground credentials: 'At that time he wanted to be hip, and not square, because he was such a fucking square. He wanted to show he was with everyone.'[288]

The fallout from Epstein's confession was private as well as public. Cilla Black, the former Cavern Club cloakroom attendant who became a singer under his tutelage, was furious and feared that she would be tarred with the same brush. Relations between the two had been deteriorating for several months, with Black becoming resentful that Epstein was not paying her enough attention; now, in her eyes, he appeared to be damaging his reputation, and bringing his clients down with him.

The 19 July 1967 edition of *Queen* magazine carried a feature by Nik Cohn titled The Love Generation. It quoted various leading show business figures on their opinions regarding drugs – among them McCartney, Epstein, Eric Clapton and Donovan. The magazine was seen by Home Office minister Alice Bacon, who quoted from it during a parliamentary debate on soft drugs on 28 July: 'I believe that at present we are in danger in this country – I am not speaking only of cannabis but also of some other drugs which have been mentioned, particularly LSD – of some people misleading young people by not only taking drugs themselves, but trying to influence the minds of young people and trying to encourage them to take drugs.

'I do not often read the magazine *Queen*,' she continued, 'but I was at the hairdresser's yesterday. This magazine was passed to me to while away the time when I was under the hair dryer. There is a very long article in it called The Love Generation with statements by various people who are pop singers and managers of pop groups. I was horrified at some of the things I read in it. For instance, Paul McCartney says among other things: "God is in everything. God is in the space between us. God is in that table in front of you. God is everything and everywhere and everyone. It just happens that I realised all this through acid, but it could have been through anything. It really does not matter how I made it… The final result is all that counts."'

Bacon went on to quote Epstein from the article. 'The manager of the Beatles said in this article that there is a new mood in the country and: "This new mood has originated from hallucinatory drugs and I am wholeheartedly on its side." The only person with any sense at all quoted in the article seems to be a little pop singer called Lulu, who said: "People talk about this love, love, love thing as if you had to be on drugs before you can be part of it. In fact, love is far older than pot and goes right back to Jesus. I'm a believer." This may sound amusing to honourable members, but young people take quite seriously what pop stars say. What sort of society will we create if everyone wants to escape from reality?'[289]

Shares in Northern Songs fell sixpence during the controversy. Two of the three stockbrokers who dealt in the shares stated a belief that the fall was connected to McCartney's confession. The *Queen* article also prompted a reaction from American evangelist Billy Graham, who was in Britain to make a religious film with Christian singer Cliff Richard. Dr Graham said that he was praying for McCartney. 'My heart goes out to him. He has reached the top of his profession and now he is searching for the true purpose of life. But he will not find it through taking LSD. There is only one way and that is through real Christian experience.'[290]

ANOTHER PERSON willing to talk about getting closer to God

through LSD was George Harrison. Unlike McCartney, however, his dedication was genuine, enduring and plentiful.

'Up until LSD,' Harrison told *Rolling Stone* in 1987, 'I had never realised that there was anything beyond this state of consciousness. But all the pressure was such that, like the man said, "There must be some way out of here."

'I think for me it was definitely LSD. The first time I took it, it just blew everything away. I had such an overwhelming feeling of well-being, that there was a God, and I could see him in every blade of grass. It was like gaining hundreds of years of experience within twelve hours. It changed me, and there was no way back to what I was before. It wasn't all good, because it left a lot of questions as well. And we still had to continue being fab, you know? And now with that added perspective. It wasn't easy!'[291]

His spiritual journey began in April 1965, while filming the Indian restaurant scene in *Help!* at Twickenham Film Studios. 'There were a few Indian musicians playing in the background,' he said. 'I remember picking up the sitar and trying to hold it and thinking, "This is a funny sound." It was an incidental thing, but somewhere down the line I began to hear Ravi Shankar's name. The third time I heard it, I thought, "This is an odd coincidence." And then I talked with David Crosby of the Byrds and he mentioned the name. I went and bought a Ravi record; I put it on and it hit a certain spot in me that I can't explain, but it seemed very familiar to me. The only way I could describe it was: my intellect didn't know what was going on and yet this other part of me identified with it.'[292]

Harrison's fascination with India began just weeks after the Dental Experience. A direct line can be drawn between the two incidents. Harrison realised that other worlds existed beyond the one he had known; that neurological and psychological doorways could be thrown open; and that a higher spiritual plane, beyond the thrills of sex, music and fame, could be within reach.

'With the after-effects of the LSD that opened something up

inside me in 1966, a flood of other thoughts came into my head, which led me to the yogis,' he said in 1987. 'At that time it was very much my desire to find out. It still is, though I have found out a lot. I've gone through the period of questioning and being answered, and I feel I've got to the point where there isn't anything really that I need to know.'[293]

Like Lennon, Harrison recognised the Dental Experience as a turning point. He remained intrigued by LSD after the second trip in Los Angeles, and took the drug again upon their return to Britain. 'The third time I did it with a guy in England,' he recalled, 'and I thought "Ooh, I can't do this anymore, this is too much." I had a slight fear of it, as well. Then I was into India and meditating and all that, and after that I realised so many things, and one of the things I'd heard about was fear. They said, "Look fear in the face and it won't bother you anymore." So I thought, well, I really do have a bit of a fear left over from this acid stuff, and I can't go through the rest of my life fearing it, so I'd better take it again.'[294]

Harrison later claimed that the shared experience of LSD brought him and Lennon closer. In the Beatles' earliest days he had been treated almost as a younger brother within the band, but the drug proved to be a leveller. 'After taking acid together, John and I had a very interesting relationship. That I was younger or I was smaller was no longer any kind of embarrassment with John… John and I spent a lot of time together from then on and I felt closer to him than all the others, right through until his death. As Yoko came into the picture, I lost a lot of personal contact with John; but on the odd occasion I did see him, just by the look in his eyes I felt we were connected.'[295]

This wasn't just a drug-infused camaraderie, however. According to Harrison it lasted beyond the peak of the Beatles' LSD period, and was particularly evident during their time in Rishikesh in 1968. Of the group, he and Lennon were the most committed to Transcendental Meditation, remaining in India after the others' interest waned.

'The very first time we took LSD, John and I were together,' Harrison recalled in 1987. 'And that experience together, and a lot of other things that happened after that, both on LSD and on the meditation trip in Rishikesh – we saw beyond each other's physical bodies, you know? That's there permanently, whether he's in a physical body or not.'[296]

Cynthia Lennon noticed the positive changes in Harrison's personality. 'Previous to George's experiences with LSD and the subsequent flower power explosion, he had been the most tactless, blunt and often pig-headed of the four Beatles,' she said. 'George of course was the youngest and least mature, but to me he was the one Beatle who altered most in character and temperament over the years. He grew up very quickly, changing from a tactless youth into a sensitive, thinking individual. The rough edges were smoothed down and self-discipline became the cornerstone of his character. This was never more evident than in India.'[297]

For a time, Harrison was as infatuated as Lennon with LSD. 'I think George was pretty heavy on it,' Lennon said in 1970. 'We were probably both the most cracked.' However, while Lennon's use declined after he began to suffer psychological damage, Harrison largely stopped when it ceased to provide the thrills and promise it once had.

'We just seemed to be taking it all year, down at John's house, round at Ringo's house, and I got to the point where I could drive this Ferrari around Hyde Park in peak hour traffic on acid and it wasn't working anymore. All it did was give me a pain in the neck ... The good stuff – the carpet flying up in the room and the chairs getting bigger and smaller, all that Roman Polanski movie stuff – stopped happening after I started to understand more about relativity and time and space. The fun had gone out of it, so I stopped doing it.'[298]

The turning point came on 7 August 1967, during a Californian holiday George and Pattie took with Alexis Mardas and Neil Aspinall. On their penultimate day they went to see Pattie's sister Jenny Boyd, who was living in San Francisco. While there they decided to visit the city's hippie district of Haight-Ashbury, which McCartney had been to that April.

On the journey they took LSD, which began to take effect as they arrived. They left the car and began exploring the neighbourhood on foot. The Harrisons were a striking pair, even among the beautiful people of San Francisco: Pattie wore beads, a minidress with kaleidoscopic red, yellow and orange swirls, pink sandals and round sunglasses, while George had on a blue denim jacket, psychedelic red and brown trousers, moccasins and heart-shaped sunglasses.

As they went inside a shop they noticed they had attracted a following. 'They had recognised George as we walked past them in the street, then turned to follow us,' said Pattie. 'One minute there were five, then 10, 20, 30 and 40 people behind us. I could hear them saying, "The Beatles are here, the Beatles are in town!"'[299]

For Harrison the area was far from the hippie utopia he had anticipated. 'I went there expecting it to be a brilliant place, with groovy gypsy people making works of art and paintings and carvings in little workshops. But it was full of horrible spotty drop-out kids on drugs, and it turned me right off the whole scene. I could only describe it as being like the Bowery: a lot of bums and drop-outs; many of them very young kids who'd dropped acid and come from all over America to this mecca of LSD.'[300]

As more and more people gathered, those at the centre began to feel the burden of expectation upon them. 'They were so close behind us they were treading on the backs of our heels,' said Pattie. 'It got to the point where we couldn't stop for fear of being trampled. Then somebody said, "Let's go to Hippie Hill," and we crossed the grass, our retinue facing us, as if we were on stage. They looked at us expectantly − as if George was some kind of Messiah.

'We were so high, and then the inevitable happened: a guitar emerged from the crowd and I could see it being passed to the front by outstretched arms. I thought, Oh, God, poor George, this is a nightmare. Finally the guitar was handed to him. I had the feeling that they'd listened to the Beatles' records, analysed them, learnt what they'd thought they should learn, and taken every drug they'd thought the Beatles were singing about. Now they wanted to know where to go next. And George was there, obviously, to give them the answer. Pressure.'[301]

Photographs from the day show a happy and harmonious scene with little indication of tension. Harrison, cigarette in mouth and wearing his heart-shaped sunglasses, sat strumming chords on an acoustic guitar, surrounded by smiling and clapping onlookers. He also played while walking, flanked by his wife, Taylor and Mardas, and trailed by a crowd of followers.

As they moved on he was offered some STP, a powerful hallucinogenic which had become infamous after five thousand high-dosage tablets had been given away weeks earlier at the Summer Solstice Celebration in Golden Gate Park. The delayed onset of its effects meant a number of users had taken extra hits and ended up in hospital.[302]

Harrison declined the STP, but his response was seen as a snub. 'I could see all the spotty youths,' he recalled, 'but I was seeing them from a twisted angle. It was like the manifestation of a scene from an Hieronymus Bosch painting, getting bigger and bigger, fish with heads, faces like vacuum cleaners coming out of shop doorways... They were handing me things – like a big Indian pipe with feathers on it, and books and incense – and trying to give me drugs. I remember saying to one guy: "No thanks, I don't want it." And then I heard his whining voice saying, "Hey, man – you put me down." It was terrible. We walked quicker and quicker through the park and in the end we jumped in the limo, said, "Let's get out of here," and drove back to the airport.'[303]

The crowd began to grow hostile as they returned to the limousine, and those outside began rocking the vehicle as their faces pressed against the windows. The narrow escape increased Harrison's resolve to move away from LSD.

'That was the turning point for me – that's when I went right off the whole drug cult and stopped taking the dreaded lysergic acid. I had some in a little bottle – it was liquid. I put it under a microscope, and it looked like bits of old rope. I thought that I couldn't put that into my brain any more.

'People were making concoctions that were really wicked – ten times stronger than LSD. STP was one; it took its name from the fuel additive used in Indy-car racing. Mama Cass Elliot phoned us up and said, "Watch out, there's this new one going round called STP." I never took it. They concocted weird mixtures and the people in Haight-Ashbury got really fucked-up. It made me realise: "This is not it." And that's when I really went for the meditation.'[304]

The Beatles' use of LSD declined during the Summer of Love. On 25 August 1967, they travelled to Bangor in north Wales to study Transcendental Meditation. The next day they were among 300 people attending an introductory seminar given by Maharishi Mahesh Yogi. Afterwards he joined the Beatles for a press conference, during which the band stated their belief in meditation.

They also renounced drugs, although in truth the claim was largely spurious. McCartney spoke on behalf of the group: 'You cannot keep on taking drugs forever. You get to the stage where you are taking 15 aspirins a day, without having a headache. We were looking for something more natural. This is it. It was an experience we went through. Now it's over and we don't need it any more. We think we're finding other ways of getting there.'[305]

Shortly afterwards, Harrison gave an interview to the *Melody Maker* in which he chiefly discussed drugs, meditation and religion. 'A hippie is supposed to be someone who becomes aware,' he said. 'You're hip if you know what's going on. But if you're really hip you don't get involved with LSD and things like that. You see the potential that it has and the good that can come from it, but you also see that you don't really need it.'

The interview also contained the first recorded reference to the Dental Experience. 'I needed it the first time I ever had it. Actually, I didn't know that I'd had it. I'd never even heard of it then. This is something that just hasn't been told. Everybody now knows that we've had it, but the circumstances were that somebody just shoved it in our coffee before we'd ever heard of the stuff. So we happened to have it quite unaware of the fact.

'I don't mind telling people I've had it. I'm not embarrassed. It makes no difference because I know that I didn't actually go out and try to get some. For me, it was a good thing but it showed me that LSD isn't really the answer to everything. It can help you go from A to B, but when you get to B, you see C. And you see that to get really high, you have to do it straight. There are special ways of getting high without drugs – with yoga, meditation and all those things. So this was the disappointing thing about LSD.'[306]

LSD continued to influence Harrison until the Beatles' final days. The last song they recorded, I Me Mine, was written by Harrison about revelations regarding the ego that he had discovered through tripping. 'Suddenly I looked around and everything I could see was relative to my ego, like "that's my piece of paper" and "that's my flannel" or "give it to me" or "I am". It drove me crackers, I hated everything about my ego, it was a flash of everything false and impermanent, which I disliked. But later, I learned from it, to realise that there is somebody else in here apart from old blabbermouth. Who am "I" became the order of the day. Anyway, that's what came out of it, I Me Mine. The truth within us has to be realised. When you realise that, everything else that you see and do and touch and smell isn't real, then you may know what reality is, and can answer the question "Who am I?"'[307]

THE INNER LIGHT | 155

THE ONE BEATLE who seemed wary of publicly discussing his drug use was Ringo Starr. A devoted family man during the 1960s, Starr had the lowest drug consumption of all the Beatles. He was happy to smoke cannabis and drop acid with his bandmates, but proved reluctant to discuss it in public. His wife Maureen never took LSD, and cigarettes and Scotch were the main drugs of choice in the Starkey household.

Pete Shotton, who had been elevated to co-manager of the Apple Boutique, credited Starr with reining in his bandmates' more fanciful ideas, providing them with some much-needed clear-headedness, particularly after the death of Brian Epstein. 'The Beatles' plodding and unassuming drummer often seemed – during the heady days of that Summer of Love – to be the one member of the group whose feet were still firmly planted on the ground,' he said. 'Their public disavowal of LSD notwithstanding, the ambitions of John, Paul, and George were to turn increasingly grandiose and utopian – especially after the sudden departure of the one person who'd formerly been able to keep the Beatles more or less in line.'[308]

When *Life* magazine broke the news of the Beatles advocating LSD, Starr kept his opinions mostly private. 'In those days, we felt everyone should be doing it,' he said in *Anthology*. 'I felt they should all be smoking grass and taking acid. I was twenty-seven years old and that's what I was doing. It was the drug of love – love towards our fellow man or woman.'[309]

In 1977, during more turbulent times, Starr was interviewed at his Hollywood home by Elliot Mintz; the results were first broadcast on the syndicated radio show Inner-View. Asked about his use of psychedelic drugs, Starr reacted defensively.

'I didn't go any further than acid,' he said. 'It was very important at the beginning. And the first time I took it was in Los Angeles. I mean, I never talk about this shit. It's like religion or politics, it's nothing to do with you or anyone else out there, okay? I've taken several substances into my body. And that's it, get off my back. I won't talk about it. I don't think it's anything to do with you. I mean, I started on acid, I think it was very important at the time, I'm glad I took it. I don't ask anyone else to take it because I took it – because that's the problem we have. And I don't want someone else's brain on my brain if they damage it.'[310]

He had been more forthcoming in a *Melody Maker* interview published in December 1967. He saw drugs as having had a positive influence on pop music, saying: 'It made a lot of difference to the type of music and the words. It gave one more scope and other things to talk about. The words were relevant to a lot of people. Some get it but others didn't and they just mentioned certain things. It's been a good experience for everybody, because it's brought out new styles and a lot of people who weren't getting anywhere came out and said it and they got somewhere.'

He did, however, indicate a hope that young people would not try to emulate the Beatles' drug use. 'I hope not,' he said, 'but by all reports, some of them are. Sometimes it worries me, but people are going to do what you say anyway. If someone else says it, they'll do it. They're just a sillier sort of person.'[311]

Nonetheless, the Beatles remained a major influence on young people. Geoffrey Ellis, the chief executive of NEMS, often fielded calls from fans wishing to meet the group or be given an autograph or memento. On one occasion he took a call from a persistent young man who had recently arrived in England from Canada, who insisted on speaking to Epstein or the Beatles but would not reveal the purpose of his visit. The anti-drugs Ellis reluctantly agreed to meet the man, who finally declared his reason for being in London: 'I've got a lot of LSD for them.'[312]

Ellis immediately called NEMS's solicitor, David Jacobs, who agreed to speak to the Metropolitan Police. Two officers from the drug squad arrived within an hour and promised to investigate, although Ellis heard nothing further. The Beatles and Epstein remained unaware of the incident.

JOHN LENNON'S early LSD experiences lessened his anger and made him more amiable, although the many months of chemical abuse had gradually taken their toll on his body and spirit. His ego destruction had left him with little sense of self, and he often experienced the horror of bad trips. He became a vegetarian but rarely ate, and in a short time his physical and mental health began to suffer. LSD made Lennon listless and fatigued. Paranoid at the prospect of a police raid, he began hiding his acid and pot in the garden at Kenwood.

This decline was rarely seen in public, however, and Lennon's appetite for drink and drugs did not often affect his appearance. As Shotton remembered: 'John always boasted a remarkable tolerance for stimulants and intoxicants of every description.'[313] Yet sometimes the mask slipped. At the launch party for *Sgt Pepper* he looked pale and gaunt, with glazed eyes and slurred speech. A journalist, Ray Coleman of the *Melody Maker*, expressed concern to Epstein at Lennon's physical state. 'Don't worry. He's a survivor,' Coleman was told.[314]

Mike Love of the Beach Boys recalled seeing pictures of Lennon in 1967 which gave him cause for concern: 'One particular time I thought he was very unhappy. This was just before they met Maharishi and I saw a picture of them in the paper and I said: "God, that guy's really in trouble, very unhappy." I felt sorry about it. I even looked at a picture of him one time and I thought he's going to die, or something. I just had this feeling, somehow. And then they met Maharishi and that feeling sort of cleared up.'[315]

Meditation spurred Lennon to greatly reduce his LSD intake, and he discovered for the first time in many months that he was able to enjoy himself without drugs. The harrowing effects of bad trips also contributed to his declining use. 'I had many,' he told *Rolling Stone*. 'I stopped taking it 'cause of that. I mean I just couldn't stand it. I dropped it for I don't know how long. Then I started taking it just before I met Yoko. I got a message on acid that you should destroy your ego, and I did. I was reading that stupid book of Leary's and all that shit. We were going through a whole game that everybody went through. And I destroyed meself. I was slowly putting meself together after Maharishi, bit by bit, over a two-year period. And then I destroyed me ego and I didn't believe I could do anything. I let Paul do what he wanted and say, [let] them all just do what they wanted. And I just was nothing, I was shit.'[316]

Lennon's vituperative *Rolling Stone* interview was conducted in New York City in December 1970, shortly after the completion of his debut solo album *John Lennon/Plastic Ono Band* and his involvement with primal therapy. The album, Lennon's masterpiece, showed the artist stripped bare: in turns paranoid, wounded and angry, railing against targets including fame, the Beatles, religion, drugs, his family and the media. In the interview he was similarly irascible, detailing the many grievances he felt at the disintegration of the Beatles and Apple, and reshaping the band's historical narrative in the wake of the split.

He later expressed bitterness at the slapdash approach he felt the other Beatles had given his songs when he was feeling mentally diminished. Paul McCartney, in particular, was targeted for sabotaging Lennon's compositions at a time when he was unable to fight his corner. 'He subconsciously tried to destroy songs, meaning that we'd play experimental games with my great pieces, like Strawberry Fields – which I always felt was badly recorded. That song got away with it and it worked. But usually we'd spend hours doing little detailed cleaning-ups of Paul's songs; when it came to mine, especially if it was a great song like Strawberry Fields or Across The Universe, somehow this atmosphere of looseness and casualness and experimentation would creep in. Sub-conscious sabotage. *He'll* deny it 'cause he's got a bland face and he'll say the sabotage doesn't exist. But this is the kind of thing I'm talking about, where I was always *seeing* what was going on... I began to think, Well maybe I'm paranoid. But it's *not* paranoid; it's *absolute* truth.

'The same thing happened to Across The Universe. It was a *lousy* track of a great song and I was so disappointed by it... The guitars are out of tune and I'm singing out of tune 'cause I'm psychologically destroyed and nobody's supporting me or helping me with it and the song was never done properly.'[317]

ON 15 FEBRUARY 1968, John and Cynthia Lennon, George and Pattie Harrison, and Pattie's younger sister Jenny Boyd travelled to Maharishi Mahesh Yogi's ashram in Rishikesh, India, to study Transcendental Meditation. They were joined a few days later by McCartney, Jane Asher and the Starkeys, along with their assistants and dozens of uninvited reporters. The Beatles arrived more than two weeks after the beginning of the meditation course, which was attended by 70 other students and was scheduled to end on 27 April. Other celebrities in Rishikesh at the time included Donovan, Mike Love and actress Mia Farrow.

No drugs or alcohol were allowed during the spiritual retreat, and swapping medication for meditation gave the Beatles several weeks of total sobriety, for the first time in many years. The relative calm of India took the band away from the public eye, allowing them a temporary escape from the problems with the ailing Apple Boutique, continued press speculation over the future of the group, and the writing-recording-release cycle of creation.

The experience was not, however, a happy one for John and Cynthia. Having reluctantly put his drug usage on hold, he became intoxicated by thoughts of Yoko Ono, who wrote almost daily to the intrigued Beatle. Each morning, unknown to his wife, Lennon would walk to the post office to check for letters from Ono. Cynthia had hoped that their stay in India would bring back their lost closeness, but it was not to be. Lennon was aloof, only occasionally speaking to her, and in their second week in Rishikesh moved into a separate bedroom. For the rest of their stay they barely communicated.

Ono was largely uninterested in the teachings of Maharishi, and her continuing communications helped Lennon retain some semblance of normality, even hope. He certainly found her more interesting than learning about cosmic consciousness. 'We had a kind of romantic exchange of letters when I was in India. She started telling me I was the only one who could solve my problems. Yoko gradually brought me back to a sense of realism. She wasn't impressed at all by this mysticism thing. She went through a vague period of pretending to do it but she thought it was all very phoney.'[318]

Back in Weybridge, meanwhile, remnants of his previous world were close to the surface. 'While we were in India my mother had found a stash of LSD he'd hidden at home,' Cynthia said, 'and had flushed it down the loo. When he discovered what she'd done he was furious, but he couldn't confront her without admitting that he used it, so he had to keep quiet.'[319]

Lennon left Rishikesh on the morning of 12 April 1968. He had become disillusioned with one guru he thought could reveal the mysteries of life, only to fall back on another one: LSD. He was also back to his old skirt-chasing ways. At the end of the month he and Derek Taylor accepted an invitation to meet French actress Brigitte Bardot, the object of many of the Beatle's teenage fantasies, who was staying at a London hotel.

Lennon asked Taylor for something to smoke to ease his anxiety. The press officer only had some LSD, so they shared a small pink microdot pill at the Apple offices on Wigmore Street. As they prepared to leave, a staffer from one of the Apple shops popped in to see if they had anything to smoke. 'We told him we had a little acid,' recalled Taylor. 'He said he'd already had a little of that.' Even at this early stage the Apple empire was teetering on the cusp of chaos.

Taylor made his way up to Bardot's hotel room, while Lennon, fearful of being spotted, crouched on the floor of his Rolls-Royce outside. Inside the suite Taylor found Bardot dressed in black leather, looking every inch a star, and accompanied by a handful of female companions. She expressed disappointment that the other Beatles had not come; Taylor, his brain befuddled with the acid, gibbered something about being in danger and being watched. Bardot was utterly perplexed, but nonetheless invited the two men inside.

A restaurant table was booked for dinner, but Lennon and Taylor were in no fit state to move. 'Suddenly everyone was standing up, ready to go,' Taylor said. 'This was terrible! For a start, neither of us was capable of eating anything at all; we weren't even sure we could stand up … Please don't think us bourgeois, we begged, but we are both married and this is getting out of hand and… oh, Christ. What a mess. Brigitte was not best pleased.'[320] She and her friends left Lennon and Taylor in the hotel room, and were surprised to find them still there when they returned several hours later. Lennon made some amends by playing new White Album songs to Bardot on a guitar, while Taylor slunk off to her bed alone. Shortly afterwards the two men were politely but firmly asked to leave.

A few days later, Taylor and his wife Joan invited Lennon, Pete Shotton and Neil Aspinall to stay overnight at their house in the Surrey countryside. According to Shotton, the property had been used as a hideaway by one of the Great Train Robbers, and that night police officers were monitoring the house from nearby trees, having received a tip-off that the fugitive was planning to return. A reluctance to blow their cover meant that Lennon narrowly avoided his first drugs bust.

After the Taylor children had been put to bed, the partygoers dropped acid, smoked several joints and went rowing on the large lake adjoining the house. Late in the evening, Taylor handed Lennon another tab of LSD, telling him: 'This one's really special. Split it with Pete.' Lennon failed to hear those final four words, and swallowed the entire tab. Taylor, alarmed at the effect such a strong hit might have on even a seasoned LSD user like Lennon, took Shotton aside and told him to look out for Lennon. 'Listen Pete, that's fantastically strong stuff. John is going to go off on one hell of a trip. We'd better stick close by him.'[321]

Taylor's instincts were correct. Lennon noticed the pair looking worried, which fuelled his paranoia. He suffered a bad trip in which his ego was shattered and he became consumed by self doubt. Taylor and Aspinall spent several hours persuading him to recount his life story, reminding him that he was a great artist, and going through Beatles songs line-by-line to demonstrate the extent of his contributions.

'The children woke early next morning and saw him slowly unfolding from a crucifixion stance on the floor, cross-legged and cross-armed and crying like a man, thin as a twig, straggly long hair all over the place,' Taylor recalled.[322] After rowing on the lake, they also wrote a lengthy essay, titled Thoughts On LSD, recounting the reassurances from the night before. 'By the time John and I finally left,' Shotton said, 'John's spirits had been lifted considerably.'[323]

Thoughts On LSD was later given by Taylor to a magazine editor looking for a written contribution from Lennon. She returned it with a note attached which Taylor paraphrased thus: 'I don't know whether you have ever read our magazine or what you could have been thinking of when you enclosed the enclosed, but it is quite unsuitable and indeed unpleasant.'[324] He later conceded that she had a point.

Lennon credited the evening at the Taylors', and a subsequent acid trip with Yoko Ono, for helping him break out of the chronic malaise that had beset him for nearly two years. 'He pointed out which songs I'd written, and said, "You wrote this, and you said this, and you are intelligent, don't be frightened." The next week I went down with Yoko and we tripped out again, and she freed me completely, to realise that I was *me* and it's alright. And that was it. I started fighting again and being a loud-mouth again and saying, "Well, I can do this," and "Fuck you, and this is what I want," and "Don't put me down. I did *this*".'[325]

He returned from the Taylors' house uncharacteristically enthused with family life. 'Christ, Cyn, we've got to have lots more children,' he told his wife. 'We've got to have a big family around us.'[326]

Cynthia, to John's bewilderment, burst into tears. 'All I could blurt out was that in no way could I see us as he did,' she wrote. 'One trip did not guarantee a secure future and it was no use using the promise of a large family to solve our problems. I was so disturbed by John's outburst that I even suggested that Yoko Ono was the woman for him. John protested at my crazy suggestion and said that I was being ridiculous. But nothing he said could dissuade me from my premonitions.'[327]

Lennon's behaviour became ever more unpredictable. In the first week of May, with Cynthia on holiday abroad, he spent an evening with Shotton in his music room at Kenwood. Both took LSD, smoked cannabis and made some experimental recordings. Shortly before dawn they fell into silence, which was eventually punctuated by Lennon's solemn announcement: 'Pete, I think I'm Jesus Christ.' Shotton was more than familiar with his friend's bizarre flights of fancy, but this was a revelation too far. He attempted to pour cold water on Lennon's sudden eagerness to tell the world of his new identity, perhaps mindful of the 'More popular than Jesus' controversy of 1966. 'They'll fucking kill you,' he told Lennon. 'They won't accept that, John.' Lennon grew agitated, telling Shotton that it was his destiny, and that he would inform the other Beatles at Apple.

A board meeting was hastily convened that day, attended by the Beatles, Shotton, Taylor and Aspinall. Lennon opened the meeting by solemnly telling the others that he was the second coming of Jesus. 'Paul, George, Ringo and their closest aides stared back, stunned,' Shotton said. 'Even after regaining their powers of speech, nobody presumed to cross-examine John Lennon, or to make light of his announcement. On the other hand, no specific plans were made for the new Messiah, as all agreed that they would need some time to ponder John's announcement, and to decide upon appropriate further steps.' The meeting came to an abrupt close, and all agreed to go to a restaurant. As they waited to be seated, a fellow diner recognised Lennon and exchanged pleasantries. 'Actually,' Lennon told him, 'I'm Jesus Christ.'

'Oh, really,' the man replied, seemingly unfazed by the news. 'Well, I loved your last record. Thought it was great.'[328]

Back at Kenwood that evening, Lennon and Shotton stayed up smoking cannabis and talking, and Lennon decided to invite Ono over. She arrived shortly after by taxi, and Shotton took himself off to bed. 'My ex-wife was away in Italy,' Lennon said, 'and Yoko came to visit me and we took some acid. I was always shy with her, and she was shy, so instead of making love, we went upstairs and made tapes. I had this room full of different tapes where I would write and make strange loops and things like that for the Beatles' stuff. So we made a tape all night. She was doing her funny voices and I was pushing all different buttons on my tape recorder and getting sound effects. And then as the sun rose we made love and that was *Two Virgins*. That was the first time.'[329]

Speaking in 1971, Lennon framed their early relationship in the context of drug use, evoking LSD and heroin: 'As she was talking to me, I would get high, and the discussion would get to such a level that I would be going higher and higher. And when she'd leave, I'd go back into this sort of suburbia. Then I'd meet her again and my head would go off like I was on an acid trip. And I'd be going over what she'd said, and it was incredible, some of the ideas and the way she was saying them. It was turning me on, you know. And then once I'd got a sniff of it, I was hooked. Then I couldn't leave her alone. We couldn't be apart for a minute from then on.'[330]

Ono's influence on Lennon, and her effect on the Beatles, remains controversial to this day. She did, nonetheless, bring focus to Lennon's life. He was galvanised by her, gaining confidence and embarking on a series of new artistic endeavours. His songwriting temporarily recovered the bite that had been suppressed during much of the Beatles' psychedelic era, and in person – at least temporarily – he recovered some of his natural ebullience and defiance.

Dependency may have been an underlying part of Lennon's personality from an early age, but his peak LSD period appeared to firmly embed personality traits which remained throughout much of the rest of his life. His quest for another kind of mind continued in the hope that each successive lover, guru, chemical, religion, campaign, cause or therapy might provide answers he was looking for. All fell short.

The Beatles necessarily had a reputation as family entertainers to maintain, and couldn't easily put their plans on hold while Lennon sank deeper into drug abuse. They closed ranks and took great care over the group's public image, and his troubles remained largely private. But the band was ultimately felled by forces they were unable to overcome: creative conflicts, overreaching ambition, implacable personal differences, hard drugs, and death.

PART II

4

IF YOU'VE GOT TROUBLE

With the threads of experimentation and excess running throughout the Beatles' story, it is remarkable that there were so few casualties in their inner circle. One key member, however, did not make it.

Brian Epstein took pride in enjoying the finer things in life. He set great store by presenting himself as a gentleman: polite, suave and well spoken. His self-assured manner ensured that he gained the trust of those he dealt with, from the Beatles to record labels, film producers, concert promoters and beyond, as he ascended from Liverpool businessman to pioneering music manager.

Yet there was self-doubt at his core. Since childhood he had suffered from anxiety, loneliness and bullying. During a brief spell in the army he became aware of what he called 'my latent homosexuality', and while training as an actor at RADA in London he was entrapped by an undercover policeman, arrested and charged with 'persistently importuning'.

The experience devastated Epstein. 'I am not sorry for myself,' he wrote as he awaited sentencing. 'My worst times and punishments are over. Now, through the wreckage of my life by society, my being will stain and bring the deepest distress to all my devoted family and few friends. The damage, the lying criminal methods of the police in importuning *me* and consequently capturing me leaves me cold, stunned and finished.'[331]

Epstein dropped out of RADA and returned to the family firm. He was put in charge of the record department at NEMS – North End Music Stores – in Great Charlotte Street, Liverpool. Epstein made a success of NEMS – so much so that in 1959, when the family opened a bigger store at 12-14 Whitechapel, just a short walk from the Cavern Club, he was given control of the entire operation.

By the early 1960s the young people of Liverpool would flock to the store to listen to, and occasionally buy, the latest releases. Although Epstein had little knowledge or interest in the burgeoning rock 'n' roll scene, NEMS had a policy of fulfilling any request, regardless of in which country the record had been released.

He was well known to the UK's four major record companies: EMI, Decca, Pye and Philips. He also became something of a celebrity around Liverpool, recognisable in his immaculate tailored suit, tie, cufflinks and highly polished shoes, and driving a large Ford Zephyr Zodiac. But he led something of a double life.

Epstein had grown to embrace Liverpool's secret gay subculture, taking risks and searching out dangerous encounters. On one occasion he was badly beaten and blackmailed. The police advised him to pretend to go along with the extortion attempt, and the assailant was arrested and imprisoned. Nonetheless it was a humiliating and troubling episode. Although Epstein's sexuality was an open secret to many, he remained ashamed and unhappy, and troubled by the potential risks to his reputation and that of his family.

Epstein's enthusiasm, professionalism and determination endeared him to the Beatles, whom he had first seen at the Cavern in November 1961. For much of the time when they were stomping the boards in Hamburg, he was tramping the streets of London trying to drum up interest in the group from record labels, while continuing to run the Whitechapel store. Epstein often came back to Liverpool feeling dejected at yet another London label's indifference, but his belief in the group kept him buoyant and positive.

'The amphetamine thing started around then,' said Epstein's close friend Peter Brown, who later joined the NEMS empire. 'My personal recollection of it is of having to do more and more because I was running my own shop and helping with Brian's shop when he was not there. I was going to London with Brian being there a lot of the time and it was great fun for me. I was travelling backwards and forwards and there was a lot of lost sleep.

'I was encouraged to take amphetamines and I did. Fortunately, my personality was such that they didn't get me. There's no question that Brian had much more stress than I did, and he was doing it much more and his personality wasn't the same.'[332]

Epstein was particularly close to his mother Queenie, who had been a frequent drug user. 'Brian's mum had been a pill taker,' said McCartney. 'I don't know whether it was for slimming or what. It was probably for anything – slimming, sleeping. His mum Queenie was a very nice lady, always really friendly to us, but I suspect that's where Brian got the pill thing. So Brian would take a pill if he needed to get up, like people who take coffee.'[333]

'He'd take anything,' said the Cavern Club's DJ Bob Wooler, no stranger to pills himself. 'Especially if the Beatles had them. They'd say, "Come on, Bri, be one of the lads, you're too stuffy." The pills didn't make him incapable but sometimes you could see the lesions in his eyes.'[334]

Two years after becoming their manager, Epstein steered the Beatles to America and the rest of the world. Although they enjoyed unprecedented commercial success, critical acclaim and worldwide popularity, the pressures increased commensurately.

He was always working behind the scenes, negotiating publishing and recording contracts, striking merchandise deals, arranging film contracts, checking details of tour itineraries, and a thousand other matters to which the Beatles most likely paid little attention.

Many of the deals struck by Epstein were the first of their kind. Although the Beatles' share was often far lower than it should have been, there was little precedent for what they were doing. Sometimes his ideas paid off, but often they left various third parties with a disproportionately large slice of the pie.

Epstein moved the NEMS operation to London in 1964; by that time it was chiefly a music management and promotions company, with a staff of twenty-five. They also looked after acts including Gerry and the Pacemakers, Cilla Black, Billy J Kramer and the Dakotas, Tommy Quickly, and Sounds Incorporated.

The level of detail was quite something, as NEMS's Alistair Taylor recalled: 'From day one in management all our artists had to have gig sheets which told them the date of the gig, where the band were playing, who the contact was, what equipment was being supplied, how many electrical points there were, what time they were supposed to be there, which hotel they were staying in, and so on.'[335] Although Epstein was paid handsomely for his efforts – often earning far more than the artists he represented – in a short space of time he became unable to give each of his acts sufficient attention.

But his life was more than just work. 'Brian was partying all the time,' recalled George Harrison. 'In fact if you were in London and looking for somewhere to go, you could always drop round his place. He was a bundle of fun, enjoyed his Rolls-Royces and being the toast of London. Brian was a friend and most times was great… we all helped each other out of a jam. We gave him drink and drugs, he gave us his Zephyr Zodiac and his friendship.'[336]

Being newly rich and in charge of pop music's biggest superstars left Epstein as an open target for various hustlers and blackmailers. And although he continued to keep his professional and personal lives separate, the threat of exploitation was present in both. 'Today there is another factor in my placing with other people,' he acknowledged in his 1964 autobiography, ghostwritten by Derek Taylor. 'I wield a certain amount of what, for want of a better word, is described as power. This in turn brings other problems because it is no longer easy to know whether I am wanted for what I am or for what I am supposed to have in terms of material goods or power. In other words – do people want me or do they want the Beatles through me?'[337]

'A lot of trouble came from being mucked about and blackmailed – if indeed he was really blackmailed,' said Taylor. 'He was certainly mucked about and thrown about a few rooms. This was a repeat pattern which he brought on by living too dangerously and drinking too much and there were quite a few pills knocking about.'[338]

Among his employees Epstein soon became known for his explosive and unpredictable temper. Firings and resignations were not uncommon, although many were rescinded – sometimes just minutes later – when he calmed down. On one occasion he sacked the entire staff of NEMS over the phone due to some perceived transgression.

Staff learnt to recognise his capriciousness and not to take his firings too seriously, although his mood swings inevitably cast a shadow over the company. Derek Taylor really did quit in 1964 after one too many arguments with Epstein; the pair later became friends, but never again worked together.

Although he never found a permanent partner, Epstein grew close to an American lover named John 'Diz' Gillespie, whom he brought back to England for a time. Although Gillespie initially made Epstein happy, which in turn improved the atmosphere at home and at NEMS, it was not an equal partnership. Gillespie brought back male and female lovers, argued with him and stole from the house.

Epstein faced a war on two key fronts: in addition to his turbulent personal life, he became embroiled in a drawn-out legal dispute with Seltaeb, the company which handled Beatles merchandising licences in America. The case took its toll on Epstein, who was ordered to pay legal costs when Seltaeb's founder Nicky Byrne countersued and won. The deal had given Byrne's companies the lion's share of income from Beatles merchandise, leaving just 10 per cent for NEMS and the band. The court case took three years to settle, and was finally concluded in January 1967, much to Epstein's relief.

He continued to sign up musical acts, though with decreasing success, and took over the lease for the Saville Theatre on London's Shaftesbury Avenue. He bought a town-house in Belgravia, a country retreat in Surrey, and a Rolls-Royce Phantom Five. He also developed a love of gambling, sometimes losing thousands in one sitting. But he remained financially solvent and continued living well, employing a house-keeper, cook, butler, chauffeur and personal assistant.

EPSTEIN HAD USED stimulants almost as long as he had known the Beatles. His taste for brandy and whisky often tipped over into heavy drinking, and he too became enthralled by cannabis after the Dylan confab in New York. Two years later, in the winter of 1966, he tried LSD.

His first trip was with Peter Brown, who was at Epstein's home in Chapel Street when the delivery arrived. Brown took the acid while Epstein was out of the room, and the manager insisted that he too be given a dose. They stayed in the house, a controlled and safe environment, and were later joined by Klaus Voormann and Gibson Kemp. According to Brown, Epstein 'enjoyed the experience so much that he immediately took another dose upon waking up on Sunday afternoon. I felt no regret that I had given Brian his first acid but did regret that he chose to do it so frequently and incautiously.'[339]

Epstein's often reckless drug use was becoming well known among his friends and associates. 'He secured drugs from a number of sources, both in America and this country,' said NEMS's Geoffrey Ellis. 'I was, of course, aware that he was taking drugs. He never referred to his drug-taking to me personally. Thinking back on it, I'm very glad that he didn't, because it does show that our relationship at least was one which did not involve this type of behaviour.'[340]

However, he wasn't always prepared to maintain clean lines, especially where the Beatles were concerned. On one occasion he was taken to McCartney's house by his chauffeur, Bryan Barrett, who was later sent out to collect a package from Archer Street in Soho. 'They gave me an address that was an old Peabody Trust type building,' Barrett recalled, 'so I asked a policeman if he could help me out since the Phantom Five was such a bloody great thing. I said, I'll only be a couple of minutes. I've just got to go collect a package down there. It's all set up. So up I went to collect this package. I came down with it, threw it in the car, off I went. When I got to Piccadilly, I was sniffing and I could smell it was grass. I thought, Christ, and I [had] asked a policeman to look after the car.'

Barrett brought the package to Cavendish Avenue, where he confronted Epstein. 'I told him, "Don't ever do that to me again. I've got three children and I don't want to go to prison. I don't want to get pulled for that."'[341] Epstein assured Barrett that he would have been given a lawyer, but the driver told him in no uncertain terms to never put him at risk again.

Epstein's drug use, mainly pills, began to rise in 1966 as the Beatles' touring days drew to a close. Nat Weiss, his American attorney and business partner, saw how temptations were now being openly offered. 'People are always trying to be hip by bringing around the latest drug. Access to any artist at the time consisted of, "Here's some acid. Here's some of this. Here's some of that," and all of a sudden you were members of the same fraternity.

'Brian began to get involved with Nembutals and Seconals and things like that. Brian had always taken certain amphetamines which kept him up, and suddenly the seesaw thing began. Down with the Nembutals, up with the amphetamines, until he had to go to the hospital at one point and be given some induced sleep so he could balance himself out. Depression began to set in and he found his haven in some of these downers.'[342]

It is impossible to know whether Epstein's mental health would have suffered had he not been so reliant on a variety of substances. He was locked in a cycle of depression and stress, using a range of unhealthy escapist and coping strategies including self-medication, and was often dismissive of advice and concern from others.

The Beatles' final concert took place at San Francisco's Candlestick Park on 29 August 1966. That day, Epstein was delighted to be unexpectedly reunited with Diz Gillespie. The pleasure was short-lived, however, when Gillespie stole briefcases belonging to Epstein and Weiss from their hotel.

Epstein's case contained cash, an assortment of pills, letters, photographs, Beatles contracts and other personal effects, much of which could have been devastating to his reputation if they became public knowledge. Although the case was recovered, Gillespie vanished with $8,000 plus the pills, photos and letters. Weiss cites the incident as the cause of Epstein's first major depression, leaving him anxious that his secrets would one day reach the press.

The Beatles each undertook individual projects in the late summer of 1966. One was *How I Won The War*, the Richard Lester film in which John Lennon appeared as Private Gripweed. Epstein had intended to join Lennon on the set in Almería, Spain, but never made it. On 26 September he was hospitalised in a London clinic. The press were told that it was a check-up, although it later transpired that he had accidentally overdosed on prescribed drugs. He remained in hospital for several weeks recuperating.

Mood swings continued to plague Epstein, and for long spells he would retreat to his homes and refuse to take calls. He was involved in negotiating new deals for the Beatles with EMI in the UK and Capitol in America, and was well aware that his own contract with the group was due to end in 1967.

Since the Beatles had finished touring and were mainly a studio-based band, Epstein was left with far less to do, and he worried that they would not renew his position. He mostly kept out of their way when recording, only dropping by the studio for occasional short visits. For a man who thrived on social acceptance and status, his reduced role in the group's success caused him no small degree of anguish. He arranged to hand over a controlling stake in NEMS to fellow manager Robert Stigwood, although he intended to retain control over the Beatles and Cilla Black.

Epstein worked almost exclusively from his Chapel Street home in 1967, rarely starting before three o'clock in the afternoon. Although some days were normal and his mood was fine, often the staff there would not see him for days, and he took to communicating by leaving notes outside doors. Epstein still enjoyed an active social life, and continued to gamble, but his depression, drinking and drug use often left him visibly impaired. He would use sleeping pills at nights, and uppers to get him through the days, which took a heavy toll on his moods.

In February 1967 he stayed at the Waldorf Towers hotel in Manhattan. He was due to give a radio interview to Murray 'the K' Kaufman for WOR-FM, but was found slurring his words after taking a number of Nembutal barbiturates. Nat Weiss discovered Epstein in the hotel room: 'I had to wrestle with him on the floor, throw the bottle out of the window of the hotel and just yell at him. Eventually, with coffee and things like that, we got him together and we took him to the interview.'[343] Epstein was adamant that it should go ahead, despite Weiss's and Peter Brown's protestations.

He was driven to the radio studio, where Weiss sat close to keep him from slumping over. For the opening moments he was clearly struggling to speak, and was barely coherent, though Kaufman managed to paper over the cracks. Fortunately, after a short time the stimulants kicked in and the old confident, lucid Brian returned.

Around this time Paul McCartney wrote a four-page letter to Epstein, which was given – along with diaries and other documents – to Bryan Barrett for safekeeping. McCartney's frustration with his manager, and his worry over his poor health, are both clear throughout the letter. At one point he adopts the tone of a religious sermon: '"We all have troubles, children, but our biggest trouble is ourselves." If I am right in thinking your sick periods are caused by events rather than germs, then I would like to echo the vicar. Your BIGGEST TROUBLE IS YOU TAKE IT ALL TOO SERIOUSLY!'

The third page of the letter was decorated with words and phrases cut out from newspapers. One, 'Who cares?' was annotated by McCartney with the words: 'Some people do, friends, and the time has come to listen to them.' He ended the letter with the words: 'THINK FINE, keep your pecker up, and speedy recovery.'[344]

The Beatles knew that Epstein was struggling, though due to his lengthy disappearances they were often unaware of the extent of his problems. The band were cloistered in the studio for many weeks, and often had little idea of what was happening outside. Joanne Petersen, Epstein's secretary, once told Pattie Harrison of her concerns over his pill use. 'I said why couldn't she or Peter [Brown] stop him, but she said they couldn't. I said to George that he should speak to Brian himself, but he said it wouldn't do any good.'[345]

'He'd have hellish tempers and fits and lock-outs and he'd vanish for days,' said Lennon. 'He'd come to a crisis now and then, and the whole business would fuckin' stop because he'd been on sleeping pills for days on end, and wouldn't wake up for days. Or beaten up by some docker on the Old Kent Road. So suddenly the whole business would stop and Brian would be missing.'[346]

Discussing emotional matters did not come particularly easily to the Beatles, although privately they would sometimes share their concerns. On one occasion Lennon revealed to Pete Shotton the extent to which the Beatles were concerned about their manager: 'Eppy seems to be in a terrible state. The guy's head's a total mess, and we're all really worried about him. But we just don't know what the fuck we can do about it. It's time for us to go off in our own direction, and that's that.'

Lennon then loaded a tape reel and hit play. Shotton described the harrowing recording as 'barely recognisable as that of a human voice, alternately groaning, grunting, and shrieking – and occasionally mumbling words which, even when decipherable, made no apparent sense whatsoever. The man on the tape was obviously suffering from great emotional stress, and very likely under the influence of some extremely potent drugs.' Shotton asked Lennon who it was. 'That's Brian! He made this tape for me in his house. I don't know why he sent it, but he's trying to tell me something – fuck knows what! He just can't seem to communicate with us in his usual way any more.'[347]

Another witness to Epstein's decline was journalist Chris Hutchins. 'He and I dined frequently at Overton's restaurant in St James's. He would pore over the menu, carefully choosing his dish of the evening and instructing how he wanted his vegetables cooked or his salad prepared. He would then pop a handful of pills, insisting that I join him in enjoying what he called "our little helpers". The uppers were, of course, appetite suppressants, and by the time the food arrived, neither of us wanted to eat. Time after time, the lobster and fillet steak dishes would be sent back to the kitchen with "Mr Epstein's compliments to the chef," but never an explanation as to why they had barely been touched.'[348]

Epstein was fortunate in having a handful of close friends and ever loyal assistants. Realising he was self-destructing in the city, Peter Brown persuaded him to consider buying a house in the countryside. They found Kingsley Hill, an eighteenth century mansion in East Sussex, which Epstein bought for £30,000 in February 1967.

It was sparse at first, but furnishing and decorating gave him a much-needed distraction, and a place to spend quiet weekends. Kingsley Hill became a retreat for the Beatles and others, and Epstein threw several parties there in the summer of 1967. Although the drugs continued to circulate, for a time it looked like he was back in the game.

Brown spent many nights at 24 Chapel Street, Epstein's London home, which enabled him to keep a closer eye on the manager. The arrangement had been suggested by Epstein's doctor, Norman Cowan, and approved by his mother Queenie. However, Brown found it had little outward effect. 'He languished in the house all day, sometimes not even getting out of his pyjamas for dinner. His conversation was morbid and nostalgic, that of a man who had given up. He stayed up until dawn every day and then slept until five in the afternoon, avoiding his business responsibilities.'[349]

One night Epstein withdrew to his room shortly after finishing his evening meal, behaviour which was out of character. Brown checked on him and saw he was asleep, but later realised he was unconscious. After failing to rouse him, Brown called Dr Cowan who advised him to call an ambulance. Wary of the publicity that would ensue, Brown chose instead to continue trying to wake Epstein while he awaited assistance.

Brown and Cowan were unable to revive Epstein so, with the help of Bryan Barrett, they wrapped him in a blanket and drove him to Richmond Hospital. His stomach was pumped and eventually he regained consciousness.

After groggily apologising, Epstein insisted he had accidentally taken one pill too many, and pleaded for the others to not
tell anyone. Brown returned to Chapel Street where he made a
sad discovery: 'On Brian's night table, next to an empty bottle
of pills, was a suicide note I had not noticed before. It said, in
part, "This is all too much and I can't take it anymore." A short
will and testament followed, in which he left his house and business and money to his mother and [brother] Clive. I was also a
small beneficiary.'350 The next day Brown took the note to the
hospital and confronted Epstein, who expressed gratitude that
nobody else knew. Epstein took the note which he vowed to
burn, although he never did.

For several spells in 1967 he rested and recovered at the
Priory Hospital in Roehampton, yet he rarely stayed for long.
He felt deep distrust towards psychiatry and initially refused
treatment for his poor mental health. Eventually he capitulated,
and in May agreed to see a psychiatrist, Dr John Flood. He
noted that Epstein was suffering from 'insomnia, agitation,
anxiety and depression', and he was admitted back into the
Priory where he was put into heavy sedation and fed intravenously, in a bid to cure him of his dependency on pills.
According to Brown, although initial attempts to induce sleep
were fruitless, 'He finally succumbed to a massive amount of
drugs and was kept in an induced sleep for nearly a week. When
he was revived he called me in London to say that the beneficial
effects were marginal at best.'351

A steady stream of visitors came to the Priory, and many
found Epstein argumentative and irascible. There were
moments of joy, such as the time he first heard the finished *Sgt
Pepper*. The Beatles had a special acetate disc pressed and sent to
him, and a portable record player was set up in his bedroom.
Epstein was thrilled and overwhelmed by what he heard. He
was also sent a huge bouquet of flowers by John Lennon, with a
note which read: 'You know I love you, I really do.' The gesture
reduced Epstein to tears.

Epstein left the Priory on 19 May. That evening the *Sgt Pepper* press party was held at Chapel Street. The event was a success, and his mood was buoyed further by his house-warming party at Kingsley Hill on 28 May. The old Brian appeared to have returned: confident and controlled, and happy to be joined by so many close friends. He was drunk at the party, though not excessively so.

Epstein's moods began to improve in the weeks that followed. The success of *Sgt Pepper* and the pending worldwide satellite broadcast of *Our World*, in which the Beatles premièred All You Need Is Love, gave him new focus, as did the renegotiation of the band's contracts.

EPSTEIN'S FATHER Harry died of a heart attack on 27 July 1967. Brian was badly shaken and returned to Liverpool to comfort his devastated mother Queenie at the funeral. Afterwards he invited her to stay with him at Chapel Street.

Queenie arrived on 14 August and her presence had an immediate effect. She woke him each morning, he started keeping normal hours and going out to work, and he took her out each night to a restaurant or play. Although he continued using pills, he did so discreetly, and his friends were delighted to see the change in him.

Even so, his positivity did not endure. The last Beatles recording session Epstein attended was on Wednesday 23 August, at the independent Chappell Recording Studios in London. The band were working on the *Magical Mystery Tour* song Your Mother Should Know. 'He came in to hear the playbacks looking extremely down and in a bad mood,' recalled studio engineer John Timperley. 'He just stood at the back of the room listening, not saying much.'[352] The next day Queenie left London to return to Liverpool.

On the evening of 24 August the Beatles met Maharishi

Mahesh Yogi for the first time, and the following day took the train to Bangor in north Wales to embark upon a ten-day course of Transcendental Meditation. Epstein wished to spend the weekend in East Sussex, but intended to follow them to Bangor in the week.

He invited Peter Brown and Geoffrey Ellis to stay with him in East Sussex over the bank holiday weekend. His personal assistant Joanne Newfield and the singer Lulu were also invited, but both had prior engagements. Undeterred, Epstein departed London on the afternoon of 25 August and drove to Kingsley Hill, where he was joined by Peter Brown and Geoffrey Ellis.

Epstein had also requested the company of a young man with whom he hoped to become better acquainted, but the man did not show. Although largely in good spirits, Epstein was nonetheless disappointed at the prospect of having to spend a long weekend with two friends he saw frequently, and after dinner – during which he drank considerably – he chose to drive back to London.

A London taxi, containing four friends of friends whom Epstein had also invited, arrived at Kingsley Hill shortly afterwards. Although surprised that the host had left, they stayed the night, partying with Brown and Ellis before leaving the next morning.

Although Epstein had promised to return to East Sussex for breakfast on the Saturday, he did not arrive. That afternoon he called Brown, who noted that he sounded befuddled and distant: 'He said he'd been sleeping all day and was still feeling drowsy. I said he'd better not drive back. If he got the train down to Lewes I'd meet him there. He agreed that was best, but he was still too dopey to start off. He was always drowsy when he woke up after taking sleeping pills.'[353]

Epstein's Spanish butler, Antonio Garcia, and his wife Maria had not seen him since his return to Chapel Street on Friday night. By Sunday morning they were starting to worry.

Garcia was unable to get through to Kingsley Hill, but did

manage to speak to Joanne Newfield. She urged him not to worry, but in the early afternoon decided to go to Chapel Street. She went upstairs to Epstein's bedroom door, knocked and called his name, but received no reply. She then tried the intercom from her office, but again heard nothing.

Newfield was unable to contact Dr Cowan, who was in Spain. She managed instead to get through to Peter Brown, who suggested she call his own doctor, John Gallway, who lived close by. Newfield also spoke to Alistair Taylor who agreed to come over. Dr Gallway arrived 15 minutes later, and he and Garcia broke open the bedroom door. Newfield followed them as they entered the room.

'The curtains were drawn and John Gallway was directly ahead of me. I could just see part of Brian in the bed and I was just totally stunned. I knew that something really bad had happened. Then I think John Gallway told me, "Just wait outside." I stood in the doorway. A few minutes later John Gallway came out. I've never seen a doctor so white. We were all white and we knew that Brian had died.'[354]

Gallway informed Peter Brown of the death, and Brown immediately called Epstein's lawyer friend David Jacobs. Geoffrey Ellis phoned Epstein's brother Clive in Liverpool, before he and Brown set off for London.

Stunned by the discovery, those at Chapel Street went to the study to have a brandy. A decision was made to defer calling the police until they were sure no illegal substances were inside the house. Alistair Taylor checked the room but found just one cannabis joint in a drawer.

Within minutes of the police being informed, reporters started to assemble outside the house. Taylor attempted to put them off, claiming that Epstein had merely gone out for a drive and that there was no story. But soon headlines across the world were announcing the death of Brian Epstein at the age of thirty-two.

The Beatles were still in Wales with Maharishi Mahesh Yogi,

who earlier that day had given them personal mantras for meditation. When word came that Epstein had died, McCartney immediately set off for London. Clearly shellshocked, Lennon, Harrison and Starr spoke briefly to reporters before they too left Bangor. 'I don't know what to say,' said Lennon. 'We've only just heard, and it's hard to think of things to say. But he was just… He was a warm fellow, you know, and it's terrible.'

'I knew that we were in trouble then,' he reflected in 1970. 'I didn't really have any misconceptions about our ability to do anything other than play music. And I was scared. I thought, "We've fuckin' had it."'[355]

Lennon continued to feel partly responsible for Epstein's demise, saying 'I introduced him to pills, which gives me a guilt association for his death.'[356] He also confessed that his own problems caused him to lose sight of Epstein's plight. 'Whenever somebody dies, you think, "If only I'd spoken a bit more to him, he might have been a bit happier." I felt guilty because I was closer to him earlier, and then for two years I was on me own. I was having me own problems, internal, for those two years. And we didn't see him hardly at all, and I had no idea of the kind of life he was living, or anything … And with the four of us and him, it was heavy people. And there would be an atmosphere, and we'd gradually break it down, and turn him on to acid and all that jazz. Or try and straighten him out – which was what we were trying to do. But he didn't. He died instead.'[357]

AN INQUEST WAS HELD in Westminster on Friday 8 September. Recording a verdict of accidental death, the coroner Gavin Thurston said that Epstein's death was due to poisoning by Carbrital, a bromide-based sedative.

Traces of antidepressants, barbiturate and bromide were found in Epstein's blood. Thurston noted that Epstein had been taking sleeping pills for some time and had 'perpetual trouble with insomnia'. The pathologist, Dr Donald Teare, stated that the amount of barbiturate was 'a low fatal level', and that 'Mr Epstein must have been taking bromide in some form, presumably by Carbrital, for a long time. This level can only be achieved by the continued use of Carbrital.'

He also expressed a belief that the levels of drugs found in Epstein's body might have made him 'careless, injudicious'. A police inspector noted that 17 pill bottles had been found in the house, including eight in the bathroom and two in a briefcase.[358]

Those closest to Epstein were united in the belief that his death was accidental, although there were some mutterings of suicide. Certainly he had been considering taking his own life. Some weeks after his death Joanne Petersen was asked to sort through some paperwork and possessions at Chapel Street. 'I found a book that I used to leave letters in for Brian to sign or he'd leave things in for me to sign. I opened the book and to my absolute horror I found the suicide notes, one to Queenie and one to Clive. Only they were dated some time much earlier, maybe six, seven, eight weeks before he died.

'They were just one-page notes and I was really shocked about finding these. They said something to the effect of, "Don't be sad. Don't be unhappy. I'm OK. Take good care of yourself. I love you." They were very short.'[359] Petersen concluded that Epstein may have been considering suicide before the death of his father, but decided he could not inflict any more pain upon Queenie. She gave the notes to Peter Brown, who returned them to the Epstein family in Liverpool.

'I've never thought Brian committed suicide,' said Starr. 'I've always thought Brian took his downers – that were probably prescribed by a doctor – then woke up and took some more. His night out is well documented. I feel that happened with Keith Moon, as well; just one too many downers: "I can deal with it." And to Jimi, Jim Morrison – all those people; I don't think any of them set out to die.'[360]

Alistair Taylor concurred: 'I know that Brian didn't commit

suicide and my proof is what was on that bedside table when I first walked into Brian's room after he died. There were about eight bottles of prescribed drugs with chemists' labels on. They were all half full and all the lids were screwed back on. Now if you were going to commit suicide you don't just half do the job and screw the lids back on the bottle. That's why I have fought all these years with the argument that Brian didn't commit suicide. It was an accidental overdose.'[361]

Without their manager's restraining influence, the Beatles were free to indulge their every grandiose fantasy, sometimes to their detriment. They postponed a planned trip to India, and instead threw themselves into the *Magical Mystery Tour* film and EP. The project was conceived by McCartney, who also contributed half of the soundtrack's six new songs.

McCartney became *primus inter pares* in the Beatles' final three years, and his efforts to bring direction to the rudderless group were artistically and commercially fruitful. He wrote a run of singles from the 1967 Christmas chart-topper Hello, Goodbye through to 1969's Get Back, motivated an increasingly listless band during the *Let It Be* and *Abbey Road* sessions, and was a driving force in the establishment of Apple Corps – a company which would surely have greatly benefited from Epstein's guidance.

His dominance may have caused resentment, arguments and a series of stalemates, yet without his focus and enthusiasm the group might never have scaled such heady heights in its latter years.

5

WHAT YOU'RE DOING

Although blues, jazz and folk musicians had for generations sung of the pleasures and pitfalls of cocaine, at the dawn of the Sixties it was used recreationally by only small numbers of people in Britain and the USA.

Yet the stimulant found its way to the Cavern Club during the Beatles' time there. An American R&B singer named Davy Jones was booked to perform at the venue on 8 December 1961, followed by an evening show at the Tower Ballroom in New Brighton, Wallasey, a short ferry ride across the Mersey from Liverpool. Jones, whose talents went beyond singing to encompass comedy, tap dancing, impressionism and acrobatics, was given star billing at the Tower Ballroom. He was backed at both venues by the Beatles, who additionally performed their own sets.

It is likely that the band first encountered cocaine on this occasion, with Jones as the supplier. One person who definitely did partake – albeit unwittingly – was Bob Wooler, the Cavern's disc jockey and showtime announcer. Wooler was not normally one of life's experimenters, and did not find the experience a pleasant one.

'Alan Ross, who was a local compère, brought Davy down to the Cavern, and that was when I had cocaine for the first and only time in my life,' he said. 'I told Davy Jones about my sinuses, and he said, "This'll clear it." Alan Ross gave me a smile of approval, I tried it… and nearly hit the roof. There was laughter galore, and I rushed out into Mathew Street, trying to breathe the effects out. I remember [Cavern doorman] Pat Delaney saying, "What's wrong, Robert?" and I said, "Nothing, I'm just a bit giddy." The Beatles welcomed Davy Jones with open arms, so I'm sure the drug-taking didn't stop with me. That is the common factor with the Beatles – whatever was going, they wanted to be a part of it.'[362]

They were almost certainly acquainted with it by 1964. A scene in *A Hard Day's Night* has the Beatles' handlers Norm and Shake impressing upon them the importance of behaving. As Shake passes bottles of cola around the train carriage, Norm gives them a pep talk: 'Now look, I've had a marvellous idea. Just for once, let's all try to behave like ordinary respectable citizens. Let's not cause any trouble, pull any strokes, or do anything I'm going to be sorry for…' As he speaks, the Beatles do their best to distract him: Starr grabs his camera and points the lens at Norm, McCartney nods with mock sincerity, and Lennon holds a cola bottle to his nose and takes a sniff.

Trying to get a 'snorting coke' gag past the mid-Sixties film censors would be daring for any actor and director. The Beatles got away with it, as so often, by virtue of their charming wit and sheer boldness, not to mention the likelihood that the majority of their young fans wouldn't have spotted the reference. Besides, the band could have innocently protested, it was actually a Pepsi bottle, not Coke! What's the problem?

THE STIMULANT PROPERTIES of the coca plant have been known to mankind for thousands of years. The leaves, chewed or drunk in coca tea, have long been used in traditional and religious customs throughout South America.

Like tobacco, the coca leaf was introduced to Europe in the sixteenth century, but its use only became widespread after 1858, when Italian neurologist Paolo Mantegazza travelled to South America and observed its effect on the native populations. He published a scientific paper extolling the positive effects of coca on cognition and physical health, noting that it could be used to treat 'a furred tongue in the morning, flatulence, and whitening of the teeth'.

The psychoactive cocaine alkaloid was first isolated from the coca plant in 1855 by German chemist Friedrich Gaedcke. Four years later an improved purification process was developed by Albert Niemann, a PhD student at the University of Göttingen, Germany, who gave the alkaloid the name cocaine.

A number of commercial products soon followed, including coca wines, medicines and tonics. An early success was Vin Mariani, a mix of Bordeaux wine and coca leaves, whose fans included Queen Victoria, the Shah of Persia, and US presidents William McKinley and Ulysses S Grant. Pope Leo XIII loved Vin Mariani so much he appeared in an advertisement for it, and awarded a Vatican gold medal to its creator.

But it was soon eclipsed by Coca-Cola, a non-alcoholic alternative which went on sale in North America in 1886. Coca-Cola was marketed as an 'intellectual beverage' and 'brain tonic' which could cure ailments including morphine addiction, impotence, nerve disorders, indigestion and headaches, and initially contained two key ingredients: cocaine and caffeine.

Cocaine became something of a wonder drug, and was used in toothache drops, toothpastes, hair care treatments and as a local anaesthetic, and was sold in various forms including powder, cigarettes and an injectable solution. Yet fears of negative health and social repercussions soon emerged. By the turn of the twentieth century it had become fashionable to snort cocaine powder, and hospitals were reporting cases of nasal damage. In the United States cocaine use was often associated with black men, and there were racist fears that it had caused an increase in sexual assault and violence. A headline in the *New York Times* from that era read: 'Negro Cocaine "Fiends" Are a New Southern Menace'. In 1903 Coca-Cola bowed to public pressure by removing all but a trace amount of cocaine from their drink.

In 1912 the US government reported five thousand cocaine-related deaths in one year. President William Taft declared cocaine to be public enemy number one, and in 1914 the Harrison Narcotics Tax Act tightly regulated its distribution and sale. In areas where prohibition was introduced, cocaine powder inevitably entered the black market.

Cocaine became fashionable in high society during the Twenties and Thirties, and was sometimes referred to as the 'champagne of drugs'. The flamboyant actress and hedonist Tallulah Bankhead famously joked: 'Cocaine isn't habit-forming – and I know because I've been taking it for years!' Musicians including Hank Williams, Woody Guthrie, Bob Dylan and Johnny Cash popularised songs about cocaine, but over time its use fell out of fashion, and by the 1950s it was largely considered a problem from the past.

UNCHARACTERISTICALLY, Paul McCartney was the first of the Beatles to regularly take cocaine. He used the drug at the peak of the Swinging London scene, 'for about a year around the time of *Sgt Pepper*. Coke and maybe some grass to balance it out.'[363]

Once again his source was art dealer Robert Fraser, whose initial connection was American interior designer Bill Willis. 'I discovered cocaine in Italy, turned Robert on to that and then he turned the Rolling Stones and the Beatles on to it,' Willis recalled. 'Nobody was taking coke in those days. Then I had a regular supply of absolutely pure cocaine. Once I was staying in Mount Street with Robert and we'd had so much coke. He went off to his gallery and I decided I would redecorate the apartment. I moved all the sculpture and furniture round the way I liked it, then I passed out.'[364]

Cocaine was one of many drugs favoured by Fraser, who used it heavily from 1966. He would visit the *Sgt Pepper* sessions, often bringing two test tubes, one with cocaine and the other a speedball – a mixture of coke and heroin. Fraser freely offered the drugs to his hosts, and although the Beatles wisely kept away from the speedballs, some of their studio guests and entourage did indulge.

It was curiosity that led McCartney to cocaine. 'Once or twice with Robert I said, "What's that you're doing? Coke?" I felt very lucky, because he introduced it to me a year before most people were doing it. That was '66, very early. The film industry went mad on it a few years after that.'[365]

In 1965 McCartney had witnessed a man injecting cocaine at the home of John Dunbar and Marianne Faithfull. 'Suddenly he pulls out a big red rubber tube thing and he tightened his arm up, putting a tourniquet on. And he's tapping, and he's got needles and he's got spoons and he's got a little light. And I'm going, "Uhhhhhh!" You get the kind of shock of horror through you, I thought, "My God, fucking hell! How did I get here? I'm in a room with a guy who's shooting up!" He had a big rubber tourniquet, which smacked to me of operations. I'd always been fearful of red rubber as a kid. And me mum was a nurse, so enemas and things, it was all red rubber. Very frightening sort of thing to me, not pleasant at all, that shit. We couldn't look at him.'[366]

McCartney wrongly assumed the man, known as Sandy, was using heroin. The following week he was told by Dunbar that Sandy had died. The news profoundly shocked McCartney, but it turned out to be one of Dunbar's more twisted jokes. 'I was probably kidding,' he said. 'I do remember that Sandy nearly died. What he would do is, in those days you could get this National Health coke from [London pharmacy] John Bell and Croyden which was totally utterly pure, like if you spilled some it took like ten minutes to settle, each flake would flutter down, it would be like all over the room. And also when it's finished, it's actually not finished, it's all over the glass phial. You just wash it out and shoot it up. And he totally OD'd and I remember it was really unpleasant. He was in really bad shape, on coke. Fixing, mainlining an overdose of coke. But he didn't die.'[367]

Despite his natural caution, McCartney remained open to new sensations and experiences. And while the memory of red rubber remained a chilling one, other childhood remembrances may have led to an affinity with coke. 'To this day, I swear as kids in Liverpool we were given cocaine to deaden the gums. People say no, that will have been Novocaine, but I think that was much later. I recognise the smell from the dentist; it's a medical smell coke can have. Anyway, that was my first thought about it.'[368]

McCartney used the drug fairly regularly towards the end of 1966 and in the early months of 1967. The only other drug he was using regularly was marijuana; his LSD intake was limited to just a couple of trips during the *Sgt Pepper* sessions. 'I liked the paraphernalia,' he said of cocaine. 'I liked the ritualistic end of it. I was particularly amused by rolling up a pound note. There was a lot of symbolism in that: sniffing it through money!'[369]

Lennon, Harrison and Starr were initially wary of cocaine, and surprised at McCartney's uncharacteristic eagerness. 'I know the other guys were a bit shocked at me and said, Hey, man, you know this is like, "now you're getting into drugs. This is more than pot." I remember feeling a little bit superior and patting them on the head, symbolically, and saying, "No. Don't worry, guys. I can handle it." And as it happened, I could. What I enjoyed was the ritual of meeting someone and them saying,

"Have you seen the toilets in this place?" And you'd know what they meant. "Oh no, are they particularly good?" And you'd wander out to the toilets and you'd snort a bit of stuff. Robert and I did that for a bit. It wasn't ever too crazy.'[370]

McCartney reportedly kept a supply of pharmaceutical grade cocaine in a jar on a mantelpiece at his Cavendish Avenue home, which he would share with visitors. One guest in 1967 was Prince Stanislas Klossowski de Rola, known to all as Stash, who had been living with the Rolling Stones' Brian Jones until a drugs bust left him temporarily homeless. McCartney promised to let de Rola stay for the duration of his subsequent trial, although the Beatle's tolerance found a limit when his cocaine supply began to swiftly diminish.

De Rola's time at Cavendish Avenue came to an abrupt end one weekend when McCartney was visiting Liverpool. The singer called his London home and demanded that all guests leave, after hearing that people were coming by and helping themselves to the drugs. Brian Jones, whose spiralling use was damaging his physical and mental health, broke repeated promises to replace what he took from McCartney's coke jar.[371]

McCartney's confidence was buoyed by the success of *Sgt Pepper*. Although naturally blessed with boundless fire and enthusiasm, his most creatively rich period and his dominance over the group began at a time when his cocaine use was at a peak. McCartney's ambitions and talents rapidly matured and converged as he steered complex multimedia projects spanning art, television, film, music and business. He also consulted with playwright Joe Orton on a proposed script for the Beatles' third film, performed with the Beach Boys and John and Michelle Phillips in America, and on his journey back to England came up with the loose concept for *Magical Mystery Tour*. He was far from the only creative mind in the group at that time – each of the Beatles was firing on all cylinders in the months leading up to the Summer of Love – but McCartney's ideas and actions were among their most enduring, daring and effective. It is also notable that *Sgt Pepper*, often considered to be the band's most LSD-influenced album, was primarily steered by a Beatle who was using cocaine more often than acid.

The increased alertness, energy, self-confidence and euphoria that cocaine releases were all evident in his prolific songwriting, restless experimentation and perfectionism around this time. The recording of Penny Lane began with McCartney using a late-night session to lay down the backing track almost alone, taping three piano parts and harmonium, with Starr's tambourine the only other Beatle contribution. It was a taste of the working practices that came to dominate the White Album and *Abbey Road*.

The first public acknowledgement of McCartney's cocaine use came in a 1984 *Playboy* interview. 'If you start the most-dangerous list with heroin or morphine – we know there's no way out of that; you've got to be suicidal to get into that in any form – then I think marijuana comes toward the bottom of the list,' he said. 'Cocaine is above marijuana in harmfulness. I used to do coke, mincing his words, but it got too fashionable, too fashionable, darling, amongst the record execs. I couldn't handle all that, being in the bogs with all those creeps!'[372]

THE SHORT-LIVED INTENSE high of cocaine is often followed by edginess, depression and desire for repeat doses. Recreational use can also give feelings of anxiety, tremors and heart palpitations, while longer-term use can lead to addiction, intense cravings, psychosis, depression and organ damage.

Eventually McCartney grew tired of the low moods he experienced during comedowns. 'I'd been in a club in London and somebody there had some and I'd snorted it. I remember going to the toilet, and I met Jimi Hendrix on the way. "Jimi! Great, man," because I love that guy. But then as I hit the toilet, it all wore off! And I started getting this dreadful melancholy. I remember walking back and asking, "Have you got any more?" because the whole mood had just dropped, the bottom had dropped out, and I remember thinking then it was time to stop it.

'I thought, this is not clever, for two reasons. Number one, you didn't stay high. The plunge after it was this melancholy plunge which I was not used to. I had quite a reasonable childhood so melancholy was not really much part of it, even though my mum dying was a very bad period, so for anything that put me in that kind of mood it was like, "Huh, I'm not paying for this! Who needs that?" The other reason was just a physical thing with the scraunching round the back of the neck, when it would get down the back of your nose, and it would all go dead! This was what reminded me of the dentist.'[373]

McCartney's cocaine use lessened during the summer of 1967, just as the drug was gaining in popularity. 'I went to America just after *Pepper* came out, and I was thinking of stopping it. And everyone there was taking it, all these music business people, and I thought, no.'[374] By that time the novelty of the ritual and the pleasurable effects of the drug had waned, and he became more concerned about the effects on his health.

McCartney mostly stopped using cocaine when the Beatles went to India in 1968. His partner during the early White Album sessions was Francie Schwartz, who worked at Apple and spent the summer of 1968 living with McCartney at Cavendish Avenue. She recalled: 'Between April and August, when I knew what drugs he was using, he wasn't doing *any* coke. Just alcohol, street speed, marijuana and hashish.'[375] She often found speed pills in his jacket pockets, but McCartney reacted defensively. 'When I asked him what they were, he shrugged, looking away from my eyes, saying, "Oh nothing, someone at the office gave them to me. I don't use them."'[376] She also claimed that he relied on her to source his cannabis. 'He hadn't formally dumped Jane and so at first I was a secret. I stayed in the house for weeks, cleaning, reading, calling the dope dealer. I was to score for my old man. You'd think he could have taken care of it, but he didn't.'[377]

Schwartz's 1972 memoir *Body Count*, a classic tale of a woman scorned, divides Beatles fans for its portrayal of McCartney as moody, emotionally immature and serially unfaithful, existing on a cocktail of drugs and drink and prone to vituperative outbursts. 'Paul's enthusiasm for Apple was shrinking,' she wrote of her later time with him. 'Even the recording sessions were strained. He came home drunk on the nights they had recorded a John or George song… It was no wonder he felt shitty most of the time. His diet was basic Liverpool slag. Beans and toast, grilled cheese and tomato sandwiches. Lots of Scotch and Coke. A hideous drink that gets you two ways: bombed and fat.'[378]

McCartney remained the most prominent public face of the group, but behind the scenes he was far from content. His stresses were often visible to his compatriots during the making of the White Album, a time when the Apple empire morphed from wilfully structured madness into something far more chaotic. One particular target of his anger was Derek Taylor, by now installed as Apple's press officer on the lively second floor of 3 Savile Row, where information and promises were dispensed as liberally as drink and drugs.

Taylor was a genial host and the perfect conduit for the Beatles' public pronouncements, yet his tendency to drink, smoke and drop acid during office hours soon raised McCartney's ire. On one occasion Taylor gave an interview to a reporter from *Woman's Own* magazine. 'Listening to him now filling in background information on the makers of *Yellow Submarine* she thought to herself how terribly efficient he was at his job,' noted Taylor's assistant Richard DiLello. 'Shockingly efficient. What she didn't know was that the press officer was high on LSD.' Minutes later Apple's A&R man Peter Asher entered the press office, to learn that Taylor was 'pleasantly zonked out on acid and having a wonderful time. The A&R man took note of this fact. Two days later Paul McCartney informed his press officer that he did not want him artificially expanding his consciousness during working office hours.'[379] McCartney remained suspicious of the activities of Taylor's team, and sent a series of critical memos to the staff. One was a drawing of two drunk men in a bar, with the caption: 'We probably don't want a press department. Do we?'

Money was draining from Apple, with enormous costs run up by the executives, staff and guests, and few accounting records kept. There were expenses for transport, hospitality, flowers, complimentary records and press packs and much more, including enormous drinks bills. As the company's general manager Alistair Taylor noted: 'All us executives had our little bar, for entertaining. In mine, I had a bottle of Scotch, bottle of vodka, bottle of gin, bottle of brandy, some mixes, and, every week, we'd put our order in to the wine merchants. Neil Aspinall, the managing director, would put in for a bottle of brandy and a bottle of Scotch. Peter Brown would put in for a bottle of vodka, bottle of Scotch, and the mixes. I kept getting this bill from the wine merchants and it was monumental! So, I said, "I want to check these more thoroughly." I found out that Derek and Richard DiLello, the office hippie, in the press office, were having a dozen brandies, two dozen Scotches, a dozen gins and six dozen Cokes...'[380]

McCartney was determined to rein in Apple's worst excesses, but his failure to establish control led to his almost total withdrawal from the organisation during 1969. Like the other Beatles he was inexperienced in management and business operations, and soon discovered that the utopia they had envisaged was unlikely to become reality. Each of the Beatles nonetheless enjoyed the trappings of power, often issuing conflicting instructions to the hapless staff.

'I don't think I ever hated anyone as much as I hated Paul in the summer of 1968,' said Taylor. 'Postcards would arrive at my house from America or Scotland or wherever, some outright nasty ones, some with no meaning that I could see, one with a postage stamp, torn in half and pasted neatly showing the gap between the two halves. Joan received one bearing the words: "Tell your boy to obey the schoolmasters," and signed: "Patron." Far out.'[381]

JOHN LENNON BEGAN USING coke in 1968, around the time he also became addicted to heroin. The two drugs often went hand-in-hand in Britain due to the ways they were legally dispensed to registered addicts. 'The bizarre idea in England was that if you registered as a heroin addict, whether you wanted it or not, you were forced to take the same amount in pure cocaine,' the Rolling Stones' Keith Richards recalled. 'On the firm belief that you'd be more useful as a member of society instead of lying about smacked out. That would bring you up, the perfect speedball. So we were living in the place where the perfect speedball was available. Junkies would sell off the cocaine and a bit of their smack. It was easy to get, the best stuff in the world. It was never cut, none of that lowlife thing about it.'[382]

That summer Lennon and Yoko Ono attended a party held at the Vesuvio Club, in the basement of 26 Tottenham Court Road in London. The club was co-managed by Richards, Mick Jagger and 'Spanish Tony' Sanchez – photographer, personal assistant to Richards, and drug dealer to the Rolling Stones, Robert Fraser and others including, occasionally, the Beatles.

The Vesuvio opening was also a belated birthday celebration for Jagger, who had turned 25 the week before. The venue, essentially a private club for the Stones and friends, had been adorned with Moroccan tapestries, an abundance of giant cushions, tables with hookah pipes and plates of hashish, Inca-style paintings, giant photographs of the Stones, and a helium-filled zeppelin which floated at head height. The party was replete with hash cakes and large silver bowls containing punch laced with mescaline. Over the club's huge speakers played an advance copy of *Beggars Banquet*, the Stones' comeback after a couple of years in the musical wilderness, lost to psychedelia, media storms and drug busts.

Details of the night are hazy, owing to the passage of time and the vast quantities of drugs circulating, but by all accounts it was a star-studded affair. Among the guests were assorted Beatles, Stones and members of the Who, along with Fraser, Marianne Faithfull and many more musicians, artists, models, flower children and space cadets. A late arrival was McCartney, who came with an acetate disc. 'See what you think of it, Tony,' he said unassumingly to Sanchez. 'It's our new one.' The song was Hey Jude, with Revolution on the b-side, and it was an absolute showstopper.

'It just went – *boom!* – straight to the chest,' recalled Faithfull. 'It was the first time anyone had ever heard it, and we were all just *blown away*. And then, of course, we couldn't stop playing it, we just played away, mixed up with a bit of Little Richard and some blues…

'Even Mick said it was fantastic, because it *was*. I guess most people would think the Stones may have had mixed feelings at that moment, and perhaps they did. But, possibly due to the laced punch, the main feeling was one of: aren't we all the greatest bunch of young geniuses to grace the planet and isn't this the most amazing time to be alive. It was as if only with this group and at *that* moment could Paul have done it. We had a sense of everybody being in the right place, at the right time, with the right people.'[383]

The Vesuvio was just a short distance from the local police station, which was something of a gamble; so many famous faces in one place would have been manna to the drug squad, had they known. Sanchez put three heavies on the door, who were instructed not to sample any of the space cakes or punch – somewhat optimistically. 'Eventually John Lennon staggered across to me, looking as though his eyes were going to pop out of his head, and asked me if I could arrange a taxi to take him and Yoko home,' said Sanchez, who sent his doorman off to hail a cab. Half an hour passed and the man had not returned, so another was sent out, followed by a third.

By this time Lennon and Ono were becoming understandably impatient, with Lennon demanding: 'What do you mean they've all vanished? What kind of club is this?' Sanchez assumed the police were grabbing his staff as they left the building. In reality (these things being somewhat relative), the fresh air had heightened the effects of the mescaline and cannabis. One of the men was found the next day lying in a flower bed in St James's Park.

Jagger had heard Lennon shouting, and asked what the problem was. When told about the disappearing doormen he laughed and handed over the keys to his Aston Martin DB6. Sanchez gave them to his cousin, one of the few people at the party just about sober enough to drive, and told him to take Lennon and Ono to their home in Montagu Square. But the sports car, which was parked illegally outside the club, was so filled with buttons and switches that the man had trouble getting it started.

As the trio sat in the car there was a tap on the window and a policeman looked inside. 'John was doing a lot of cocaine at that time,' Sanchez recalled, 'and he was convinced he was about to be busted, so he discreetly dropped a little bottle of the stuff on the floor of the car. All three of them were totally stoned anyway, so they just stared at the policeman in terror.'[384]

Fortunately for them, the officer's intentions were to help. Sanchez's cousin explained that he had borrowed the £25,000 Aston Martin from a friend. The policeman got inside, started the car and waved them away, wishing them a safe journey. But Lennon's stresses were not over. He was unable to find his coke bottle on the floor of the car, and he was worried – not just for himself, but also for Jagger, who remained a target for the

Metropolitan Police. The erratic driving was the final straw, and after a quarter of a mile he demanded the car be stopped. 'We're getting out,' he told the hapless driver. 'I'll walk home if I have to. You find the coke and keep it.'[385]

Of the many drug references in Beatles songs, cocaine appears to have inspired the fewest lines – which perhaps reflects its niche status in their history. Two of Lennon's songs from *Abbey Road* come closest to mentioning cocaine culture. Some assume the line 'He got monkey finger, he shoot Coca-Cola', in Come Together to be about cocaine. And nestled in the long medley is Mean Mr Mustard, Lennon's breezy tale of a miserly old man and his stash of cash. The line 'Keeps a ten bob [shilling] note up his nose' might bring to mind the cocaine user with a rolled up banknote pressed to a nostril, but it would be a misplaced allusion: an expensive drug habit would be at odds with the protagonist's penny-pinching ways.

McCartney's brief episode on cocaine was reprised following the Beatles' split, and the other three also came to use the drug in the years after their break-up. Towards the end of the Sixties and beyond, cocaine became more prevalent in music, film, fashion and media, and during the Seventies it had become synonymous with Hollywood and celebrity excess. Worldwide, it is now the second most frequently used illegal drug after cannabis.

6

FIXING A HOLE

I n early 1965, while the Beatles were filming *Help!* on Paradise Island in the Bahamas, two American models attempted to show Paul McCartney their own narcotic idea of Eden.

The incident was witnessed by Richard Lester, the director of the Beatles' first two feature films. According to his biographer, Lester 'accidentally overheard two of the most beautiful women he had ever seen, dressed in identical, stunning black swimsuits, try to coax Paul into taking heroin. The combination of their sexual come-on and the enticement towards hard drugs was one of the most chillingly evil moments Lester has ever encountered, a numbing experience he will never forget.'[386]

To Lester's profound relief, McCartney spurned the women's offer. But it was just a matter of months before heroin reappeared in his life. In the mid-Sixties the drug was slowly weaving its web across the high reaches of British popular culture. And, just as he had been with the spread of LSD and cocaine, Robert Fraser was at the forefront.

Fraser was part of a wide and wealthy social circle in which heroin abuse had all but become normal. 'A lot of his friends messed around with heroin,' said McCartney. 'A lot of his lords and ladies were heroin addicts and had been for many many years. And give Robert his due, he knew I wasn't that keen. He knew I wasn't a nutter for that kind of stuff. So I did sniff heroin with him once, but I said afterwards, "I'm not sure about this, man. It didn't really do anything for me," and he said, "In that case, I won't offer you again." And I didn't take it again. I was often around it when they'd all be doing it. They'd repair to the toilet and I'd say, "I'm all right, thanks, no." One of the most difficult things about that period was the peer pressure to do that.'[387]

McCartney subsequently gave a contradictory account of his first heroin experience, suggesting that he had been an unwitting participant, and that he had smoked rather than snorted it. 'I didn't realise I'd taken it,' he said. 'I was just handed something, smoked it, then found out what it was.'[388]

As with pills and LSD before, McCartney's instinctive wariness was a natural check on dangerous temptations. 'Robert Fraser once said to me, "Heroin is not addictive. There's no problem with heroin addiction, even if it is addictive, you've just got to have a lot of money. The problem with heroin is when you can't pay for it." Which of course is absolute bullshit! You're a junkie, of course you are. This was the way he put it to me and for a second I was almost taken in but then my northern savvy kicked in and said, "Now don't go for all of this. This is all very exotic and romantic but don't go for all of it." There was always a little corner, at the back of my brain, that "knock! knock! knock!" on the door – "Stop!"'[389]

Even though McCartney was able to resist the peer pressure, he admitted it may have been a different story had he enjoyed his heroin experience. 'I was very frightened of drugs, having a nurse mother, so I was always cautious, thank God as it turned out, because I would be in rooms with guys who would say, "Do you want to sniff a little heroin?" and I would say, "Well, just a little." I did some with Robert Fraser, and some of the boys in the Stones who were doing things like that. I always refer to it as walking through a minefield, and I was lucky because had anyone hit me with a real dose that I loved, I would have been a heroin addict.'[390]

This was the *Sgt Pepper* era. Fraser had begun snorting heroin just months before, but within weeks was using it intravenously. His financial problems increased with his escalating habit, threatening the future of his acclaimed gallery. His paranoia had already been heightened by his heavy use of cannabis and cocaine, and a burgeoning heroin addiction exacerbated his unreliability.

'He certainly got his habit pretty quick,' said fellow art dealer John Dunbar. 'I kind of warned him about it – do be careful, because it's not like smoking dope, it's real easy to get stuck. And by the time he'd got a lot of connections – these were the days when you got it off a doctor and, you know, people would sell you a bit of their script for a pound a grain. In other words, it was sort of like 10p for a pill, half of which would do you fine if you weren't into it. Literally, it was more or less free.

'And he was sort of – I mean, I remember saying, "No thank you" to some more and he was going [*posh voice*], "Oh, you're so paranoid, John!" about getting a habit sort of thing. Or I'd say, "Look, I've had it for three days on the trot, it's enough," that sort of thing, and like within a month or two he was really, really bang into it. You know, shooting, and a habit.'[391]

THE GERMAN PHARMACIST Friedrich Sertürner first synthesised morphine from opium in 1803. The hypodermic syringe was invented shortly afterwards, and injectable morphine was used for pain relief during the American Civil War.

Addiction was an unanticipated side effect which increased throughout the nineteenth century, a time when opiates were readily available in the United Kingdom and America. Tinctures and elixirs were sold in pharmacies, and doctors prescribed opioid medicines for a variety of ailments.

In 1874 a London chemist, CR Alder Wright, experimented with combining morphine with various acids. He synthesised a more potent form of the drug – known as diacetylmorphine, morphine diacetate or diamorphine. It was independently re-synthesised 23 years later by Felix Hoffmann, a chemist working at the Bayer pharmaceutical company in Elberfeld, Germany. Although instructed by his supervisor to produce codeine, Hoffmann's diamorphine was discovered to be far more effective for pain relief.

Bayer named its new drug heroin. From 1898 it sold the product as 'the sedative for coughs' and a supposedly non-addictive substitute for morphine. But it soon found favour among a subculture of recreational users, and its powerfully effective painkilling and euphoric properties, combined with a lack of awareness of its highly addictive nature, led to a new social crisis.

The drug became widely used among New York jazz musicians in the Thirties and Forties, and later among the beatniks of the Fifties. Despite law enforcers' efforts to contain the problem, prohibition led to a flourishing black market.

After the First World War, a number of returning soldiers used opium and coca preparations for pain relief. In 1920 the UK government passed the Dangerous Drugs Act, which criminalised possession of cocaine and opium but enabled medical practitioners to prescribe morphine, cocaine and heroin in a controlled manner.

Six years later the government-appointed Rolleston Committee declared addiction to be a disease and that drug addicts should be treated accordingly. Doctors were able to provide treatment in a controlled manner, but were obliged to inform the Home Office. The committee also opposed the outright banning of heroin, which was rarely abused in Britain.

This conciliatory approach was in stark contrast to the prohibitionists in the United States. The 'British system', as it became known, put the treatment of addicts in the hands of doctors rather than law enforcers. Some patients were placed on withdrawal programmes, while others were prescribed pure heroin and cocaine.

The system remained in place for the next forty years, until officials noticed that it was open to abuse. There was particular concern for the rapid rise in the number of drug addicts. In 1959 there were 62 heroin addicts known to the Home Office (there would have been substantially more unregistered ones); by 1964 the number had risen to 342.[392] A younger demographic was also emerging: 11% of addicts in 1959 were under 35, rising to 40% in 1964. Perhaps more importantly, by 1964 just 6% of recently-registered addicts had begun taking the drug for pain management purposes.[393]

These numbers were still low as a proportion of the population, and the drug did not yet blight towns and cities nationwide. Like cocaine, high prices and scarcity put heroin out of reach for the majority, and in the first half of the Sixties heroin was predominantly a middle- and upper-class problem.

Addicts tended to be geographically dispersed and often isolated from one another, and there was little crossover with the speed, pot and alcohol crowds in nightclubs. The main cluster was in London, where several hundred addicts were on the books of sympathetic doctors. A branch of Boots pharmacists at London's Piccadilly Circus was commonly used for exchanging prescriptions for 'jacks' – diamorphine in soluble pill form – and the corner of Coventry Street and Haymarket became known as 'Junkies' Corner'.

The social separation of these drug users began to dissolve towards the end of 1967 and into 1968. Methedrine – the brand name for methamphetamine – began to be prescribed instead of cocaine as a drug to be taken alongside heroin, and ampoules containing injectable speed entered circulation in London.

Methedrine bridged the gap between heroin addicts and users of Dexedrine or Benzedrine pills: the capital's speed-freaks began using needles and syringes, effectively lowering the barrier to other intravenous drug taking.

Many of these users soon discovered that barbiturates – sedatives used to come down from Methedrine – could also be injected, albeit dangerously. A new wave of addiction followed, with users hooked on speed and downers either prescribed legitimately or procured on the black market. In November 1968 high street pharmacists voluntarily agreed to end the dispensing of Methedrine ampoules.

'WE KNEW people who were on H in Liverpool before we really knew anything about it, or drugs, or things like that,' John Lennon said in 1971. 'We just heard about all those famous drummers in England, the jazz drummers, and we were just being traditional musicians taking drugs, as far as we were concerned. Every musician we met, from the jazz or the rock world, was taking some kind of drug.'[394]

Addicts like Robert Fraser had no need to buy heroin on the streets. Well-placed connections were able to obtain drugs of great purity for non-registered users. Some addicts preferred not to declare their usage to the authorities, which would hinder their movements. But among those that did, many exaggerated their habits in order to deal the surplus for profit.

'Everybody eventually had their own pet junkie,' said Keith Richards, who allowed a pair of registered users to stay at his West Sussex estate in exchange for a share of their heroin. 'Anita [Pallenberg] and I installed them in the cottage across from Redlands, which was where I was living at the time. And once a week, "Steve!" Into Chichester, pop into Boots for a minute, go back home and then I'd have half of his smack.'[395]

Lady Isabella Frankau was a British psychiatrist specialising in drug and alcohol addiction, and one of a handful of doctors in England licensed to administer to addicts. She was also by far the most prolific: in 1962 alone she prescribed more than 600,000 heroin tablets – approximately 100 kilos.[396] Like others, she believed that a steady supply of pure cocaine and heroin would take addicts away from the cycle of getting high followed by withdrawal. But her generosity and readiness to accept a story were at odds with the wily nature of many of her patients.

Her private practice was at 32 Wimpole Street, a stone's throw from the Asher family home at number 57. Addicts from across the globe knew of her reputation, her tendency not to ask too many questions and occasional willingness to waive her consultation fees. Jazz trumpeter Chet Baker made a beeline for her office in 1962, on his first day in Britain.

'She was about 75 years old, white-haired, and very businesslike,' Baker wrote in his memoir. 'She didn't ask me for much information about myself. She had already heard of my antics all over Europe. She simply asked my name, my address and how much cocaine and heroin I wanted per day.'[397]

For a fee of two shillings Lady Frankau wrote a prescription for 10 grams of each of the drugs. As the barely credulous Baker noted: 'The coke was about what you would get for 500 dollars in New York, but pure. The whole script cost only about three and a half dollars. After that first day my scripts were all for 20 grams of each, and I was off and running under that old English drug system.'[398]

Lady Frankau also saw a number of unregistered users. Although her intentions were good, if naive, her ministrations directly fed into the flourishing illegal trade in heroin and cocaine. As prescription laws were tightened, heroin and other narcotics flooded into the UK from China, in no small part due to the elevated demand she had helped create. The black market junk which blighted London in the late Sixties was commonly a mixture of heroin, quinine, caffeine and other unidentified substances. Mostly originating from Hong Kong or

China, it sold for around thirty shillings a grain (around 60 milligrams).

Chet Baker was not Lady Frankau's only celebrity patient. Her client list was said to include people in high office, as well as musicians, actors, artists, writers and other influential figures. Her death in May 1967 did much to end the period of easy availability of heroin for hundreds of addicts and their customers.

Another high profile heroin user was William Burroughs, author of *Junky* and *Naked Lunch*. Burroughs lived in London from 1965 to 1974, generally keeping a low profile but remaining a key figure among the literary and artistic cognoscenti. He met McCartney several times in late 1965 and early 1966, and the author set up a tape studio in the Montagu Square flat while it was also being used by McCartney. The Beatles thought highly enough of Burroughs to include him on the cover of *Sgt Pepper*.

Michael Cooper, the album's photographer, was another heroin addict and a primary mover in Swinging London. Fraser and Cooper were among the few people in London at that time to work with both the Beatles and the Rolling Stones. Cooper photographed not only the *Sgt Pepper* cover, but also the Stones' similarly-psychedelic *Their Satanic Majesties Request*. As Marianne Faithfull remembered: 'If all wires were going to one place, they would be going to Robert, or to Michael Cooper's in Flood Street, which was also Robert, because he had backed Michael. If those were the brain centres in your body, your nervous system would be Robert. He was where you went to tell what was happening, or where you went to find out what was happening. Better than having or even being a copy of *Time Out*. Robert was a serious conductor of lightning.'[399]

THREE SONGS on *Sgt Pepper* were thought by some to contain

heroin references, although in truth each had more innocent meanings. Towards the end of the Summer of Love the artist Alan Aldridge interviewed Paul McCartney for the *Observer*, and put it to him that one of the songs was about injecting drugs: 'People have told me that Fixing A Hole is all about junk, you know, this guy, sitting there fixing a hole in his arm.' McCartney rejected the allegation, telling Aldridge: 'If you're a junkie sitting in a room fixing a hole then that's what it will mean to you, but when I wrote it I meant if there's a crack or the room is uncolourful, then I'll paint it.'[400]

The other *Pepper* songs under scrutiny were A Day In The Life and Being For The Benefit Of Mr Kite!, both by Lennon. A Day In The Life had already been banned by the BBC for the words 'I'd love to turn you on', but another cryptic line provided enough intrigue for a heroin rumour to take hold. 'Now they know how many holes it takes to fill the Albert Hall' was no more about injecting smack than Henry the Horse was a crude allusion to heroin – another allegation of the time.

Lennon was, for the time being, naive about the drug. Mr Kite!, he explained, was derived 'from a Victorian poster, which I bought in a junk shop. It is so cosmically beautiful. It's a poster for a fair that must have happened in the 1800s. Everything in the song is from that poster, except the horse wasn't called Henry. Now, there were all kinds of stories about Henry the Horse being heroin. I had never seen heroin in that period.'[401]

Nonetheless, considering John Lennon's willingness to experiment with drugs, and the pressures he and Ono felt as the press and public turned against them, it was perhaps only a matter of time before heroin found them. 'Unfortunately, he was driftin' away from us at that point, so none of us actually knew,' McCartney told *Rolling Stone* in 1986. 'He never told us; we heard rumours, and we were very sad. But he'd embarked on a new course, which really involved anything and everything.'[402]

Lennon and Ono began using heroin together soon after their relationship began in May 1968. She claimed to have first taken it in France while the Beatles were in Rishikesh, and after their return Lennon asked her about the experience.

'John was very curious,' Ono revealed. 'He asked if I had ever tried it. I told him that while he was in India with the Maharishi, I had a sniff of it in a party situation. I didn't know what it was. They just gave me something and I said "What is that!?" It was a beautiful feeling. John was talking about heroin one day and he said "Did you ever take it?" and I told him about Paris. I said it wasn't bad. I think it was because the amount was small I didn't even get sick. It was just a nice feeling. So I told him that. When you take it – "properly" isn't the right word – but when you do a little more, you get sick right away if you're not used to it. So I think maybe because I said it wasn't a bad experience, that had something to do with John taking it.'[403]

Lennon immersed himself in Jean Cocteau's book *Opium: The Story Of A Cure*, which sparked a romantic fantasy about the drug. 'He was fascinated by Cocteau's experiences with opium and how he got clean of it,' said Ono. 'The story was all about Paris in the Twenties, Picasso, Diaghilev, Erik Satie and people like that. John couldn't put the book down. He started asking me again what taking heroin was like, saying how interesting it must have been.'[404]

Lennon was one of the first British rock stars to acquire a heroin habit. George Harrison later blamed Ono for getting Lennon hooked, a suggestion she rejected. 'Of course George says it was *me* who put John on heroin, but that wasn't true. John wouldn't take anything he didn't want to take.'[405] In truth, Lennon scarcely needed encouragement, and the fact that he hadn't used heroin prior to 1968 can be attributed more to his other interests and a lack of supply, rather than any reluctance.

In his post-Sixties interviews he often spoke about the pain of his childhood and his experiences at the end of the Beatles. Heroin is a remarkably effective anaesthetic, and self-medication would have helped him cope with the Beatles' tumultuous final months. Yet it would be wrong to suggest that his lapse into addiction was an inevitable result of his creative, personal and financial pressures. Many people cope with far worse experiences without resorting to drugs, and Lennon was no stranger to adversity.

Heroin is not a sociable drug, at least not between users and non-users, and a very real barrier was erected within the Beatles. Lennon and Ono, wrapped in their warm opioid blanket, blocked out the adverse media attention, racism and public hostility they felt they were receiving, and became increasingly independent of their old friends and associates. Lennon's attitudes changed dramatically during and after 1968: he largely stopped caring about group projects, and almost the only activities that truly fired him up were his collaborations with Ono.

An exchange from the 1970 *Rolling Stone* interview reveals his mindset during this period. While Ono seeks to downplay their addiction and avoid the subject, he describes heroin as something they almost felt forced into by those at Apple and elsewhere:

> LENNON: *Heroin. It just was not too much fun. I never injected it. We sniffed a little when we were in real pain. I mean we just couldn't – people were giving us such a hard time –*
>
> ONO: *We didn't get into it so much.*
>
> LENNON: *No. But we got such a hard time from everyone. And I've had so much shit thrown at me and especially at Yoko. People like Peter Brown in our office, he comes down and shakes my hand, and doesn't even say hello to her. Now that's going on all the time. And we get in so much pain that we have to do something about it. And that's what happened to us. We took H because of what the Beatles and their pals were doing to us. And we got out of it. They didn't set down to do it, but things came out of that period. And I don't forget.*[406]

Kevin Harrington was one of the staff members at Apple. He had started at NEMS in 1966 as a 15-year-old office boy for Brian Epstein, before switching to Apple two years later. Dependable and discreet, he began working with Mal Evans as a studio assistant, looking after the Beatles' equipment and ensuring they had everything they needed. He appeared alongside Evans in the opening scene of the *Let It Be* film, and was on hand during the Apple rooftop performance – the redheaded youth holding a lyrics sheet for Lennon during Dig A Pony.

Harrington's work went beyond the confines of Abbey Road and Apple, and he often ran errands for his employers. 'One day I was asked to pick up a letter for John and Yoko from a Battersea mansion to take to where they were staying in Ringo's old flat,' he said. 'I jumped in a cab to Battersea, found the flat and knocked on the door. After a few minutes the door opened a little and a half-asleep man peered out at me. I told him who had sent me and he closed the door. A minute later the door opened again and I was handed an envelope and the door closed.'

The envelope was unsealed, and Harrington's curiosity got the better of him. 'Inside was a small folded piece of paper. I carefully pulled it open and saw white powder, which I have to admit confused me at the time. Very carefully I closed the paper back up and put it back in the envelope. It was only later when John got busted that I realised what it was. I was completely ignorant of such things at that time. But it was all part of the job I suppose.'[407]

The drugs errand was a one-off for Harrington, who was just 17 at the time. He remained convinced that the Beatles rarely used Apple staff for similar pick-ups without them knowing the nature of the contents. But the group did often use their trusted lieutenants to find and prepare drugs: 'They had friends and assistants who I'm sure would have got what was needed,' he said. 'I was a late entry into their world and they had many people over many years who would do their bidding, because if a Beatle wants something you try to get it.'[408]

One such associate was Tony Sanchez, another addict with whom Lennon regularly used cocaine and cannabis. 'John, I feared, seemed to be following Brian [Jones] into a world where drugs dominated everything,' he said. 'He called almost daily to see if I could help him get hold of dope. I promised myself that I would never become labelled as a dealer. Once he aggressively insisted I supply him with heroin. He sent his chauffeur to my flat to get it. I was so annoyed at the way he was pressuring me that I accepted the £100 proffered by the driver and gave him a jar containing two crushed aspirin.' Sanchez thought that would be the end of the matter, but the following day Lennon was back on the phone demanding more. What, Sanchez asked, happened to the previous lot? 'Oh,' replied Lennon, 'I didn't think very much of that. It hardly gave me a buzz at all.'[409]

Ono described their heroin use as 'a celebration of ourselves as artists', and references to the drug quickly found their way into Lennon's songs. The most overt was in Happiness Is A Warm Gun: 'I need a fix 'cause I'm going down' became the Beatles' most explicit drug reference to date. Lennon may have also been referring to heroin in the title of Everybody's Got Something To Hide Except Me And My Monkey, and its refrain 'The deeper you go the higher you fly'.

Years later he was asked about the words of the song, and responded with characteristic vim at the reception it had received at the time. 'What did the critics say? "A bit simplistic, no imagery in it." Perhaps I should have said: "Your inside is like a whale juice dripping from the fermented foam of the teenyboppers' VD in Times Square as I injected my white clown face with heroin and performed in red-leather knickers." Maybe then they'd like it, right?'[410]

Demo recordings of both songs were made at George Harrison's home in May 1968, shortly after the group returned from India. Lennon's early version of Happiness Is A Warm Gun, as heard on *Anthology 3*, begins with the 'I need a fix' lines, suggesting that he might actually have wanted to open the song that way (the song's eventual opening lines were later written by Lennon and Derek Taylor during an acid trip). If so, the BBC's banning of A Day In The Life for slightly ambiguous drugs references clearly hadn't cowed him. Whatever his intentions, the fact that Lennon was singing about heroin withdrawal just six weeks after being clean in India shows how quickly it seeped into his life.

It could be seen, however, to have had one positive effect. He began to move away from LSD, which had left him psychologically fragile over the previous two years. Heroin provided a more lucid, comforting high than cannabis, and was less disorientating than acid. Yet to the consternation of his bandmates, Lennon became a habitual user as 1968 progressed. 'He was getting into harder drugs than we'd been into and so his songs were taking on more references to heroin,' McCartney recalled. 'Until that point we had made rather mild, oblique references to pot or LSD. But now John started talking about fixes and monkeys and it was harder terminology which the rest of us weren't into. We were disappointed that he was getting into heroin because we didn't really know how we could help him. We just hoped it wouldn't go too far. In actual fact, he did end up clean but this was the period when he was on it. It was a tough period for John, but often that adversity and craziness can lead to good art, as I think it did in this case.'[411]

The summer and autumn of 1968 marked a tumultuous time for Lennon and Ono. Their affair began in May, and shortly afterwards both filed for divorce from their respective spouses. Ono had become pregnant in May, but it ended in miscarriage in November. Until then they worked at a dizzying pace – Lennon on Beatles recordings, and together on a range of film, recording and art projects, including a first joint exhibition, You Are Here, which opened in July at the Robert Fraser Gallery.

'My theory is that John and Yoko were so much in love that they began adding wildness to ordinary love, going for it in a big way,' said McCartney. 'From what they told us – from what we found out – it did include crazy things like heroin. It appeared to include everything and anything. I mean, if the dare was to go naked, they would go naked. If the dare was to try heroin – nothing was too much. To think of yourself as Jesus Christ was not blasphemous, it was all just larger than life. All sorts of stuff was going on. Everybody was talking about expanding your mind.'[412]

Lennon and Ono's attempts to release the experimental album *Unfinished Music No. 1: Two Virgins*, with its full-frontal nude cover photograph, were met with resistance from the other Beatles and EMI's top brass. 'We took it to Apple, where the so-called "Swinging Generation" was born,' Lennon said. 'And we got from Paul and George the most ridiculous Catholic onslaught. I mean they really gave us hell.'[413] Less controversial was *The Beatles*, the official title of the White Album. But the record was created in a time of increasing tension within the band. Their group dynamic splintered after India: Ringo temporarily quit the band, each Beatle worked independently at various times, with several of the songs essentially solo recordings.

Heroin was a major factor in the escalating problems. As Barry Miles observed of Lennon: 'He was on edge, either going up or coming down. The other Beatles had to walk on eggshells just to avoid one of his explosive rages. Whereas in the old days they could have tackled him about the strain that Yoko's presence put on recording and had an old-fashioned set-to about it, now it was impossible because John was in such an unpredictable state and so obviously in pain. Yoko sat right next to him while he played, ordering Mal Evans to fetch her food and drinks and, worst of all, adding her unasked-for comments and musical suggestions, thoroughly inhibiting the other Beatles. Most of John's attention was focused upon her instead of the other three Beatles. The Fab Four had become the Fab Five without the other three ever being asked if they wanted a fifth Beatle.'[414]

Lennon and Ono stayed at 7 Cavendish Avenue for a month during the recording of the White Album. They spent many evenings watching television while McCartney lived out his last bachelor nights in the London clubs. 'Yoko made opium cookies one night, and the three of us sat staring at each other, waiting for something to happen,' said Francie Schwartz. 'It never did, but that was one time when John read through my giggle to the sadness of waiting up for Paul.'[415]

Lennon and Ono took up the habit of reading McCartney's fan mail. One day an unsigned, typed note was with the new arrivals: 'You and your Jap tart think you're hot shit.' According to Schwartz, when Lennon and Ono opened it 'they sat puzzled, looking at each other with genuine pain in their eyes'. Shortly afterwards McCartney arrived and confessed that he was the author of the anonymous note: 'Oh I just did that for a lark...'

The house guests were dumbfounded that he would be so callous. 'It was embarrassing,' Schwartz recalled. 'The three of us swivelled around, staring at him. You could see the pain in John. Yoko simply rose above it, feeling only empathy for John.'[416] Shortly afterwards they moved out, spending a few nights in a flat owned by Peter Brown and a week with Neil Aspinall.

Eventually they took up residence at 34 Montagu Square, where their addictions took hold. Lennon's chauffeur Les Anthony described the scene to Cynthia: 'It was a complete tip. They were doing heroin and other drugs and neither of them knew whether it was day or night. The floor was littered with rubbish.'[417]

Keith Richards, himself no stranger to hard drugs, witnessed Lennon's changing behaviour at this time. 'I never knew what John was on,' he said. 'He was always on something for quite a while. I always wondered when he used to come and visit me and he'd always end up throwing up over the staircase. I should have figured that he was on something else but I just thought he'd drunk too much. We'd never sit around and talk about "what you're on". We'd always talk about music or listen to records, trying to solve the world's problems or something like that. I always thought that John was bigger than any drug that he took anyway.'[418]

In May 1968, Richards bought a house on Cheyne Walk in London's Chelsea, which he shared with Anita Pallenberg. Lennon and Ono were frequent visitors. They would take drugs together although, as Richards recalled, Lennon's tolerance was significantly lower. 'The thing was with John – for all his vaunted bravado – he couldn't really keep up. He'd try and take anything I took but without my good training ... John would inevitably end up in my john, hugging the porcelain. And there'd be Yoko in the background, "He really shouldn't do this," and I'd go, "I know, but I didn't force him!" But he'd always come back for more, wherever we were ... I don't think John ever left my house except horizontally. Or definitely propped up.'[419]

In her June 2007 appearance on the BBC's *Desert Island Discs*, Ono suggested that squeamishness and the absence of a regular supply made it easier for them to kick heroin. 'Luckily we never injected because both of us were totally scared about needles. So that probably saved us. And the other thing that saved us was our connection was not very good. The connection kept giving us a lot laced with baby powder. In fact we smelt talcum powder. We'd say: "What is this?"

'But that saved us, actually. Many rock stars had very good connections and we would visit them and they would have a big bowl of powder, and if we did something then we'd be so high. We couldn't even walk straight. We would think: "Is this what they are doing every day?" We weren't doing it that way. We didn't have a connection like that.'[420]

RELATIONS within the Beatles had been deteriorating since the White Album sessions, and they reached a nadir in January 1969, the month of the *Let It Be* recordings. It began with days of rehearsals at Twickenham Film Studios. McCartney aside, there was little enthusiasm for a mooted back-to-basics live show, and the presence of film cameras created a further strain.

Although not all the days were tense, the members were often at odds with one another. Harrison was frustrated and found McCartney bossy and domineering; Lennon was addicted, unmotivated and unwilling to be parted from Ono; and Starr, sensing the prevailing mood, appeared largely subdued. As Lennon later recalled: 'That film was set up by Paul, for Paul. That's one of the main reasons the Beatles ended … We got fed up with being sidemen for Paul.'[421]

On 14 January Lennon and Ono were interviewed at Twickenham by a reporter from Canada's CBC-TV. Lasting 30 minutes, it became known as the 'Two Junkies' interview. Lennon, in particular, is clearly high on heroin, with heavy eyelids and slow speech. During one discussion he is audibly nauseous, and the interview is briefly paused after he tells the interviewer: 'Excuse me, I feel a bit sick.' Although he appears noticeably livelier once the interview resumes, and well enough to discuss live performances, inspiration and the couple's future plans, the entire exchange stands in sad contrast to the vibrancy of his past media exchanges.

A visitor to Twickenham that same day was the actor Peter Sellers, shortly to begin filming *The Magic Christian* with Ringo Starr. Sellers was a friend to the Beatles, and their tongue-in-cheek conversation – recorded with their knowledge – took a series of subtly revealing comic turns:

> *LENNON: Remember when I gave you that grass in*
> *Piccadilly?*

SELLERS: *I do, man, it really stoned me out of my mind. Acapulco gold, wasn't it?*

LENNON: *Exactly.*

SELLERS: *That was really fantastic. I'm not selling any, right now. I'm sorry.*

LENNON: *No, which they have now given up, you know, as stated by Hunter Damier [sic] in the Beatles' actual life story.*

SELLERS: *[laughs] Well, I'm sorry about that fellas… If I'd known I was going to see you quick I would have had some on me…*

JOE McGRATH *(writer/director of* The Magic Christian*): Do you want to make the scene for the gents' lavatory?*

SELLERS: *That's a groove, as they say. Well guys, see you.*

LENNON: *Bye bye.*

McCARTNEY: *Too much, Pete.*

STARR: *Bye.*

LENNON: *Way out.*

SELLERS: *Way out.*

McGRATH: *Exit.*

McCARTNEY: *Yes.*

LENNON: *Just don't leave the needles lying around, you know, we've got a bad reputation now with John getting busted and that. I know what it's like for showbiz people. They're under a great strain and they need a little relaxation.*

STARR: *That's why he's going to bed.*

LENNON: *It's a choice between that and exercise, you know, and drugs win hand down, I say hand down.*

ONO: *Well, shooting is exercise.*

LENNON: *Shooting is exercise, oh yeah.*

STARR: *Especially for the birds.*[422]

Lennon's songwriting for the Beatles had slowed to a trickle since the release of the White Album, and on *Let It Be* his only major new song was Dig A Pony. His other contributions included the studio improvisation Dig It; a brief section of I've Got A Feeling; a live version of One After 909, one of Lennon-McCartney's earliest songs; and Across The Universe, a 1968 recording the Beatles had yet to find a use for.

His only other Beatles song of note was the Get Back b-side Don't Let Me Down, written for Ono but which could as well have been about any of his other addictions or gurus. Heroin left him placidly indifferent to the activities of the Beatles, and as more of a supporting actor than in a leading role. There was no single cause of the Beatles' break-up, but if any one drug was the main catalyst it was surely heroin.

Ono claimed the drug helped calm their overactive selves. 'We both felt it was very effective in the sense of slowing down our minds,' she said. 'If you get an upper, because we're both very up people anyway, we would just go crazy with this. So we couldn't take an upper, you know. We took a downer.'[423] And yet, although addiction had a deleterious effect on Lennon's Beatles work, it didn't do the same to his energy outside the group.

For Lennon, 1969 was an astonishingly busy year, his most active since the frenetic days of Beatlemania. In addition to his work with the Beatles, he appointed Allen Klein as his manager; formed the Plastic Ono Band; performed live in Cambridge, Toronto and London; married Ono in Gibraltar; honeymooned in Paris; made a lightning trip to Vienna; staged bed-ins for peace in Amsterdam and Montreal; changed his middle name to Ono; bought and moved into Tittenhurst Park; took holidays in Wales, Scotland, Greece, India and Denmark; was hospitalised after crashing his car; flew to the Isle of Wight to watch Bob Dylan perform; made several films; resolved to leave the Beatles; returned his MBE to the Queen; released *Unfinished Music No.2: Life With The Lions*; recorded and released Cold Turkey, Give Peace A Chance, *Wedding Album* and *Live Peace In*

Toronto 1969; made an unreleased fourth experimental album; gave an array of television, radio and press interviews; appeared in documentaries for *Man Of The Decade* and the BBC series *24 Hours*; and launched the 'War is Over' poster campaign. These were clearly not the actions of a stupefied drug zombie. His focus had merely moved from the Beatles to his new chief collaborator.

AFTER WRAPPING UP *LET It Be* at the end of January 1969, the Beatles took some time out before regrouping for *Abbey Road*, their final recorded album. Lennon and Ono holidayed briefly in Wales before driving to Scotland, accompanied by John's son Julian and Yoko's daughter Kyoko. Lennon was a notoriously bad driver who had rarely been behind the wheel since passing his test in 1965. He was poor at navigating roads and often failed to notice other traffic.

On 1 July 1969 the family was near Durness in the Scottish Highlands. The roads were narrow, the weather poor, and Lennon panicked after spotting a foreign tourist driving towards him. He lost control of his Austin Maxi car, driving it into a roadside ditch. Lennon, Ono and Kyoko sustained cuts to the face, and Ono's back was injured.

They were taken to Golspie's Lawson Memorial Hospital where Lennon was given 17 facial stitches, Ono 14 in her forehead, and Kyoko four. Lennon was hospitalised for five days. He later told reporters: 'If you're going to have a car crash, try to arrange for it to happen in the Highlands. The hospital there was just great.'[424]

Julian Lennon was treated for shock but was otherwise unhurt. He was taken to stay with Lennon's Aunt Mater in Durness, before Cynthia took him back to London the following day. When she arrived at the hospital to demand an explanation from Lennon, he refused to see her.

Although Lennon never intended to attend, 1 July was the first official day of recording for what became *Abbey Road*. The crash further delayed his return to London, and after being discharged from hospital he spent three days in Weybridge before finally rejoining the Beatles on 9 July.

Lennon's musical productivity picked up during the *Abbey Road* sessions. Mean Mr Mustard and Polythene Pam had been written in India the previous year, but he wrote the new songs Come Together, I Want You (She's So Heavy), Because and Sun King. The album, however, was dominated by others. McCartney's contributions included the concept of the tapestry of song fragments in the second half, and George Harrison provided two of his most celebrated compositions: Here Comes The Sun and Something.

There are few studio photographs of the making of *Abbey Road*, but a number of outtakes from the cover shoot exist. In each of the zebra crossing pictures Lennon walks hunched, expressionless, with his hands in his trouser pockets. However, pictures taken beforehand of the group waiting on the studio steps are even more revealing. Lennon appears pale, furrowed, haggard and at least a decade older than his 28 years.

Ono was once again pregnant at the time of the car crash; it ended in miscarriage in October. Lennon arranged for Harrods to deliver a double bed to EMI Studios, allowing her to be near him while he worked and she recuperated. She slept, read and knitted, and a microphone was suspended above the bed for her to add her thoughts during the Beatles' recording sessions, a development which would have been unthinkable in previous years. The bed became a divisive symbol among studio staff and the musicians, and was emblematic of Lennon and Ono's often inward and obstinate behaviour.

The couple's heroin use had levelled off after the *Let It Be* sessions, but their habits resumed after the road accident. According to Ono, they self-medicated to alleviate their back pain. During this time she asked her friend Dan Richter to bring

drugs to the studio. 'Yoko asked me to bring over some pharmaceutical heroin,' he recalled. 'And I said I didn't want to do that.
She said "No, no, it's OK, we've been doing it for a while."'[425]

Richter was an American mime artist whose most famous
role was the bone-throwing primate at the start of Stanley
Kubrick's *2001: A Space Odyssey*. He was also a registered heroin
and cocaine addict. 'It felt weird to be sitting on the bed talking
to Yoko while the Beatles were working across the studio. I
couldn't help thinking that those guys were making rock and roll
history, while I was sitting on this bed in the middle of the
Abbey Road studio, handing Yoko a small white packet.'[426]

Richter had arrived in London in 1965. Having previously
dabbled with heroin while living in Greece, he wanted to experiment with a regular supply of legal pharmaceutical-grade
heroin and cocaine, with the intention of detoxing once the
exercise needed to end. But reality inevitably proved different.
He soon found himself hooked, and became a patient of Lady
Frankau.

The Beatles always had a small circle of trusted assistants,
and new alliances formed as the band began to fragment.
Richter was invited, with his wife Jill and their infant son Sacha,
to move into Tittenhurst Park, the sprawling Ascot estate owned
by Lennon and Ono. He worked as their assistant, photographer, film maker and runner. He also became the couple's drug
supplier, taking a taxi to north London each day to procure their
dope, taking a cut for himself in the process.

Most registered addicts had by then been moved on to
methadone, although a few long-term users were permitted to
remain on heroin. One such person was 'an old junkie named
Janet', who was willing to sell Richter some of her large daily
dose. 'She sat in her bed in the corner of her little room; a
grimy curtain covered her only window,' he recalled. 'She
looked like an ancient rumpled bird. She didn't even bother to
lift her nightgown when she gave herself a shot. Her veins had
been ruined so she just stuck the needle in her thigh right

through it. Poor Janet's voice was more of a croak than speech. As I watched her I wondered if that would be me one day. I gave her the cash and she gave me the heroin pills. Then the cab took me back to Ascot.

'On returning to Tittenhurst, I would lock myself in my bathroom, take out a clean syringe and inject myself with enough of the drug to take the nagging sickness away. If I had enough, I might even get a bit high. Once I was comfortable, I would go up to John and Yoko's area and quietly put some outside their bedroom door then called Yoko and let her know it was there. Unlike grass and cocaine, we never used the heroin together.'[427]

ADDICTED couples often operate in tandem: obtaining drugs for one another, using together, pooling resources and providing mutual support during withdrawal and treatment – sharing and collaborating like most couples do, albeit in highly unusual circumstances. Another reason for the solidarity is to provide mutual support during the declining self-esteem, deceptions and slackening of personal moral boundaries that junkies often experience.

It can be devilishly difficult to kick a habit while with someone who is still using, a reason why many addiction recovery programmes insist that people remain single until their treatment is complete. Lennon and Ono fell into heroin use together, and would have supported each other through recovery, but the danger remained that one weak moment may have sent them both back into addiction.

In August 1969 they decided to address their heroin habits before they spiralled deeper. The effects on her pregnancy would also have been a major concern. Warned that heroin could cause a second miscarriage or leave the baby addicted, the couple chose to kick the habit. 'John said, "Right, that's it. We cut it here",' Ono recalled.[428]

They opted to get clean without professional help, withdrawing at Tittenhurst Park with the assistance of Dan and Jill Richter. 'We were very square people in a way,' said Ono. 'We wouldn't kick in a hospital because we wouldn't let anybody know. We just went straight cold turkey. The thing is, because we never injected, I don't think we were sort of – well, we were hooked, but I don't think it was a great amount. Still, it was hard. Cold turkey is always hard.'[429] The most likely date they began withdrawal was 25 August 1969. Coincidentally, in London that same day, the final studio session for *Abbey Road* took place in Lennon's absence.

Withdrawal symptoms can vary depending on the extent of a person's habit, tolerance, and their physical and emotional strength. For newer users they can be fairly mild. A running nose, sweating, involuntary twitching, restlessness and goosebumps are often the first signs, but they can be accompanied by feverish temperature changes, aching pains, insomnia, anxiety, vomiting and diarrhoea.

Milder ailments escalate to agonising proportions until a fix is acquired, or the addict undergoes medical assistance or 'cold turkey' – abrupt and complete cessation, instead of gradual reduction or weaning. Physical withdrawal normally peaks after two or three days, but the acute symptoms can last over a week. Psychological opiate addiction can endure for many more years, and former users often speak of never being free of addictive thoughts and impulses. Recidivism rates among addicts are high, and Lennon and Ono were no exceptions.

As was his custom in 1969, Lennon put his experiences into song. What he described in Cold Turkey was physical withdrawal from a full-blown addiction, sparing few details and laying himself bare before his listeners. In early September 1969 he recorded a series of acoustic guitar demos of the song. He even tried to get Bob Dylan to play piano on one recording, the day after Dylan's appearance at the Isle of Wight Festival.

'He came to our house with George when I'd written Cold Turkey,' said Lennon. 'I was just trying again to put him on piano for Cold Turkey to make a rough take, but his wife was pregnant or something and they left. But he's calmed down a lot now than what he was. I just remember we were both in shades and both on fucking junk. And all these freaks around us, and Ginsberg, and all those people. I was nervous as shit.'[430]

Lennon took his Dylan-less demos to the Beatles, suggesting they record it as the group's next single with a Lennon-McCartney songwriting credit. Unsurprisingly it was rejected outright, and Lennon elected instead to record the song with his new ad-hoc group, Plastic Ono Band.

Cold Turkey had its first public performance on 13 September at the Toronto Rock 'n' Roll Revival festival, with Lennon reading the lyrics from a sheet of paper held up by Ono. The live debut lacked the biting guitar of the later studio recording, but featured a tremulous vocal by Lennon which was presumably a throwback to the pain of withdrawal. The crowd's response to the new song was muted, and Lennon dejectedly demanded: 'Come on, wake up.'

Having kicked the drug just weeks before, Lennon was back to using heroin – or heroin substitutes – in September, and was high during the Toronto performance. A year later he told *Rolling Stone*: 'We were full of junk too. I just threw up for hours till I went on. I nearly threw up in Cold Turkey – I had a review in *Rolling Stone* about the film of it – which I haven't seen yet, and they're saying, "I was this and that." And I was throwing up nearly in the number, I could hardly sing any of them, I was full of shit.'[431]

Lennon had wanted cocaine before taking to the stage. Gene Vincent reportedly gave him a small capsule which he claimed was coke, but it didn't have the desired effect. 'When it came time to play, John was throwing up in the bathroom,' recalled

Dan Richter. 'I couldn't tell if it was nerves, heroin withdrawal or the lousy dope. I later learnt that he was always sick before a performance.'[432]

Cold Turkey was recorded at the end of September 1969, just days after *Abbey Road* was released. Gone was the chugging rhythm guitar of the demos and live version, and in its place was a searing, jagged guitar riff played by Eric Clapton. Klaus Voormann's bass and Ringo Starr's drums were mixed without echo or treble, giving a feeling of claustrophobia, and Lennon's howls and screams towards the song's end pointed the way to the primal soul-baring of his first solo album *John Lennon/Plastic Ono Band*.

The song would have been a remarkable artistic statement for any major musician of the time, but coming from a Beatle it was astonishing. In the US it was banned, a decision which Lennon later found bewildering. 'To me, it was a rock 'n' roll version of *The Man With The Golden Arm*,' he said. 'You know, it's like banning *The Man With The Golden Arm* because it showed Frank Sinatra suffering from drug withdrawal. To ban the record is the same thing. It's like banning the movie. Because it shows reality.'[433]

Given the challenging nature of the release, its modest chart performance should perhaps not have been too much of a surprise. Lennon made light of it when returning his MBE to Buckingham Palace, issuing a statement which read: 'I am returning this MBE in protest against Britain's involvement in the Nigeria-Biafra thing, against our support of America in Vietnam, and against Cold Turkey slipping down the charts. With love, John Lennon of Bag.'

Curiously, Lennon initially declined to confirm that the song was about heroin addiction. Speaking to journalist Ray Connolly in 1970, and evidently mindful of the influence of his fame, he said of the song: 'I wrote it when I was coming off drugs and it was dreadful. I'm not mentioning which drugs or it'll be another bloody scandal. I never injected anything. I don't want kids injecting ... It was the press who released the news that we were junkies.'[434]

Yoko Ono maintained that she and Lennon quit heroin with no outside assistance. That may have been true in August 1969, but several of their associates at the time – including Connolly and Apple's Neil Aspinall and Alexis Mardas – recall her and Lennon undergoing methadone treatment for addiction at the London Clinic, a private hospital in Marylebone. Ono became pregnant again in January 1970, and on 5 March checked in to the clinic for observation, remaining there for four days. At the time it was reported that she was recovering from surgery caused by 'the aftermath of a miscarriage last October'.[435]

She later dismissed suggestions that she and Lennon were being treated for heroin addiction. 'It's a myth that we went into the hospital to withdraw,' she said. 'People said, "Oh, they're privileged, probably the hospital took care of them or something." We were so totally scared, we thought, "It's an illegal thing, we can't openly go to hospital, they might arrest us or something." So we never even dreamt of going to hospital. We just cold turkeyed.'[436]

On 7 March Ray Connolly, then an *Evening Standard* columnist, visited the couple at the clinic. 'The nurse came in at one point and was going to give Yoko something, and John said, "You do know she's a junkie, don't you?" However, he would use the word "junkie" in a very loose sort of way. He didn't mean that she was an addict, but it did mean that she would dabble with drugs.'[437]

LENNON AND ONO'S time out of the junkie lifestyle gave them cause to reevaluate their friendships and associations. Under the spotlight was Dan Richter, who was still struggling with his own habit. 'As the winter of 1970 approached, John and Yoko decided to stop using heroin before they became more seriously addicted,' he said. 'I was scared because I was so entrenched in my long-term addiction and I had never succeeded in quitting,' he said. 'With the screwed-up logic of a junkie, I resented them as "chippies," the term we used for people who dabbled in the drug. Actually, John had gone through prolonged battles with addiction and alcoholism for years.'[438]

Lennon wanted Richter's family to move out of Tittenhurst Park, knowing that his presence as a drug addict would cause overwhelming temptation for them. With characteristic kindness, Lennon offered his friends a lifeline. 'I said I was trying to stop, had been to several rehabs, etc, so John said, "What would it take?" And I said if I was isolated from the world for two months and have a doctor visiting me to prescribe tranquillisers so I don't go into convulsions during withdrawal, I could do it. John said, "We'll do it then. You can have that."'[439]

Lennon and Ono granted Richter his every wish. Each day he and Jill gave Tittenhurst's housekeeper, Val Wilde, a shopping list of requirements. A local doctor, Mike Loxton, checked on Richter daily and provided medication to alleviate the physical and mental pain of withdrawal.

The doctor then helped him stabilise by prescribing measured doses of methadone. Richter went onto methadone maintenance for several years to taper down his addictions, and despite some lapses eventually found sobriety. He and his family remained at Tittenhurst before parting ways with Lennon and Ono in 1973.

Lennon and Ono, too, used methadone. They believed it to be non-addictive, and found it brought unintended complications. 'It was the wrong information that somebody gave us that there was a new drug called methadone and that gives you the same high as smack, but you don't get hooked on it,' said Ono. 'And so, "Whoopee," you know, and at that time we were totally dry.

'So most people take methadone because they want to withdraw from smack and we weren't taking smack, we weren't taking anything, so it was the silliest thing to do. So we got hooked on methadone…'

Ono described coming off methadone as 'the hardest thing that I've ever done. And I'm sure that's true for John too. After that, we couldn't get hooked on anything.'[440]

7

IN SPITE OF ALL THE DANGER

The British press had long enjoyed a symbiotic relationship with pop stars. Since the early Sixties, in exchange for close access, reporters turned a blind eye to the various infractions which, were they widely known, could have ruined a career. It was a gentlemen's agreement which held strong until the middle of the decade.

The music weeklies – among them the *New Musical Express*, *Melody Maker*, *Record Mirror*, *Disc Weekly* and *Music Echo* – maintained the sanitised style that had served them well since the 1950s: upbeat gossip on fave raves, tour hijinks, new arrivals in the charts, and chatter about cars, homes and partners.

By 1966, however, musicians were tiring of the family-friendly tone, and several stars began to falter publicly. The news that year included Scott Walker's suicide attempt, Ray Davies's depression and disillusionment with the music industry, Mick Jagger's collapse with nervous exhaustion, Bob Dylan's mysterious motorcycle accident, and Roy Orbison's sorrow over the death of his wife. Some of the more lurid details were omitted but, with the exception of Dylan, reporters were given free access to the stars within just days of the events. Drugs, too, were being openly discussed in the music press, as musicians attempted the delicate balance of appearing hip without giving away too much about their own lifestyles.

The national newspapers were also changing their coverage. The broadsheets had tended to take a detached view of the pop revolution that began in 1963, focusing mainly on business matters: record sales, film contracts, lawsuits and the like. The tabloid press were more enthusiastic, running interviews with performers, sharing trivia and titbits, and acting as a conduit between management and the fans. Yet journalists and their editors knew about musicians' off-stage misdemeanours, and the pressure to keep ahead of their rivals by reporting front page scoops inevitably led to closer scrutiny.

The *News Of The World* was a Sunday tabloid which epitomised the more sensational press. Its pages were awash with crime stories, sex scandals and celebrity gossip, and it comfortably reached over six million readers each week. In 1964 the paper reported the amphetamine craze that went hand-in-hand with the mod lifestyle, and as pop musicians began to share their positive attitudes towards drugs, its newshounds started to sniff out a larger story.

The changing media coverage coincided with a shift in the responses of the UK government and the police to drug use. New measures outlawing the use of premises for drug taking were introduced, and penalties for possession were greatly increased. Convictions for cannabis offences rose 79% in a year, and London's Metropolitan Police Service increased its activities against known users and dealers. The chief Blue Meanie was Detective Sergeant Norman Clement Pilcher, known to colleagues as Nobby, who joined the Met's drug squad in 1966. Pilcher had established strong links between the police, the media and the criminal underworld, and realised that taking down celebrities would be more effective at garnering press coverage than targeting little known dealers and users.

Scottish pop-folk singer Donovan Leitch was an early British exponent of flower power. A 1966 television documentary, *A Boy Called Donovan*, contained several party scenes in which the singer and friends appeared to be under the influence. Later in the year his transatlantic hit single Sunshine Superman contained an LSD reference in its opening lines. Its b-side, a hallucinatory fantasy titled The Trip, was even more explicit, and was also the first pop song to mention Methedrine by name.

Early in the morning of 11 June, nine officers from the drug squad, led by Pilcher, raided Leitch's Edgware Road apartment. They failed to find any acid, but did uncover a large block of hashish in the room of his friend 'Gypsy Dave' Mills. According to Mills, the cannabis was planted there by the police.

Leitch, Mills and a woman, Doreen Samuel, were arrested, and charged the following day with possession of cannabis. George Harrison and Paul McCartney insisted that the trio were represented by the Beatles' lawyer, David Jacobs. Leitch and Mills avoided jail, but were each fined £250, and Samuel was given a year's probation.

It was the first in a long series of high profile arrests and convictions which sent shockwaves through London's music scene. Many musicians were using stronger drugs than cannabis, and feared the consequences of getting caught after many months of feeling infallible. For the time being, however, the Beatles were beyond the scope of the drug squad, whose officers were content to pick the lower-hanging fruit.

An easier target were the Rolling Stones, who had cultivated a reputation as the bad boys of rock. Brian Jones had the most prodigious appetite for drugs, with an intake rivalling, and occasionally eclipsing, John Lennon's. The Stones came to view Jones as a liability, after he repeatedly failed to turn up for sessions or was unable to play.

On 29 January 1967 the *News Of The World* ran the first of what promised to be a series of articles lifting the lid on drugs in the pop world. The first focused on Donovan, who was considered unlikely to offer much in the way of defence. A friend of the singer, Suzanne Lloyd, went on the record about her own drug use, and the paper offered interpretations of some of his more far-out lyrics, along with those of the Mothers Of Invention and the Move. The double-page feature concluded with a trail for the following week's exposé, which promised to unmask 'The Beat Groups Who Use LSD'.

The second feature, published on 5 February, spoke of LSD parties hosted by the Moody Blues, and named the Who's Pete Townshend and Cream's Ginger Baker as users. Yet more sensational was an encounter with a Rolling Stone at Blaises nightclub in London. Two journalists from the paper spoke to the band member at length about his use of pills, hashish and LSD, and witnessed him knocking back half a dozen Benzedrine tablets before inviting a friend and two girls back to his place 'for a smoke'. The reporters were naturally delighted with their scoop.

At the time of its publication, Mick Jagger was enjoying an Italian holiday with Marianne Faithfull. Leafing through the papers, he was astonished to see a large photograph of himself alongside the article, which named him as the pill-popping, dope smoking nightclub hedonist. The story was completely untrue: unlike Jones and Richards, Jagger was yet to try LSD, and took pains to control his public image.

Back in London, the band's managers, Andrew Loog Oldham and Allen Klein, feared it would cause problems for future international tours, and Jagger's lawyers issued a libel writ against the *News Of The World*. In the newspaper's offices the journalists realised their error: they had actually spoken to Brian Jones, and were potentially facing punitive costs in damages and fees.

Obeying the principle that attack is the best form of defence, two reporters were sent to find evidence to derail the lawsuit. Jagger's and Richards's telephones were tapped, their homes were put under surveillance, and paranoia began to rise within the Stones camp.

ON FRIDAY 10 FEBRUARY, Jagger, Richards and Faithfull attended the orchestral overdub session for the Beatles' A Day In The Life. Robert Fraser had suggested a trip to the country, and a party was arranged for the weekend at Redlands, Richards's thirteenth century thatched cottage in West Wittering, Sussex. It was to be Jagger's induction to LSD.

David Schneiderman, the likely supplier of the Beatles' LSD-laced sugar cubes in New York two years before, was a recent arrival in London, and had been dispensing Owsley Stanley's strong 'California Sunshine' microdot pills around the clubs and parties. A chance encounter with Richards led to Schneiderman, whom Fraser dubbed the 'Acid King', being invited to Redlands. Jagger, Richards, Faithfull, Fraser, Michael Cooper and a handful of others were at the party, although Brian Jones and Anita Pallenberg failed to show.

On the Sunday morning the guests were given microdots with their breakfast tea. Schneiderman, who carried an attaché case filled with a variety of substances and false passports, also passed around cigarettes dipped in DMT. The guests partied in the grounds and nearby woodlands, and later took a trip to the beach.

The drugs were wearing off as the sun began to set, and the guests settled down to relax in the large living room. The evening was briefly enlivened by the unexpected arrival of George and Pattie Harrison, who had been invited during the 10 February session. George later said he had found the party boring, and just before 8pm he and Pattie bade their farewells. As they drove home, unknown to them, a group of 18 officers from the local police force were assembled at the end of the Redlands driveway, armed with a search warrant.

Someone in the Stones' circle had tipped off the *News Of The World* about the weekend. The newspaper, knowing that a successful raid could put an end to Jagger's libel action, had notified the Metropolitan Police in London. The drug squad, however, reportedly decided against making martyrs of Jagger and Richards, fearing it might counterproductively make cannabis more attractive to the nation's youth. Instead, the newspaper approached Chichester Police with their intel.

Harrison believed he and Pattie had been spared arrest by officers wary of upsetting the apple cart: 'I was at that party, and the funny thing about it was that they said in the newspapers later: "Another internationally famous pop star and his wife escaped moments before the net closed in." I left there about 7pm, so it showed me they were waiting until I had gone because they were still climbing the ladder, working their way up. They didn't want to get to the Fabs yet.'[441]

In fact, it appears that the police were unaware that a Beatle had been at Redlands, and the timing was little more than coincidental. Nonetheless, a subsequent *News Of The World* report mentioned that 'one pop star and his wife drove off and so quite unwittingly escaped the net,' suggesting that the newspaper was informed of their presence shortly thereafter.

When the police launched the raid there was confusion and little resistance from the blissed out party guests. In the search that followed, officers discovered four white amphetamine tablets inside a velvet jacket owned by Jagger. Heroin tablets and eight capsules of methamphetamine hydrochloride (speed) were found on Robert Fraser, and an ashtray containing cannabis detritus implicated Richards as the householder. The pharmacopeia owned by Schneiderman curiously avoided close scrutiny. The Acid King absconded to Spain shortly after the raid, under another false identity, and eventually surfaced in New York.

The trials of Jagger, Richards and Fraser took place in June 1967. All three were found guilty: Jagger was sentenced to three months for amphetamine possession; Richards was given a one-year sentence; and Fraser, who had pleaded guilty, received six months for heroin possession. Aside from the predictable outrage and upset from the Stones' loyal fans, one intersection of press and establishment came to their defence. In July the editor of *The Times*, William Rees-Mogg, published the famous editorial 'Who breaks a butterfly on a wheel?', in which he argued that the sentence handed to Jagger (curiously, the only person mentioned) for a minor first offence was punitive, vindictive and disproportionate.

The appeals were brought forward and Richards's conviction was overturned, while Jagger's was reduced to a conditional discharge. Defiant, they recorded a stopgap single, We Love You, accompanied by a promo film which mocked the court proceedings. Lennon and McCartney performed uncredited backing vocals on the song and its b-side, Dandelion.

Ringo Starr summed up the generational divide in a *Melody Maker* interview published that December: 'Judges are old men. And I'm not saying all old people are bad. But some judges think it's a great joke. They're trying to "kill" the pop people. But as soon as they grab one of them the news is all over everywhere, so they're spreading it. They haven't caught on to that yet. They think it's great, you know, if the police raid a place. But 50 million people have read about it again and a couple of thousand will say, "I'll try drugs." So they're building the case for it, more than against it, because of their silly attitude.'[442]

The convictions may have destabilised the Rolling Stones, but support and resistance swiftly flourished. A number of public protests, concerts and demonstrations took place over the summer, some centred on the Fleet Street offices of the *News Of The World*. On 16 July a rally was held in London's Hyde Park. Posters advertised it with the words 'Legalise Cannabis – The Putting Together of the Heads'. A week later *The Times* ran the Soma-sponsored advertisement, signed by the Beatles and Brian Epstein, calling for the drug to be legalised.

Meetings were held to find a way to support those arrested on drugs charges. They led to the formation of Release, an underground organisation set up by Caroline Coon and Rufus Harris. It provided legal advice and welfare assistance, and distributed a card containing the number of an advice line, instructions on what to do if arrested, and a brief overview of a person's legal rights. In time, Release came to handle a third of all of Britain's drug busts. In 1972 it was given charitable status, and later received government funding. At first, however, Release was a shoestring operation, with a 24-hour helpline run by volunteers.

THE SUCCESS of *Sgt Pepper* and the worldwide satellite broadcast of All You Need Is Love helped the Beatles sidestep the controversy over their admission of LSD use and endorsement of cannabis, and their cross-generational popularity remained strong. But the tabloid press, so supportive in the earlier years, began to turn on the group as they embraced such unconventional practices as meditation and became mired in their first critical failure, the *Magical Mystery Tour* film. In 1968 Lennon and Ono received the lion's share of press opprobrium, which ranged from dismay at a perceived betrayal to outright racist hostility.

As the Beatles' reputation showed the first signs of tarnishing, the police began to pay more attention to their activities. Emboldened by his success with other rock stars, Norman Pilcher set his sights on bagging a Beatle. According to Donovan Leitch, there was an attempted raid of Kenwood in early 1968. Lennon received a tip-off and disposed of the drugs he was keeping, including several ounces of hashish. By the time the police arrived, the house was clean and they left without finding anything. Pilcher reportedly told Lennon: 'We'll get you next time.'[443] There is no known police record of the incident, and Lennon never publicly discussed it, so some scepticism may be warranted, not least because the drug squad was not averse to planting evidence.

On 16 February 1968, detective constable Donald Speirs led

a raid on Alexis Mardas's home in London's Westmoreland Place, where Pattie Harrison's sister Jenny Boyd had been staying. She was co-managing the Apple Boutique with Pete Shotton, and the previous day had flown to Rishikesh with the Beatles.

In her basement bedroom they found a Moroccan hookah pipe which was taken away for analysis, and was later found to contain traces of cannabis resin. A warrant for Boyd's arrest was issued in her absence. On 23 April, the day after she arrived back from Rishikesh, Speirs returned to Westmoreland Place and made the arrest. 'She said she had only just got back from India on the day before and did not know about the search,' Speirs later stated in court. 'I said the analysis showed cannabis resin had been in the pipe. Miss Boyd said she used to smoke cannabis, but had stopped smoking it now that she had taken up meditation.'[444]

Boyd appeared at Bow Street magistrates court on 20 June, where she pleaded not guilty and was given one year's conditional discharge. Mardas, as the owner of the property, was fortunate not to be charged at all. The police may not yet have been targeting the Beatles themselves, but they were getting ever closer.

PAUL MCCARTNEY's readiness to discuss his drug use may have left him susceptible to police attention, but during the late Sixties he appeared to have been given a free pass. Nonetheless, he remained a prolific smoker of cannabis, and his Cavendish Avenue home saw many scenes of debauchery, legal and otherwise.

In 1968, during a break from the White Album sessions, he and Francie Schwartz were returning from a trip to Liverpool, travelling at speed. The car was pulled over by a policeman who issued them with a ticket. The floor of the car was covered with marijuana, but the starstruck officer chose to turn a blind eye. 'Paul delivered a piece of Beatlecharming bull about how the cop didn't really have to give us the ticket, how we could all be friends if we tried, and the policeman smiled engagingly,' said Schwartz. 'He took a second look at me. I must have had a stupid stoned smile, because he handed me the ticket fast, as if he didn't want to think twice about what had really been going on in that car.'[445]

Schwartz was jettisoned by McCartney not long after their return to London, and another American, Linda Eastman, assumed her place. McCartney had first met the New York photographer in May 1967 at the Bag O'Nails, and four days later she attended the press party for *Sgt Pepper*. They first got together in June the following year while McCartney was on an Apple promotional junket in Los Angeles.

The LA party also included label boss Ron Kass, McCartney's childhood friend Ivan Vaughan, and Apple employee Tony Bramwell. Eastman had a Victorian drawstring bag filled with grass, which she liberally passed around. McCartney had found someone who enjoyed cannabis as much as he did, a mutual enthusiasm which helped strengthen their early bond.

Eastman accompanied the Apple delegation to LAX as they prepared to fly back to England. She and McCartney sat slightly apart from the rest of the group in the VIP area; Tony Bramwell described them as 'like Siamese twins, holding hands and gazing into each other's eyes'.[446] But their reverie was interrupted when FBI officers burst into the lounge. 'There's a bomb warning on your flight,' one told McCartney. 'Do you know of any Caucasian male with a grudge against you?' McCartney knew of no such person, but the officers wanted to search their luggage to check for any suspect devices.

'Out of the corner of my eye,' said Bramwell, 'I noticed Linda very swiftly aiming a neat little backward kick with her heel. Her square vanity case, which she had placed on the floor beneath her seat, skidded to the row of empty seats and, fortunately, came to rest exactly underneath one of them.' Eastman stood up and said farewell, informing the FBI men she was bound for New York and was not with the Apple contingent. 'She smiled at us all and sauntered off through the door of the VIP lounge as if she had all the time in the world, and as if there wasn't enough marijuana packed into her vanity case to get a herd of elephants stoned.'[447]

Paul and Linda married the following year, and remained near-constant companions until her death in Tucson, Arizona, in April 1998. During their time together they endured drug busts in Sweden, Scotland, the United States, Japan, Barbados and England, caused by a mix of carelessness and planted evidence. But that was in a future chapter, a different career. McCartney was fortunate to remain below Norman Pilcher's radar in London. Two of his compatriots were not so fortunate.

JOHN LENNON WAS WELL aware of the establishment's changing attitude towards the Beatles. 'In a way we'd turned out to be a Trojan horse,' he said. 'The "Fab Four" moved right to the top and then sang about drugs and sex and then I got into more and more heavy stuff and that's when they started dropping us.'[448] Pilcher could well have chosen any of the group for his first strike, but McCartney, Harrison and Starr had appeared far less eager – in the public eye, at least – to upset the apple cart.

'There's two ways of thinking, that they're out to get us, or it just happened that way,' Lennon said in 1970. 'After I started *Two Virgins* and doing those kind of things, it was like, well, it seemed like I was fair game for the police. There was some myth about us being protected because we had MBEs. I don't think it was true, it's just that we never did anything. I mean the way Paul said the acid thing – he never got attacked for it. I don't know if that was protected, because he was sort of openly admitting that we had drugs. I don't really know about that. I don't think we were ever protected in England. I just think nobody ever really bothered about us.'[449]

After Lennon's marriage to Cynthia broke down, she and their son Julian had moved to 34 Montagu Square. They stayed there for three months from June 1968, after which they swapped residences with Lennon and Ono and moved back to Kenwood.

On the morning of 18 October 1968, Pete Shotton happened to call round to see Lennon at Montagu Square. Shotton had witnessed plenty of outlandish behaviour over the years, and considered himself largely unshockable, but was nonetheless taken aback to see Lennon using a vacuum cleaner. Lennon revealed that he had received a phone call thirty minutes earlier tipping him off that a police raid was imminent.

'It's genuine,' Lennon told Shotton. 'They're definitely coming. It was one of the drug squad that phoned me – I suppose he's hoping for a pay-off... Anyway, I've just about finished hoovering all the carpets. You know what those cunts are like – they'll bust you if the fucking dog smells something in the rug. They'll hoover up all the minuscule bits and put them under a microscope, and bust you for it even if the stuff's been there for three years. Since fucking *Jimi Hendrix* used to live here, Christ knows what the *fuck* is in *these* carpets!'[450]

The tip-off followed a warning from the *Daily Mirror*'s Don Short three weeks before. 'A friend of mine from Fleet Street gave me a call after he'd overheard a cop in a pub saying how he was going to get the Beatles,' Lennon said in 1973. 'Which meant me. I mean, he's not about to bust Ringo or Paul. I was really up for grabs what with *Two Virgins* and living in sin with a foreigner and all.'[451]

Lennon and Shotton swept through the apartment, checking clothes, cupboards, cabinets and drawers for anything that might have contained traces of illegal substances. Ono had shut herself in the bedroom upon Shotton's arrival, unhappy at his presence, and as Lennon cleaned out the room an argument between the couple escalated. Shotton made his excuses and left. In addition to his discomfort at being the subject of their quarrel, he was keen to avoid becoming embroiled in a drugs bust. He took with him the bag from the vacuum cleaner, disposing of it in a nearby bin before making his way to 3 Savile Row. By the time he arrived, word of the raid had reached Apple.

At 11.55am two detective sergeants, three detective constables and two police dog handlers – yet no dogs – arrived at 34 Montagu Square. With Shotton gone and the flat clean, Lennon and Ono had gone back to bed. They were half undressed – 'feeling very clean and drugless' – when the entryphone rang. Ono opened the door, but quickly slammed and locked it after a female officer declared that they had a search warrant. 'We ran back in and hid,' Lennon said. 'Neither of us was dressed, really; we just had vests on and our lower parts were showing.'[452]

The police believed that at least three people – Lennon, Ono and an unidentified other – lived on the premises. The raid had been planned in the hope of busting a party in full swing, although it is unclear why they thought midday would be the most appropriate time. 'It is not unusual when executing search warrants for premises occupied by members of the entertainment world to find that there are large numbers of people present taking part in unusual parties,' Pilcher later told the home secretary, James Callaghan. 'In this case it was found that only two persons were present, and both were in a state of undress.'

An officer attempted to open a bedroom window to gain entry at the back of the property, but it was held shut by Lennon. 'I don't care who you are, you're not bloody coming in here,' he told the policeman. Ono held the window shut while Lennon got dressed and attempted to stall the officers. 'He was saying, "Just open the window, you'll only make it worse for yourself." I was saying, "I want to see the warrant." Another guy comes on the roof and they showed me this paper, and I pretended to read it – just to try and think what to do.'[453]

Lennon admitted defeat after the police began forcing open the front door, eight minutes after they had arrived. Once the officers were inside, and had established that Lennon and Ono were alone, there was a 30-minute wait for the sniffer dogs.

A call to Apple was answered by the company's telephonist Laurie McCaffery. Lennon declined to reveal his identity, but she patched the call through to Neil Aspinall's office. 'John called me and said, "Neil, think about all your worst paranoias – because they're here",' Aspinall recalled.[454] He sent Peter Brown, who was looking after Lennon and Ono's personal affairs, to Montagu Square. Brown found the couple ashen faced, frightened and chain smoking. He attended to their immediate needs and arranged for their lawyers to arrive. By this time several reporters and photographers were outside.

The sniffer dogs, labradors named Yogi and Boo-Boo, arrived at 12.35pm, and the search got underway. The dogs found cannabis resin in a leather binocular case and a suitcase. Lennon initially claimed he had forgotten about the drugs due to their chaotic lifestyles: 'I'd had all my stuff moved into the flat from my house, and I'd never looked at it. It had just been there for years. I'd ordered cameras and clothes – but my driver brought binoculars, which I didn't need in my little flat. And inside the binoculars was some hash from last year. Somewhere else in an envelope was another piece of hash. So that was it.'[455]

However, he later suggested that at least some of the cannabis was put there by the police. 'We were planted,' he said in 1980. 'Believe me, I'd cleaned the house out, because Jimi Hendrix had lived there before in this apartment, and I'm not stupid. I went through the whole damn house.'[456]

Lennon and Ono were arrested and charged, then escorted from the property. Ono emerged first, accompanied by the female detective constable. Lennon came out shortly after, flanked by two male officers. They were taken separately to

Paddington Green police station and formally interviewed in the presence of their lawyers.

Paul McCartney, at home in Cavendish Avenue, was informed of Lennon's plight. He phoned the chairman of EMI, Sir Joseph Lockwood, to see if any establishment influence could be exerted. Sir Joseph called Paddington Green and spoke to Lennon, who by that point was feeling more composed. 'Hello! This is Sergeant Lennon,' he answered. 'Can I help you?'[457]

By 3pm they were released, leaving by a side door to avoid reporters, and went briefly to the home of their solicitor Nicholas Cowan. Lennon and Ono were each bailed for £100 and were made to pay a surety sum of £100, ahead of their appearance at Marylebone Magistrates' Court the following morning.

Lennon and Ono attended the court hearing, which lasted just five minutes. Norman Pilcher read the two charges against them, for drug possession and obstruction. They were remanded on bail, and their case was adjourned until 28 November. The court register noted the two charges thus:

'Having in his/her possession a dangerous drug to wit, a quantity of cannabis resin without being duly authorised at 34 Montague [*sic*] Square W1 on 18-10-68 Con. To Regs 3 Dangerous Drugs (No 2) Regs 1964 and Sec 13 Dangerous Drugs Act 1965 AND Wilfully obstructing Norman Pilcher, a constable of the Metropolitan Police force, then exercising his powers under the Dangerous Drugs Act, 1965 on the 18th, October 1968 at 34 Montague Sq W1. Contrary to Section 13 (3) Dangerous Drugs Act. 1965.'[458]

The couple's car was not waiting outside the court. They huddled together in the scrum of reporters, police and the public, with Lennon doing his best to protect his pregnant girl-friend before their transport arrived. A photograph of the scene, taken by a Daily Mirror photojournalist, was used on the rear cover of their 1969 album *Unfinished Music No. 2: Life With The Lions*.

Two days after the court appearance, Labour MP Arthur Lewis tabled a written question to James Callaghan, questioning the manpower and expense incurred by the raid. Pilcher was summoned to the House of Commons, where he denied that the police presence had been excessive. 'The officers involved in executing the search warrant were: two detective sergeants, two detective constables, one woman detective constable, and the two dog handlers,' he said. 'It was found on this occasion that at least five officers were required because of the difficulty in gaining entry to the premises and the fact that the premises consisted of two floors with numerous rooms that were in a very untidy condition.'[459] Pilcher also revealed that the total weekly salary of the officers who took part was £178, 14 shillings and sixpence.

The answer did not placate Arthur Lewis, who on 30 October submitted a follow-up question, asking the home secretary 'to what extent the Metropolitan Police notified the press and publicity services of their intention to raid the private residence of John Lennon; and whether he will give an assurance that the police do [*sic*] notify the press of intended action, either of arrest or impending court action.'[460]

Callaghan ordered a full report into the events of 18 October. The Met denied it had leaked news of the raid to the press, and suggested that a neighbour may have been responsible. 'The fact that police officers were attempting to effect an entry into the residence of Lennon and Cox [Ono] is of immense news value to the press and of likewise publicity value to Lennon himself. The police officers involved have been questioned and strongly deny being responsible for any leakage of information. Police do not notify the press, or any other body of their intended actions.'[461]

This was relayed to parliament by Callaghan on 7

November. 'The police do not make public their intention to search premises or make an arrest, and the normal practice was followed in this case,' he told the House of Commons. 'The first pressmen arrived forty minutes after the police had knocked on the front door.'[462] Nonetheless, Lennon remained convinced that the reporters had been tipped off by Pilcher. 'There was a question raised in the Houses of Parliament,' he told the BBC in December 1980. 'Why do they need 40 cops to arrest John and Yoko? I mean that thing was set up. The *Daily Mail* and the *Daily Express* were there, before the cops came. He'd called the press.'[463]

A FORENSIC ANALYSIS of the substances seized during the raid was prepared by senior scientific officer Michael Ansell. His report revealed that, in addition to the cannabis, three Omnopon tablets – a mixture of morphine, papaverine and codeine – had been found.

> Statement of MICHAEL ANSELL, M.A.
>
> Occupation of Witness: Senior Scientific Officer
>
> On the 22nd October, 1968, I took possession of the following sealed items:
>
> Description: One binocular case containing binoculars and herbal mixture.
>
> Result of Analysis: 12.43 grammes (191.8 grains) of Cannabis resin.
>
> Description: One tin containing herbal mixture.
>
> Result of Analysis: Traces of Cannabis resin.
>
> Description: One envelope containing herbal mixture.
>
> Result of Analysis: 1.77 grammes (27.3 grains) of Cannabis resin.
>
> Description: One cigarette case.
>
> Result of Analysis: Traces of Cannabis resin.

Description: One box containing a phial of brown tablets.

Result of Analysis: Three 'OMNOPON' tablets. Containing a total of 30 milligrammes (1/2 grain) Morphine.[464]

Lennon and Ono were back at Marylebone Magistrates' Court on 28 November, standing side by side in the dock to answer the charges against them. First up was the obstruction charge, to which both pleaded not guilty. This was accepted by the prosecuting lawyer John Frisby and the charge was dropped.

The charge of cannabis possession was then read out. Ono entered a not guilty plea, which was accepted, and the charges against her were withdrawn. She stepped down from the dock after a request to remain by Lennon's side was denied by the magistrate, John Phipps.

Frisby outlined the prosecution's version of the events of 18 October, followed by a speech by Lennon's lawyer Martin Polden, who worked for Release. He claimed that Lennon had been drug-free since embracing Eastern philosophies earlier in the year, but his lifestyle and lack of tidiness meant he had forgotten about some of the substances. 'There was no question of either of them indulging,' he told the court.

Lennon pleaded guilty to the charge, thus avoiding a lengthy spell in court, and was fined £150 plus costs. The magistrate also warned that he could face a year's imprisonment were he to be convicted again. After leaving court he expressed relief, saying he had anticipated a raid for some time. 'It was better when it happened,' he said. 'It's been building up for years – thinking something would happen. Now, the fear has gone a bit. Now you know what it's like, it's a bit different. And it's not too bad; a £150 fine.'[465]

He later claimed that the guilty plea was to protect Ono from deportation. 'The only reason I pleaded guilty was because I thought they'd send Yoko away because we weren't married. And I thought – what's the word? – they'd throw her out of the country. So I copped the plea. And the cop said to me, "Well, we've got you now, so it's nothing personal, you know".'[466]

However, in 1972 Polden stated in a letter that Lennon's primary motivation had been to protect Ono from the emotional pressure of the trial. 'The alleged offence took place at a time when she was expecting a baby and was experiencing physical and emotional difficulties,' the lawyer wrote. 'The impact of the proceedings needless to say added to her burdens.

'What Mr Lennon did not want to do, at the time, was to aggravate her condition and he sought my advice as to what course he should adopt in this regard. The facts of the case were such that I considered Mr Lennon to have a good defence but for the presentation of the same it would be essential to call her as a witness. I was obliged to explain to him that the only course open that would obviate the need for her appearance as a witness would be for him to plead guilty.'[467]

Lennon and Ono left Montagu Square shortly after the bust. Living in central London had left them wide open to unwanted attention from fans, and their heroin habits gave them need to avoid further police scrutiny. In November 1968 they moved back once again to Kenwood, which Cynthia and Julian had recently left. The house gave them some much needed stability after several tumultuous weeks.

Ringo Starr was fortunate to avoid guilt by association. The most he had to endure was a legal tussle with the building's owners. On 19 February, Brymon Estates served a writ against him in London's High Court. Five injunctions were applied for, the main one of which was to prevent Starr from allowing 'one John Lennon and/or one Yoko Ono Cox or either of them' to use 34 Montagu Square. A second injunction prevented Starr from allowing the property to be used for any 'illegal, immoral or improper purpose'.

A hearing was scheduled at the High Court for 28 February, but the case was dismissed by Mr Justice Donaldson within a matter of minutes. Starr's lawyers gave a statement saying:

'The case against Ringo Starr was adjourned indefinitely on the basis of Ringo giving undertakings in respect of his own use of the flat. Ringo Starr was not required to give any undertakings in respect of John Lennon's and Yoko Ono's use of the flat.'

THE SECOND BEATLES drugs bust took place less than six months after Lennon and Ono's. This time the target was Kinfauns, the home of George and Pattie Harrison.

Unlike the mob-handed approach of the Montagu Square raid, and doubtlessly mindful of the criticism he had received in parliament, Norman Pilcher was careful to choose a time when the bungalow was likely to be empty. It was no accident that he chose Wednesday 12 March 1969, the day of Paul McCartney's wedding to Linda Eastman.

What Pilcher did not know was that none of the other Beatles had been invited to McCartney's wedding. George was at Apple, and Pattie was preparing to go to a Pisces-themed party at the Chelsea home of artist Rory McEwen. That day she went into London and bought a new dress at the shop of designer Ossie Clark.

On returning to her car she found a cigarette packet attached to the windscreen, with a name and number written on it. Pattie threw the packet into the car and drove home. When she arrived she discovered a small block of hashish inside. She left the packet in her handbag. It was later discovered by the police and found to contain four grains of cannabis resin.

As she awaited George's return that evening, her attention was caught by the sound of several cars drawing up outside. Knowing there were too many for it to be her husband, she initially assumed it was the newlywed McCartneys wanting to party. She opened the front door and was confronted by several policemen, one policewoman and the sniffer dog, Yogi. The back doorbell also rang, indicating that the house was surrounded.

Norman Pilcher introduced himself as the leader of the squad, and handed over a search warrant. 'In they came, about eight policemen through the front, another five or six through the back and there were more in the greenhouse,' she said. 'The policewoman said she would follow me while the others searched and didn't let me out of her sight.'[468] Pattie, who assumed they were looking for heroin or cocaine, denied that there were any drugs in the house.

She called 3 Savile Row and spoke to George: 'It's your worst nightmare. Come home.' Harrison promised to return, and said in the meantime he would send someone over to help. The police overheard Pattie asking him 'Where in the living room?', raising suspicion that they were discussing drugs. George also spoke to a police officer on the telephone, and was asked if any drugs were on the premises at Kinfauns. 'No, there is nothing there,' Harrison replied. 'There is only the stuff I got on prescription on top of the fridge.'

Shortly afterwards Harrison called Pete Shotton, who was at his own home in Esher. 'Pete, this is serious,' Harrison said. 'I'm in London, at Apple, and I've just heard that the drug squad's raided my house. Since Pattie's all alone there, would you do us a favour and just keep her company until I can get home?'[469] Shotton sped over to Kinfauns where he was accosted by two police officers who demanded his name and address, after which he was permitted to enter. Pattie, grateful to see a friendly face, poured them each a drink while the search continued. Shotton realised to his horror that he was carrying two joints in a cigarette packet, which the sniffer dog failed to notice.

As the police searched the entire house, some of the officers took it upon themselves to play Beatles records in the living room. Eventually Pilcher appeared carrying a block of hashish, which he claimed had been found by Yogi in one of George's shoes. Pattie protested, saying they always kept their cannabis in a pot on the living room table, and that Pilcher's discovery had been planted.

As they waited for George to return, some of the officers requested cups of tea. Others chose to watch television, while another asked if the Beatles were making any new music. 'Yes,' Pattie replied tersely, 'but you're not going to hear it.'[470]

When Harrison arrived home at around 10pm, with Derek Taylor, Mal Evans and Martin Polden, he was aghast to see the police making themselves comfortable in his home. 'The police made a rush for the door as I went inside,' he said. 'There were several of them, I didn't count them, and they had been sitting down drinking coffee and playing records. It was like a party where there are too many people around and when I went in they all stood up, put their hats on and became policemen again.'[471]

According to Shotton, Harrison grew furious, and began railing at the officers. Paraphrasing Jesus in Matthew 8:20, he told them: 'The foxes have got their lairs, and the birds have their fucking nests – but man doesn't have anywhere he can fucking go without people breaking into his house!'[472] He was arrested by Pilcher and the charges were read out. Two pieces of evidence were produced. 'That one's mine,' he said, 'but I've never seen this one before in me fucking life! You don't have to bring your own dope to me house, I've got plenty meself! And you didn't have to turn this whole fucking place upside down – I could have shown you where the stuff was if you'd asked me!'[473]

'I'm a tidy bloke,' he later told *The Sunday Times*. 'I keep records in the record rack, tea in the tea caddy, pot in the pot box. This was the biggest stick of hashish I've ever seen and something I'd obviously know about if I had seen it before.'[474]

The Harrisons were taken to Esher police station to be fingerprinted. The local staff were astounded to see them being marched in by London officers. It took them over thirty minutes to find and use the fingerprinting machine, but eventually the

Harrisons were formally charged and released on bail, after Taylor put up a bond of £500.

That evening, to lift their moods, they decided to go to the Pisces party, where George attempted to solicit help from Lord Snowdon. Elsewhere at the party, Snowdon's wife, Princess Margaret, was in conversation with Pattie's younger sister Paula. To Pattie's horror, Paula had lit a joint and was handing it to the princess. 'I leapt at her and said, "Don't!" When I told them what had happened, Princess Margaret and Lord Snowdon beat a hasty retreat.'[475]

THE HARRISONS APPEARED at Esher and Walton Magistrates' Court for a preliminary hearing on 18 March, and returned for the full trial on 31 March.

Extra police officers had been stationed at the court for the trial, but the case attracted little public interest. There were around a dozen people, mostly teenagers, in the public gallery. The Harrisons arrived in a chauffeur-driven white Mercedes and walked into court hand in hand.

Like Lennon they pleaded guilty on the advice of their counsel. Michael West, for the prosecution, noted that the couple had been of hitherto impeccable character, and had cooperated fully with the police search. Pattie had shown them pills to which she was entitled, but was unable to account for the hashish found in her handbag, saying someone had left it on her car.

Pattie had told the officers about the cannabis in a white box on the living room table, and confirmed that she and her husband had discussed it on the telephone. The court also heard that other items, including a home-made metal pipe used for smoking cannabis, had been found in a cabinet.

West also noted that a box containing 217 grains of cannabis resin and 228 grains of marijuana had been discovered. In a different room a box containing 36 grains of cannabis was found, along with a cigarette roller containing traces of the drug. The sniffer dog had discovered another 304 grains in a bedroom wardrobe.

'It is infrequent to find quite as much of the drug as one found in this case,' West told the court. 'There is something like 570 grains which would result, when used, in a large number of cigarettes. It would be wrong to draw the inference that there was any intention to sell them. It is quite clear on the evidence that this was for personal consumption and no more than a private supply.'

Martin Polden, representing the couple, confirmed that Pattie had assisted the police once her initial shock had subsided. He told the court that a phial found in her handbag had been give to her by a stranger in Chelsea, and the long pipe had been a gift from a San Franciscan friend. The Harrisons, he said, had no idea the pipe contained traces of cannabis.

Speaking of the drugs found in the wardrobe, Polden said: 'The couple cannot explain this find. They know nothing about it to this day. The large amount of cannabis found does not indicate that theirs is a household of corruption and debauchery. There is no question of addiction.' He also argued that the case could negatively affect George's work abroad, particularly in the United States. The Beatles, he said, often needed to conduct business overseas.

The magistrates retired for a 15-minute consultation, after which their chairman, Eric Causton, announced that George and Pattie would both be fined £250, plus ten guineas each in costs. Thanking the magistrates, Polden referred to the pipe which had been a gift from San Francisco, saying it was no more than an ornament. Causton replied saying the Harrisons would be permitted to keep it. Upon leaving court George Harrison remarked: 'I hope the police will leave us alone now.'

'I remember that when we came out of court, all that people talked about was how big our hats were,' he later said. 'I said to a policeman, "Can I have my pipe back now, then?" It was the big Indian pipe with feathers and coloured strings that had been given to me in Haight-Ashbury. They gave it back but one cop came up and said, "Don't take it back because there are people around here who will bust you again if you do because they know there are traces of cannabis resin in the pipe."'[476]

The organisation Release had helped both Lennon and Harrison avoid severe punishments, but was still operating on a shoestring budget. Hoping to gain some financial help, Caroline Coon contacted Derek Taylor, and a meeting was arranged with Harrison at Apple where she made a presentation detailing the running costs of Release. Also present were Peter Asher and Barry Miles. Towards the end of the meeting Harrison opened his desk drawer and handed Coon a cheque.

Expecting little more than a token gesture, Coon thanked Harrison and left the office without looking at the amount. As she reached the front door she was astounded to find it was for £5,000 – slightly more than the national average house price, and three times the typical annual salary. Harrison's generosity allowed Release to buy larger premises, and ensured their ability to continue providing legal assistance. A photocopy of the cheque was displayed on a wall in their office for many years.

Later in 1969 a party was held at Release to thank Harrison and other benefactors. He and Eric Clapton attended early in the evening, but left to watch BB King at the Albert Hall. Soon after Norman Pilcher arrived at the party with several officers, demanding to know where Harrison and Clapton were. Drugs were quickly hidden. Told that the celebrities had gone, the disgruntled police departed, and the partygoers began rolling up once again.

As for Harrison, he once again publicly vowed to give up smoking cannabis. 'This business has suddenly pinpointed a little thing in my life,' he said. 'It's ridiculous. I don't need pot, it's not important to me.' But he remained avowedly on the side of those who wanted to challenge the system: 'Those who think it's a low down dirty thing to do to smoke pot will be further convinced they're right and we're wrong. But it will strengthen the others who follow us.'[477]

The Beatles were entering their final months. The band's endgame was no less turbulent than any of their momentous preceding years, but was mercifully free of further police attention. However, there were still scares.

EMI's security guards had become friendly with the local constabulary, due to the near-constant presence of Beatles fans outside the studio gates at Abbey Road. The main doorman, John Skinner, would sometimes invite officers into the building for a cup of tea and a chat. Occasionally they would go inside the control room to observe a Beatles session, which would understandably make the musicians nervous.

During one of the final *Abbey Road* sessions, when the Beatles were assembling the album's long medley, an unaccompanied policeman walked unannounced into the studio control room. The Beatles, who disliked having outsiders in their sessions, were spooked by the officer's presence. John Lennon looked especially perturbed, as session engineer Geoff Emerick remembered. 'He was trying to contain his nerves, but after the bobby left, Lennon gave Mal a right bollocking: "It's your job to keep people out of here!" he shouted at the hapless roadie.'[478]

Lennon's concern was not misplaced. While they never again fell victim to Norman Pilcher's mob, the Beatles' problems with substances and the law lasted decades and transcended international borders, resulted in court cases, more arrests, a prison term and rehab, and even attracted the ire of the FBI and the US presidency.

Norman Pilcher never achieved his aim of snaring all four Beatles. Nor did he manage to eradicate drugs from music. The press and political scrutiny of his methods led him to adopt a lower profile as the Sixties ended, and in 1972 he left the Metropolitan Police. Later that year five members of the drug squad, including his former boss DCI Victor Kelaher, were charged with conspiracy to pervert the course of justice in connection with a long-running drugs case. Charges of perjury were also levelled at Pilcher and the four detectives from Kelaher's team.

Pilcher was on an ocean liner bound for Australia, where he had hoped to start a new life. He was arrested as the ship docked in Fremantle on 11 November 1972, and spent a week in an Australian jail before being extradited to Britain.

The trial took place the following September at the Old Bailey. Three of the defendants, including Pilcher, were found guilty of perjury, although the conspiracy charges failed to stick. Justice Melford Stevenson told him: 'You poisoned the wells of criminal justice and set about it deliberately. What is equally bad is that you have betrayed your comrades in the Metropolitan Police Force, which enjoys the respect of the civilised world – what remains of it – and not the least grave aspect of what you have done is to provide material for the crooks, cranks and do-gooders who unite to attack the police whenever opportunity occurs.'[479]

Pilcher was sentenced to four years in prison, of which he served two. He was released on parole in the summer of 1975, after which he retreated from the public eye, living a quiet life in a suburb of Tonbridge in Kent. It was an ignoble end to an often vindictive and malfeasant career.

PART III

8

NO BED FOR BEATLE JOHN

As the sun set on the Sixties, each of the Beatles was forced to contemplate an existence without the others. For Lennon and Harrison, the most independent of the four, the adjustment was the least problematic, as they already had new collaborators and projects to command their attention. McCartney, who never wanted the Beatles to split, struggled the most before his solo and Wings output became bolder and successful. Starr scored some early solo hits, and guested on many of his former bandmates' releases, but had diminishing commercial returns as the years wore on.

Coming down from the greatest party of the twentieth century was never likely to be easy, and each of the Beatles struggled in some way after the group's demise. The excitement and experimentation of the Sixties gave way to a darker strand of hedonism, with career highs and lows punctuated by self-medication, addiction and domestic turmoil.

John Lennon was perhaps the Beatle most likely to fall back into self-destructive behaviour. He and Ono both used methadone in the Seventies to control their opioid addiction, and both relapsed into heroin use at times.

The repercussions from the Pilcher raid went further than Lennon anticipated, and for many years he struggled to gain residence in the US. 'It's just strange when you hear people are snorting in the White House and that stuff, you know, after the misery they put a lot of people through,' he said in 1980. 'I have a record for life because the cop who bust me and Yoko, and also bust Brian Jones and the Stones – he was scalp-hunting and making a name for himself. And I have a record for life. I have problems getting in countries because this guy bust me.'[480]

The first indication came in May 1969, when an application for a travel visa to the United States was refused – he and Ono were left standing in the dock at Southampton, unable to board the QE2 ocean liner. Attempts later that month to stage a bed-in for peace in New York were similarly foiled.

They travelled instead to Canada, where their passports were seized and they were forced to attend an immigration hearing. Ono, who had not been convicted on drugs charges, was not prevented from entering the US. Lennon was granted a temporary visa to Canada, but was unable to obtain a non-immigrant waiver to enter the US. They left the country before the hearing took place, choosing instead to return to England to wait for formal permission to enter.

It was a long wait for Lennon. In August 1971 he was granted a six-week temporary visa, the first of many, which allowed him to work in the US. He and Ono first moved into the elegant St Regis Hotel on Manhattan's East 55th Street, taking two adjacent suites on the seventh floor. In October they relocated to a two-room loft apartment at 105 Bank Street in Greenwich Village, where they felt more at home as artists and campaigners. Their involvement in radical left-wing and anti-war politics, and their support for countercultural drug advocates such as David Peel and John Sinclair, had done little to endear them to the authorities, and their case was being monitored at the highest level.

1972 was an election year in the US. President Richard

Nixon saw Lennon as a threat to the war effort in Vietnam, and feared that he was planning a series of rallies to mobilise voters and campaign for legalisation of marijuana. On 1 March 1972 the Immigration and Naturalization Service wrote to Lennon and Ono demanding that they leave the US voluntarily within 15 days or face deportation hearings, with Lennon's 1968 conviction used as a basis for the order.

Lennon continued to fight the government's extradition efforts, winning a series of temporary reprieves. He also began to withdraw from political campaigning, fearing that it would jeopardise his chances of remaining in the US. The strategy worked. The FBI, which had been monitoring Lennon and had assembled a 300-page dossier, ended its surveillance in August 1972. An internal memo noted that he had fallen out of favour with some of the radical activists he had been associated with: an FBI informant wrote that 'Rennard Davis, Stewart Albert, Jerry Rubin and John Lennon are heavy users of narcotics,' but that Rubin and Davis 'are apparently at odds with Lennon due to his excessive use of drugs, which are referred to in the vernacular as "downers". Source advised that Lennon appears to be radically orientated, however he does not give the impression he is a true revolutionist since he is constantly under the influence of narcotics.'[481]

Key to Lennon's success was his lawyer, Leon Wildes, who sued the attorney general and other officials, and uncovered evidence that Nixon's efforts were politically motivated to make an example of the former Beatle. Wildes used a number of arguments and technicalities to defer the order against Lennon. At one point, noting that the law specified that convictions for possession of 'narcotic drugs or marijuana' were grounds for deportation, he asked Lennon whether cannabis resin was the same as marijuana. 'Oh, no,' Lennon replied. 'Much better than marijuana.' Wildes duly testified that hashish was not marijuana and was therefore exempt from the ruling. Unfortunately for Lennon, the tactic was unsuccessful. 'While this argument has some technical appeal,' the Board of Immigration Appeals mentioned in its summation, 'we are not persuaded.'[482]

Nixon's resignation in August 1974 effectively halted the deportation efforts, and in October 1975 the New York State Supreme Court overturned the order. 'The courts will not condone selective deportation based upon secret political grounds,' Judge Irving Kaufman said. 'Lennon's four-year battle to remain in our country is testimony to his faith in this American dream.' In July 1976 his victory was finally sealed when he received the Green Card which conferred permanent residence.

But the long fight had taken its toll. The 1972 album *Some Time In New York City* was a critical and commercial failure. It was followed by *Mind Games*, on which Lennon jettisoned the political sloganeering but ended up treading musical water. He and Ono were having marital problems during the sessions, and she suggested he take up with one of their assistants, May Pang.

IN SEPTEMBER 1973 Lennon and Pang relocated to Los Angeles, and a month later he began work on the *Rock 'N' Roll* album. The alcohol-fuelled early sessions were produced by Phil Spector, whose behaviour became increasingly erratic as work progressed. Lennon was normally impatient and disciplined in the studio, hating delays or retakes, but after surrendering creative control to Spector was forced to endure endless takes as the maverick producer worked his magic at the recording desk.

The sessions started late afternoon and would go on into the early hours of the next morning. Lennon, off the leash without Ono, abandoned his Beatles-era vow of sobriety in the studio. He drank to hide his nerves and insecurity, egged on by Spector, who typically swigged from a bottle of brandy throughout the sessions. According to studio engineer Roy Cicala, Lennon often drank a bottle of Dewar's Scotch whisky a day.

The hired musicians partied hard too, seizing the opportunity to kick back and indulge at Lennon's expense. 'By the end of those evenings almost everyone was roaring drunk,' Pang said. 'At three in the morning, when the sessions were dismissed, the A&M parking lot resembled an alcoholics ward on a binge.'[483] Eventually they were all kicked out of A&M Studios after a bottle of whisky was emptied onto a mixing console. Spector vanished soon after with the session tapes, leaving Lennon to finish the project off a year later in New York.

Lennon had been a lousy drunk since his teenage years, and had changed little in the time in between. Ono had evidently helped keep his drinking under control, and from New York urged Pang to do the same. Pang found Lennon delightful and attentive while sober, yet after just a few drinks he became confrontational, and with more became angry, melancholy, jealous, violent or aggressive.

The 18-month separation from Ono came to be known as the Lost Weekend, after the 1945 film starring Ray Milland as an alcoholic writer. Lennon's heavy drinking was punctuated by the occasional acid trip, and cocaine and cannabis were never far away.

There were a number of notorious public incidents, one of the first occurring on 12 January 1974. Lennon and Pang started the night at Lost On Larrabee, a small restaurant off Santa Monica Boulevard, accompanied by Jim Keltner, his wife Cynthia, guitarist Jesse Ed Davis and his girlfriend Patti Daley. Lennon was drinking brandy alexanders, a potent mix of cream, dark crème de cacao and brandy that briefly became his drink of choice during the Lost Weekend.

After three rounds of drinks they ordered dinner, and Lennon left to use the bathroom. There he found a supply of Kotex sanitary pads, one of which he taped to his forehead before returning to the table. He and Davis grew more belligerent as the drinks continued to flow, and the restaurant manager threatened to have them ejected.

Lennon continued to wear the sanitary pad to the Troubadour, where soul singer Ann Peebles was performing. According to legend, Lennon taunted a waitress, asking: 'Do you know who I am?' Her alleged response was blunt: 'Yes, you're some asshole with a Kotex on your head.'[484]

The night ended with a police visit to Lennon's West Hollywood apartment. LAPD officers had been alerted to Patti Daley's screaming after Lennon knocked Davis unconscious with a Coke bottle. They entered carrying shotguns and flashlights, looking for a homicide which had not occurred, but it was enough to sober up the terrified Lennon.

Another infamous night at the Troubadour cemented the legend. Comedy duo the Smothers Brothers gave two shows on 12 March, at 9pm and 11pm. Lennon, Pang and the singer Harry Nilsson arrived shortly before the second set, the men drinking brandy alexanders and becoming boisterous and combative. They serenaded the packed venue with a drunken barbershop-style version of Peebles's hit song I Can't Stand The Rain while waiting for the show to begin. A photographer inside the venue took some snaps of their table, before Lennon shouted 'Fuck you!' in his direction. When the photographer confronted Lennon, he said he had aimed the insult at a nearby waitress. She turned to Lennon and told him: 'Well, fuck you!'[485] The tone was set for the night.

As Tom and Dick Smothers began their performance Lennon started heckling, egged on by Nilsson. Tommy Smothers eventually ended the show, saying: 'There's a narrow line between bad taste and vulgarity, and you've managed to cross it.' The Troubadour's manager Chris Walsh, and the Smothers Brothers' manager, Ken Fritz, arrived at the table to try to resolve the incident, but Lennon landed a punch on Fritz's jaw and the manager responded in kind. Lennon's table was overturned in the fracas, leaving broken glass everywhere.

Lennon was thrown out, but he fought with the doorman and two bystanders. A photographer, Brenda Mary Perkins, attempted to take some Polaroid pictures but Lennon swung at her, his fist allegedly landing on her right eye. She filed charges, which left Lennon fearful of deportation, but they were dropped due to insufficient evidence.

Another time, Lennon told Nilsson: 'I'd love to get some girls and some acid and fuck 'em.' It was almost dawn and the pair had been up all night. Against the odds, Nilsson managed to find two willing participants, and the singers got in his Volkswagen jeep and drove to the girls' house.

'John's eyes were bugging out and he was rubbing his hands together,' said Nilsson. 'It went on for almost two days — that was the real "Lost Weekend" — we didn't even know where the hell we were after the first day. We just kept doing it. At one point it got stupid — sucking our toes, massages, music in the background, cool water, and I'm laughing. John was on a roll, and we were laughing uncontrollably. Neither of us could stop laughing, and finally I said, "I can't take any more pleasure, John. I can't take any more pleasure. Stop! It's gotta stop!"'[486]

Indeed it had. The pair agreed they ought to use their time more productively and, during a pause in the Spector sessions, started work on a Nilsson album, *Pussy Cats*. This was not a new idea: they had decided to work together one drink-sodden night in LA in late 1973. 'We were sitting around drunk and he said, "Let's do an album",' recalled Nilsson. 'I said, "Sure, man." So he announced it to the room. Joni Mitchell was there, Phil Spector, Barry Mann. "I'm gonna produce Harry Nilsson." So I just thought, "Oh he's drunk, he'll forget about it." Then about six months later we were sitting around in Ringo's room talking, and we were both sort of at loose ends.'[487]

They decided to rent a beach house near Santa Monica, where all the album's musicians would live during the recording. A pattern was set of working from early evening until midnight, after which most of the residents went out to party. On returning home they stayed up drinking and taking drugs, then recovered in the afternoon by the pool before the cycle repeated.

'The only time we ever had our own place was when Harry

rented the beach house, and even that wasn't our own place really,' said May Pang. 'We had Ringo, Keith Moon, Harry and Klaus Voormann living there, and they fell into the "boys back in England" behaviour. Mal Evans was even in LA basically reassuming the role of procuring anything for the boys.'[488]

The first recording session took place on 28 March 1974 at Burbank Studios in Los Angeles. Around midnight, as work was drawing to a close, Paul and Linda McCartney arrived unexpectedly, as did Stevie Wonder and producer Ed Freeman. Lennon and McCartney greeted each other and made small talk, and a jam session ensued. McCartney was canny enough to see that this was not the best time for a reunion, and chose to play Starr's drums and sing harmony. The other performers were Nilsson on vocals, Wonder playing an electric piano, Jim Keltner on drums, sax player Bobby Keys, guitarist Jesse Ed Davis, Linda McCartney playing an organ, and May Pang on tambourine.

The recording opens with Lennon offering Wonder a line of cocaine: 'You wanna snort, Steve? A toot? It's going around.' The words were used for the bootleg that followed, *A Toot And A Snore In '74*. It is the last known session to feature Lennon and McCartney together, although its historic importance is greater than the quality of the music. 'I'm afraid it was a rather heady session, shall we say,' said McCartney. 'I ended up getting on drums for some unknown reason. Then we just jammed. But I don't think it was very good.'[489]

Four days later the McCartneys and their children visited the Santa Monica house. Lennon was still in bed, so Paul whiled away the time at a piano, even playing a medley of Beatles songs with vocal accompaniment from Nilsson and Starr. At one stage Nilsson offered McCartney some PCP, a powerful hallucinogenic also known as angel dust.

'What is it?' he asked.

'It's elephant tranquilliser,' came Nilsson's reply.

'It is fun?'

Nilsson paused before answering in the negative.

'Well, you know what,' McCartney told him, 'I won't have any.'[490]

The heavy drinking, drugs and lack of sleep were affecting Nilsson's voice, and during the *Pussy Cats* sessions one of his vocal cords became ruptured. Fearing the cancellation of the sessions, he chose to power through rather than tell Lennon. The decision exacerbated the damage to his voice, which never recovered. 'We were all so blitzed at the time, it was a pretty heavy drinking bunch,' he said. 'The bugaboo was always liquor, a combination of liquor and coke... all kinds of controlled substances and uncontrolled substances.'[491]

The cover of *Pussy Cats*, released in August 1974, contained a clue to the chaos of its creation: children's building blocks showing the letters D and S were placed either side of a rug, spelling out the word 'drugs'. 'That was just word play, which John always loved,' said Pang. 'It was called *Pussy Cats* to contrast the image of them being bad boys actually.'[492]

A month after the album sessions began, Lennon returned to New York to mix the recordings without distraction. 'It got a little near the knuckle, that's when I straightened out,' he said. 'That's when I realised, there's something wrong here, you know? This is crazy, man! So then, I suddenly was the straight one in the middle of all these mad, mad people.'[493] The party was drawing to a close.

LENNON'S LOST WEEKEND lasted until February 1975, when he reunited with Ono and moved back to the Dakota, their home in Manhattan. Speaking to *Rolling Stone* in June, he described the time as 'a year that manifested itself in most peculiar fashion. But I'm through it and it's '75 now and I feel better and I'm sittin' here and not lyin' in some weird place with a hangover... I feel like I've been on Sinbad's voyage, you know, and I've battled all those monsters and I've got back.'[494]

He withdrew from public life shortly afterwards to bring up his second son Sean. By the end of his life Lennon was keen to present himself as a clean-living family man, largely pure of mind and body: 'A little mushroom or peyote is not beyond my scope, you know, maybe twice a year or something,' he told *Playboy* in 1980. 'But acid is a chemical. People are taking it, though, even though you don't hear about it anymore. But people are still visiting the cosmos... I've had bad trips and other people have had bad trips, but I've had a bad trip in real life. I've had a bad trip on a joint. I can get paranoid just sitting in a restaurant. I don't have to take anything.' Lennon was similarly dismissive of cocaine: 'I had a lot of it in my day, but I don't like it. It's a dumb drug. Your whole concentration goes on getting the next fix. I find caffeine easier to deal with.'

Challenged by interviewer David Sheff on his chain-smoking, Lennon's response revealed some curious attitudes to physical health: 'Macrobiotic people don't believe in the big C,' he said. 'Whether you take that as a rationalisation or not, macrobiotics don't believe that smoking is bad for you. If we die, we're wrong. We don't buy the establishment version of it at all.'

Although he was careful not to promote drug-taking, Lennon was dismissive of the US government's war on drugs. 'They're so stupid,' he said. 'They're always arresting smugglers or kids with a few joints in their pocket. They never face the reality. They're not looking at the cause of the drug problem. Why is everybody taking drugs? To escape from what? Is life so terrible? Do we live in such a terrible situation that we can't do anything about it without reinforcement from alcohol or tobacco or sleeping pills? I'm not preaching about 'em. I'm just saying a drug is a drug, you know. Why we take them is important, not who's selling it to whom on the corner.'[495]

Lennon's final album, *Double Fantasy*, was produced by Jack Douglas, who had first worked with Lennon on *Imagine*. 'After the sessions, John never left immediately,' Douglas said of *Double Fantasy*. 'He'd always sit in the control room and usually took a little grass. He had this old opium pipe, it was probably 500 years old, and he'd say to me, "Is it all over?" 'Cause he would never do anything if we were working. And I'd say, "It's over, John." And he'd sit back and put his feet up on the console and he'd load up the pipe and sit back and light up… And he'd start talking, you know, reminiscing about things. We'd listen to the radio and if a Beatles song came on, he'd talk about it. But the one thing – the overwhelming feeling about the things that he was saying was that he loved the guys in that band more than anybody else, you know?'[496]

9

DON'T BE CARELESS LOVE

P aul McCartney was hit hardest in the months that followed the Beatles' break-up. Unaccustomed to life without the band to which he'd belonged since his teenage years, with bruised confidence and without the routine and purpose of project work, he seemed adrift. Feeling washed up at 27, he struggled to sleep at night, hit the whisky during the daytime, chain smoked unfiltered Senior Service cigarettes and self-medicated with marijuana.

He was eventually dragged back to earth by Linda, his wife of barely a year, who had watched her husband change from a confident, successful rock 'n' roller to a despondent, unmotivated depressive.

The pair found gradual solace in simple domesticity, spending weeks in their Scottish farm, where eventually Paul's songwriting muse returned. He would document this period in the song Every Night, on his 1970 album *McCartney*: 'Every night I just want to go out, get out of my head,' went the refrain. 'But tonight I just want to stay in and be with you, and be with you.'

McCartney later credited Linda with bringing him back into line when he sought comfort in drugs and alcohol. 'I was lucky to have Linda because she did ground me,' he said in 2001. 'There were certain things I was going off on that she could pull me back from. Drinking and drugging and getting crazy. I just got into the habit, like you do. And when you're single you don't even think, is this a good idea? It's just what you do. Linda would say, "Are you sure you want to do that tonight?" And I'd go, "Oh, there's an alternative?" She reminded me there was this real life there that I liked a lot.'[497]

To say the McCartneys were fond of weed is something of an understatement. It was right there in their joint album *Ram*, in the hazy, bucolic sound of the countryside, and in lyrics such as 'When I fly above the cloud, when I fly above the crowd, you could knock me down with a feather,' and 'Hands across the water, heads across the sky.'

Cannabis was also a core ingredient of Wings, his first post-Beatles band. 'We weren't Bob Marley and the Wailers by any means,' recalled original drummer Denny Seiwell. 'We enjoyed a bit of the herb for the creative conscious, you know what I'm saying?'[498]

On their early tours, Wings had a strict system. They would typically each take a small amount of drugs with them, and further supplies would be sent from the McCartneys' MPL organisation in London to an agreed destination in each new country. Before crossing international borders they would throw any remaining substances from the bus, to ensure they could get through customs checks with no difficulty.

The system worked until their 1972 Wings Over Europe tour arrived in Sweden. Unknown to the group, the Swedish authorities had been surveilling them since their arrival in the country. A call from Linda to MPL, arranging for two cassette cases filled with weed to be posted to Gothenburg, had been recorded. In it, she was heard to ask where the package should go. 'Send it to Gothenburg,' Paul was heard to say in the background. 'To the hotel.'[499] The package, containing seven ounces of marijuana, was addressed to Seiwell.

On 10 August, following a performance at the city's Scandinavium Hall, armed police and sniffer dogs appeared in the auditorium. As Wings attempted to return to the dressing room their way was blocked, and Paul, Linda and Seiwell agreed to be taken to a local police station for questioning, along with the tour secretary Rebecca Hines, who had collected the package from the hotel's front desk.

The seven ounces were only meant to last them for the final two days of the tour's Swedish leg. During three hours of questioning the trio admitted to using the drug, but persuaded the police that it was for their own personal use – thus avoiding a more serious charge of intent to supply.

They were not placed under arrest, and were eventually released after depositing 9,000 krona in preliminary fines, and signing a written pledge to not use cannabis again in the country. The pledge lasted less than a day. On the tour's next stop, in the southern Swedish city of Lund, Wings scored fresh supplies.

The case brought much publicity to the band, and the McCartneys became outspoken advocates of the drug. The day after the bust the *Daily Mail* published an interview headlined 'Why I smoke pot – by Paul', in which the unrepentant singer argued that his drug use had no bearing on his music or commitment to his family.

'At the end of the day,' he said, 'most people go home and have a whisky. Well, we play a gig and we're exhausted, and Linda and I prefer to put our kids to bed, sit down together and smoke a joint. That doesn't mean we're heavily into drugs or anything. You can't expect us to pretend we don't smoke for the sake of our fans.'[500]

FIVE WEEKS LATER, on 19 September, a police constable in Scotland decided to pay a visit to the McCartneys' aptly-named High Park Farm in Campbeltown, Scotland, while the family was away. PC Norman McPhee had recently completed a drugs identification course in Glasgow, and in the light of the Swedish bust decided to take a look around the property.

In a greenhouse he spotted plants which looked like marijuana. Returning later with seven colleagues and a search warrant, he discovered a total of five cannabis plants. Three days after the raid McCartney was charged on two counts of possession and one of cultivating cannabis. A not guilty plea was submitted *in absentia* to all three charges, and a trial was set for 8 March 1973.

The two drugs busts, although with potentially catastrophic consequences for McCartney's freedom and ability to tour, brought some welcome publicity for Wings. 'The police action against us was an excellent advertisement,' one unnamed member of Wings was quoted as saying. 'Our name flies now all over the world.'

Yet if McCartney's lawyers had advised him to keep out of trouble, he was not paying much heed. December 1972 saw the release of Wings' single Hi, Hi, Hi, which was promptly banned by the BBC for its unguarded allusions to sex and drugs. A broadcasting ban was little bother to McCartney, who was well aware that controversy helped to sell records, yet to release such a song with two recent drugs busts and a pending trial could be considered somewhat cavalier.

Prior to the Scottish trial, McCartney's barrister John McCluskey noticed some procedural errors in two of the charges. A meeting was called with the prosecutor, Iain Stewart, during which it was agreed that the two charges of possession would be dropped if the one of cultivation was accepted.

Paul and Linda arrived in Scotland by private plane. McCluskey noted that, although Paul appeared to take the trial seriously, Linda appeared 'stoned out of her mind'[501] and insisted on wearing McCluskey's bowler hat throughout the proceedings.

In court McCluskey argued that McCartney had been given the seeds by fans, and had planted them without knowing what they were. No effort had been made to conceal the plants, he noted. Doubtlessly mindful of Lennon's travails in America, he added that a conviction could jeopardise future international tours.

Sheriff Donald McDiarmid summed up by first suggesting a punitive reaction would be in order. 'I take into account that the seeds were sent to you as a gift,' he said, 'but I also take into account that you are a public figure of considerable interest to young people and I must deal with you accordingly.' A charge of £100 was levied, which the multi-millionaire musician was generously given 14 days to pay – a decision greeted with laughter in the courtroom.

Outside, a relaxed and unrepentant McCartney joked with reporters, describing the sheriff as 'a great guy' and saying he believed cannabis to be less harmful than alcohol. Linda giggled at her husband's side, apparently still stoned.

McCartney may have twice eluded major penalties for his pot-smoking, but the habit was starting to affect his creativity. The quality of his Seventies output varied wildly, and his drug consumption often left him struggling to complete songs. 'In songwriting,' he later said, 'the amount of times I have got stuck on a word that really didn't matter... It was absolutely inconsequential what the word was – it could've been "boot" or "chump". It did not matter, y'know. And you just totally come to a grinding halt, so the song never gets finished. I had a lot of that through substance misuse.'[502]

WINGS HAD a fluctuating line-up throughout the Seventies, with the McCartneys and Denny Laine, formerly of the Moody Blues, as the only permanent members. Henry McCullough, a gifted guitarist with a penchant for heavy drinking, joined in 1972, but quickly yearned for greater freedom of expression. His fluid, improvised solo on the ballad My Love was particularly widely admired, but behind the scenes things were discordant.

During the making of the 1973 television special *James Paul McCartney*, McCullough drank heavily, argued loudly with his wife, and ended the night barefoot and lost in Liverpool. On another occasion, while filming a *Top Of The Pops* appearance, he threw up on stage. He left Wings after two years, following a drunken row with McCartney just days before the *Band On The Run* sessions. McCullough, incidentally, can be heard on Pink Floyd's *The Dark Side Of The Moon*, speaking the words 'I don't know; I was really drunk at the time.'

Wings contracted to the core of Paul, Linda and Denny Laine for *Band On The Run*, which was recorded at EMI's studio in Lagos, Nigeria. It took them time to adjust to the hot climate, basic facilities and reduced line-up. To add to the adversity, they experienced antagonism from suspicious local musicians, and a mugging at knifepoint from which the McCartneys were lucky not to have been murdered; their biggest losses were cameras and cassettes containing demos for the album.

Shortly afterwards, however, McCartney collapsed outside the studio after complaining of chest pains. 'We carried on making the album but the stress caught up with me because a couple of days later I began to feel a bit odd and then fainted. Linda thought I had died. She had a point – when I came around even I was convinced I was going to die. We got a cab to the hospital where the doctor said I had been smoking too much and suffered a bronchial spasm.'[503]

In August 1974 two new arrivals joined Wings: guitarist

Jimmy McCulloch and drummer Geoff Britton. McCulloch was another talented young musician with a tendency to overindulge, and was prone to mood swings when intoxicated. He co-wrote and sang the songs Medicine Jar and Wino Junko, which warned of the dangers of excess. McCulloch left the band in 1977, and two years later was found dead in London at the age of 26. An autopsy revealed he had died of heart failure due to morphine and alcohol poisoning.

The combative Britton, meanwhile, was a teetotal, non-smoking karate fanatic who was never shy of making his opinions heard. This was perhaps Wings' most volatile incarnation, with a dangerous mix of headstrong personalities threatening to overshadow the business of music-making. McCartney's refusal to give the other members contracts, instead insisting on paying them session rates, further amplified the discontent.

Britton was ejected from Wings during the *Venus And Mars* sessions. His replacement, Joe English, was a New Yorker battling a heroin addiction, who overdosed on a handful of occasions while in the band. Outwardly, Wings' reputation was of a fairly wholesome group, seemingly leagues away from the likes of Led Zeppelin or the Rolling Stones, but behind the scenes they could easily rival their peers in rock 'n' roll indulgence.

On 2 March 1975, days after the final recording sessions for *Venus And Mars*, the McCartney family were in Los Angeles. A stoned Paul was driving their silver Lincoln Continental when he took an illegal right turn and ran a red light at Santa Monica Boulevard and Midvale Avenue. A police patrol car pulled them over, and while leaning into the car detected a strong smell of marijuana. Paul, Linda and their children Heather, Mary and Stella were all ordered out of the car while a search took place. A plastic bag containing 17 grams of grass was discovered underneath the passenger seat, along with the smouldering remains of a joint.

Paul had experienced difficulty entering the United States

after the busts in Sweden and Scotland. This time Linda, a US citizen, took the rap, insisting that the drugs were hers alone. She was arrested on suspicion of possessing marijuana and taken to a police station, while Paul took the children back to their rented home in Coldwater Canyon.

Linda was released on bail set at $500, and appeared a week later at Los Angeles Municipal Court where she was ordered to complete a six-month drug diversion programme. She complied with the ruling and the charges were dismissed in November, at a court hearing where her attorney Richard Hirsch revealed that she had undergone drug counselling from a psychiatrist in England. Paul, meanwhile, always insisted that the drugs had been planted by the LAPD.

Paul and Linda made great efforts to give their children a relatively normal upbringing, sending them to local state schools, keeping them close on tour and maintaining a strong family bond. 'Anyone who was likely to get crazy, it would be on their own time, in a hotel room,' said McCartney. 'It would be somewhere where the kids weren't. They were very respectful, and the kids never really saw any kind of hedonistic behaviour.'[504]

Nonetheless, there were times when the children were exposed to the band's more reckless tendencies. During the 1975-6 Wings Over The World tour they travelled by private jet, and the musicians whiled away the long hours drinking, smoking and gambling. For the most part this was tolerated by the McCartneys, although the line was drawn after Paul discovered that for several weeks some band members had taken turns to control the jet, with the permission of the easy-going Texan pilots. A livid McCartney banned the band from entering the cockpit after one musician sent the plane into a dive, throwing the passengers around the cabin and putting their lives in danger.

Wings Over The World cemented McCartney's position as the most successful solo Beatle. The tour took in 31 North

American shows, 25 in Europe and nine in Australia, won critical plaudits, and led to the 1979 television film *Wings Over The World*, the 1980 movie *Rockshow*, and the triple live album *Wings Over America*.

The studio follow-up, *London Town*, meanwhile, was partly recorded in the Virgin Islands, on board a yacht equipped with mobile recording facilities. The sessions were relaxed and the pace leisurely, although Wings made themselves unpopular for violating a 10pm ban on amplified music.

On another occasion they were unexpectedly visited by three US Customs officials who boarded the yacht but improbably failed to find any illegal substances. But their reputation was enough to prompt a letter from Peter Baker, who had arranged the boat hire, saying: 'Please make sure that no drugs, illegal drugs or narcotics of course are taken on board or used on board any of the three yachts now on charter to you and the group. Apart from anything else, illegal actions are specifically excluded from the charter agreement and could give us valid grounds for advising the owner to conclude the charter.'

BY THE SUMMER of 1979 McCartney was growing tired of Wings, and recorded his second solo album *McCartney II* alone in Sussex and Scotland. However, the band regrouped for a short British tour at the end of 1979, ending with a show at London's Hammersmith Odeon on 29 December. Unbeknown to all, it was their final show.

Japanese officials had denied McCartney a visa in 1975, citing his earlier convictions for drug possession. Five years later, however, he was granted entry to the country for 11 Wings concerts over 18 days.

In early January 1980 the band undertook some cursory rehearsals in Sussex which left them underprepared, but on 12 January the McCartney family flew on Concorde to New York, booking into the luxurious Stanhope Hotel by Central Park. There, Paul and Linda scored half a pound of marijuana which they chose not to dispose of before continuing to Japan.

Paul phoned the Dakota while in New York, asking if he could see John Lennon and offering to bring round some 'dynamite weed'. Yoko Ono took the call and said it was not convenient, which McCartney took as a snub. He told her about the looming Japanese tour, also disclosing that they were to stay in the presidential suite at Tokyo's Okura Hotel – the same base used by the Lennons while in Japan.

Wings had a sizeable Japanese fanbase, and the tour was due to net the musicians a significant financial sum. Their management had worked hard to secure the visas to enter the country; McCartney even had to sign an affidavit pledging that he no longer used cannabis, and his application was personally approved by the minister of justice.

Furthermore, the band had been sternly instructed by their tour managers not to enter the country with even the slightest trace of drugs, and it was let known that drugs could be procured through contacts at US Army bases in Japan. Everyone knew they needed to behave with the utmost responsibility. Well, almost everyone.

The band arrived at Tokyo's Narita Airport on 16 January 1980. Denny Laine and drummer Steve Holley arrived on an earlier flight; it took Laine five hours to clear customs due to his own past drugs conviction. Eventually they left the airport and waited on the tour bus for the others.

The McCartneys had travelled from New York with guitarist Laurence Juber. They spent two hours going through paperwork with Japanese immigration officers before being allowed to make their way to customs with their luggage. Officials made random spot checks, opening bags and doing cursory searches. Inside McCartney's beige canvas suitcase was found, lying on top, a clear plastic bag containing 219 grams of the New York marijuana. According to Juber, McCartney turned white.

The clearly-surprised official appeared to consider returning the bag to the suitcase, but knew he had no choice but to alert his supervisors. Juber and the McCartneys were ushered into a separate area, and Paul was taken into a room for questioning. The luggage was checked again, more thoroughly, with musical instruments being taken apart in case drugs were hidden inside. Eventually Linda, the children and Juber were allowed to leave, while Paul remained behind.

'We were about to fly to Japan and I knew I wouldn't be able to get anything to smoke over there,' he later said. 'This stuff was too good to flush down the toilet. So I thought I'd take it with me. I was so warned against doing it. But I thought, "What the hell!" I was incredibly cavalier about the whole thing.'[505]

McCartney's entrenched belief in cannabis as a harmless drug, coupled with the privileged status he and the Beatles had enjoyed for years, may have made him feel somehow above the law, but equally he was under no misapprehension as to the severity of being caught. And if he felt confident that, like before, he could escape with a fine, he was in for a rude awakening.

'In America, President Carter had come out and said he thought cannabis should be decriminalised. Maybe I was thinking, "Hey, it's no big deal." In my mind, I was only doing what everyone else was doing. It was like nicking sweets from the school tuck-shop and I happened to be the one who got my collar felt.'[506]

McCartney was arrested, handcuffed and taken to Tokyo's Kojimachi police station for further questioning. There, he confessed his guilt and apologised for breaking the law. He was then transferred to the Metropolitan Jail, where he was issued with prisoner number 22 and had his personal belongings confiscated. His appointed legal representative, Tasuku Matsuo, informed him he was facing up to seven years in prison.

The rest of Wings were shocked to hear of the bust. Their initial excitement at arriving in Japan soured once it became clear that the tour would be cancelled. With their hotel under siege from journalists they hotfooted it to Kyoto, and thereafter went their separate ways.

Linda remained at the Okura Hotel, looking after the children and awaiting news. She was eventually allowed, alone, to visit her husband. He chose not to tell her he was potentially looking at years in prison. 'If I'd known what Paul was really facing, I'd have fallen apart,' she said. 'They told me he might be detained for a few days or weeks, and people caught with less pot were in Japanese prisons for years. Well, they made sure I didn't hear the word "years".

'At first I thought he'd be out the next day, that it would all be taken care of with a fine or something. Then the days went by, with the kids and me in a Japanese hotel, and we didn't know what was going to happen.'[507] In New York, Linda's father Lee Eastman dispatched his son John to Tokyo to help arrange Paul's release, and worked hard to arrange legal representation.

McCartney had trouble sleeping in his small cell on the first night, and it took several days to acclimatise to the new environment. Each morning the lights came on with the sun, and Prisoner 22 rolled up his tatami mat, sat cross-legged and waited for the warders to inspect his cell. Breakfast was miso soup and three bread rolls; supper was a bowl of rice.

Fearful of being sexually assaulted while in prison, he slept with his back to the cell wall. 'I can remember that the first thing I expected was rape,' he later said. 'That was my big fear. Right? Wouldn't that be yours? So I slept with me back to the wall. I didn't know what was going to happen, you know?'[508]

On day two he was taken back to Kojimachi, where he was interrogated by police for six hours. He continued to maintain that the drugs were for his own personal use, and argued that marijuana was relatively harmless, but the words had little effect. The next day prosecutors requested a further ten days to question McCartney.

By now a Japanese media ban on his music had been

enacted, and the press began to turn against him. His request for a guitar to be brought to his cell was refused. He was, however, visited by Donald Warren-Knott, the British consul in Japan, who found McCartney calm and relaxed. 'Yes, OK, he knew the packet had been found,' recalled Warren-Knott. 'Yes, it was his. And it shouldn't have been there. I didn't press too closely, because it's not my business to enquire into those sort of details. I suspect – personal view – that a package was slipped in while they were packing. I don't know whether he fully intended to use it while he was in Japan. If he did, he'd be very foolish, given the circumstances of his previous arrests.'[509] McCartney made just one request: that he be given a reasonable vegetarian diet including fruit.

Linda visited for a second time on 22 January. She found Paul in high spirits, laughing and cracking jokes, which in turn helped lift her own mood. McCartney was starting to bond with several of his fellow inmates, particularly one from a neighbouring cell who was also inside for smuggling drugs.

When offered a private bath McCartney chose instead to use the communal one, and led his fellow inmates in a singalong of songs including the Beatles' Yesterday. He was becoming used to the routine inside the jail, which allowed him two cigarettes per day and a brief exercise period. He counted the days inside by picking bits of plaster off the wall to keep a tally.

George Harrison and his wife Olivia sent a telegram to Paul and Linda at the hotel: 'Thinking of you all with love. Keep your spirits high. Nice to have you back home again soon. God bless. Love, George and Olivia.' Ringo Starr spoke to reporters at Heathrow while on his way to France, seemingly with little sympathy for his former bandmate: 'It's the risk you take when you're involved with drugs. He's just been unlucky.'

John Lennon, meanwhile, became gripped by developments in McCartney's situation, scouring newspapers and flipping through television channels to search for the latest news reports. Like others, he wondered why McCartney would be so reckless when entering Japan. 'People wrote in from all round the world,' McCartney later said. 'There were messages from Teddy Kennedy and John and Yoko, and people the Japanese respected. So I think that carried some weight in my defence.'[510]

A fanciful conspiracy later emerged that Yoko Ono, upset by the McCartneys' use of the Okura presidential suite, had pulled strings with a relative working with the Japanese customs authorities to engineer the arrest. Ono denied the story and McCartney gave it little credence. 'There is a story people have put to me that I was framed, which actually makes more sense to me as time goes on,' he said. 'But I don't think I was. I think I was just stupid, and I paid the penalty. This is life.'[511]

McCartney was still awaiting trial, but it was becoming clear that the Japanese authorities did not want the embarrassment of bringing him to court. The Eastmans and Tasuku Matsuo had kept up the pressure, as had Donald Warren-Knott on behalf of Britain's foreign office.

On 25 January McCartney was released after nine nights in prison. It was declared that, because his visa had been cancelled upon his arrest, he was an illegal alien and should be deported immediately. The police issued a statement which read: 'Charges were not brought against Mr McCartney because he had brought in the marijuana solely for his own use and already he has been punished enough.'

Upon leaving he was given back his possessions, although his wedding ring was missing. With no time to make a complaint, the distraught McCartney asked for a paperclip to wear in its place. He was put on the first available flight to Amsterdam, where he was finally reunited with his family.

'I've been a fool,' he told a reporter on the aeroplane. 'What I did was incredibly dumb. I was really scared, thinking I might be imprisoned for so long and now I have made my mind up never to touch the stuff again. From now on, all I'm going to smoke is straightforward fags [cigarettes] and no more pot.'[512]

Back home, McCartney wrote a 20,000-word account of his

time in prison, titled *Japanese Jailbird*. It was intended as an *aide-memoire* for when his children asked for the details, but not meant for wider circulation. 'I would have liked to have written about it while I was there,' he said in 2014. 'That would have actually made it easier. But you weren't allowed writing materials – I think in case you stuffed the pencil up your nose or something. So I had it all in my brain; my brain was bursting with all these details. So when I got back, each morning I used to go and write for a couple of hours. It was good 'cause all the details were fresh. I gave a copy to each of my kids. It was cathartic. I never knew what that word meant, but it was that: it got rid of it.'[513]

THE JAPAN TOUR'S cancellation effectively brought an end to Wings, although they limped on until Denny Laine's departure in 1981. McCartney later agreed with speculation that the drugs bust may have been part of a subconscious desire to break the band up. 'There might have been something to do with that, because I think I was ready to get out of Wings. I think also, more importantly, we hadn't really rehearsed much for that tour, and I felt very under-rehearsed. I cannot believe that I would have myself busted and put in jail nine days just to get out of a group. I mean, let's face it, there are easier ways to do it than that – and also having to pay a million pounds to the promoters in default. I think the only thing; it might have just been some deep, psychological thing. It's a weird period for me.'[514]

McCartney turned 40 in 1982, the year he enjoyed critical and commercial success with the *Tug Of War* album. He also made a series of life changes which included taking up running and painting, and giving up cigarettes. Cannabis, however, remained a perennial, at least well into the next century.

The family fell foul of the law once again in January 1984, on a two-week holiday in Barbados. Cannabis, although illegal, was widely tolerated and openly sold on the island, and the couple had bought some on the beach outside their rented villa. One evening, when they were with 10cc's Eric Stewart and his wife Gloria, local police raided the villa and discovered ten grams of marijuana on Paul and seven more on Linda.

Police inspector Alan Long said: 'We received a tip-off that they were in possession of marijuana. Four uniformed officers went round to the McCartneys' holiday villa with a search warrant. Mr McCartney freely admitted his guilt and accompanied the officers to the police station.'[515]

The next day, precisely four years after the Japan bust, they appeared before Judge Haynes Blackman at Holetown Magistrates Court in Barbados. They pleaded guilty to possession and were each fined BD$200. Outside the court Paul told reporters: 'I've got absolutely no grudges and no complaints. It was a small amount of cannabis and I intended to use it, but the police came to my place and I gave them ten grams of cannabis. Linda had another small carton of cannabis in her handbag.'[516]

Their holiday ruined, the couple and their children immediately flew back to England, although the island's chief immigration officer Kendrick Hutson stressed that they had not been deported and were free to return. At Heathrow Airport they went through customs unimpeded, and Paul spoke to reporters, making clear that his views on cannabis remained unchanged: 'Can we get one thing straight? Whatever you think, or whatever you think I've done, this substance cannabis is a whole lot less harmful than rum punch, whisky, nicotine and glue, all of which are perfectly legal. I would like to see it decriminalised because I don't think, in the privacy of my own room, I was doing anyone any harm whatsoever.'[517] Asked if he would continue to smoke pot, McCartney winked and said: 'Never again.' When questioned if he was serious, he replied: 'Probably not.'[518]

The McCartneys were then driven a short distance to their private plane. As they prepared to board they were asked to return to the customs hall. Marijuana had been found in Linda's luggage. According to a witness: 'They cleared customs with their heavy luggage through the "green" channel. Shortly afterwards, a camera bag and a shoulder bag, which had apparently been left behind accidentally, were presented for clearance by a British Airways employee through the "red", something to declare, channel. In the camera bag, cannabis was found inside a film canister together with a reefer cigarette, while in the shoulder bag there was another reefer and there were traces of cannabis at the bottom of the bag.'[519]

Linda immediately took responsibility, and was arrested and charged at the airport's police station. She was immediately released on unconditional bail and ordered to appear at Uxbridge magistrates court a week later.

Paul was in the public gallery for the 13-minute hearing, during which Linda pleaded guilty and was fined £75. She later claimed the bags had been thoroughly searched by police in Barbados and were declared clean, so she felt no need to check further.

Having now faced drugs charges on six occasions in six different countries, and having experienced visa problems and Paul's spell in prison, the McCartneys had become the subject of much prurient interest from the tabloids.

The Sun newspaper ran an interview with Denny Laine, serialised over four consecutive days from 31 January, titled 'The Real McCartney'. The revelations included that they smoked joints 'the way ordinary people smoke cigarettes'; that they had smuggled cannabis through airports in the hood of their toddler James's coat; and that Paul's colossal habit hampered his creativity and left him unfocused. 'That's why Paul's albums take ages and ages to make,' Laine said. 'He just cannot be decisive about anything.'

Later in 1984 Paul and Linda gave an interview to *Playboy* in which they spoke openly about their recent travails. 'I've never wanted to be seen talking about marijuana for publication,' said Paul. 'Why? Because I've got four kids and it looks like I'm advocating it. I'm not. But after this last bust in Barbados, with people saying, "Naughty boy, shouldn't do that!" as a 42-year-old man, I feel I now have the right to reply. If anyone had told me in the Sixties that 20 years later we'd still be talking about whether pot was worse than this or that, I'd have said, "Oh, come off it, boys…" For me, pot is milder than Scotch. That doesn't mean I've turned around and advocated marijuana. I haven't. I'm really only saying this is true for me. I mean, in Barbados, where I was on holiday, I was in a room miles away from anyone. It never interfered with anyone. No one was watching me except one manservant at the place.

'I also want to say that there are things that marijuana is more harmful than: air, for instance. I advocate air every day. Water, orange juice – I'd advocate that and a good vegetarian diet any day of the week. But as I say, in print, you're put in a corner; they make you sound like the bloody high priest of pot. It's stupid, you know. I can take pot or leave it. I got busted in Japan for it. I was nine days without it and there wasn't a hint of withdrawal, nothing.'[520]

In 1986 McCartney and Ringo Starr were among the performers on a charity album, *It's A Live-In World*, in aid of the drug and alcohol rehabilitation organisation Phoenix House.

McCartney's contribution was the light reggae Simple As That, a poor song even by McCartney's wildly variable Eighties standards. 'I know it isn't easy to refuse,' goes the opening verse. 'A lot of thoughts are flying through your head. Tell me this before you have to choose: Would you rather be alive or dead?' In the chorus he appears incredulous than anyone could ever succumb to drug addiction: 'It's as simple as that. Would you rather be alive or dead? It's as simple as that, it's so simple. It makes you wanna cry.' Indeed.

But his love of cannabis endured. In September 1999 a

listening party for the *Run Devil Run* album was held in the Manhattan Centre in New York City. During the event McCartney was seen smoking up a storm with actors Woody Harrelson and Laurence Fishburne. Afterwards his publicist Geoff Baker handed a photo of the trio to *High Times*, encouraging them to publish it. They did, under the heading 'The Three Stoners.'

In the early years of the twenty-first century, however, the seemingly unthinkable happened: McCartney announced that he'd finally quit cannabis. The catalysts appear to have been his ill-fated marriage to Heather Mills ('She's violently against it'[521]) and the birth in October 2003 of their daughter Beatrice.

'I don't smoke the stuff these days,' he said in 2004. 'It's something I've kind of grown out of. But I was doing a fair bit back in those days. Someone said to me the other day, "I can have a clear conversation with you these days because you're not always stoned." When I look back at some of the work I've done which I don't like, maybe some of that was written when I was stoned.

'That's the problem with being high – everything seems great. You think anything can be turned into a song. Pick up a newspaper and choose the first phrase that jumps out... "The decline of the orang-utan." Wow! Fucking great title for a song. By the time you're finished, you think you've got your next single. Only next morning you realise it's a load of old tripe. Personally, I'm much happier being straight and writing straight. I've tried the other way. Been there, done it. Never again.'[522]

McCartney's marriage to Mills ended in divorce in 2008. Seven years later he confirmed that giving up cannabis had not been temporary. 'I don't do it any more,' he said. 'Why? The truth is I don't really want to set an example to my kids and grandkids. It's now a parent thing... Instead of smoking a spliff I'll now have a glass of red wine or a nice margarita. The last time I smoked was a long time ago.'[523] With abstinence seemed to come renewed energy: on and off the stage he cut a sprightly figure, undertaking a series of world tours, putting out some of the best music of his post-Beatles career, and collaborating with stars including Kanye West and Rihanna. 'It's a bit befuddling,' he said of cannabis. 'It's actually more important at my stage of the game to be unfuddled.'[524]

10

THE ANSWER'S AT THE END

Just as McCartney had done in Scotland, George Harrison found solace in nature in the first months after the Beatles' split. In January 1970, as the band completed their final recordings for *Let It Be*, he and Pattie purchased Friar Park in Henley-on-Thames.

The 120-room ornate neo-gothic mansion was in stark contrast to the simplicity of their Kinfauns bungalow, and they worked hard to restore the house and gardens to their former glory. After the caves had been excavated, a party was thrown in which Pattie's 14-year-old brother Boo was given the task of rolling and distributing joints for the guests. This lasted until a false alarm of a police raid, and Boo threw the bag of marijuana into some bushes. Some of the guests spent the rest of the night unsuccessfully scouring the area for the drugs.

Friar Park became a retreat and refuge, a place of safety and isolation. In the 62-acre grounds Harrison could tend the sprawling gardens, explore the caves, grottoes and underground passages, and lose himself in meditation. 'Sometimes I feel like I'm actually on the wrong planet, and it's great when I'm in my garden,' he said. 'But the minute I go out the gate I think: "What the hell am I doing here?"'[525]

Although he continued to perform with Lennon and Starr, Harrison formed close alliances with other musicians including Bob Dylan, Ravi Shankar, Jackie Lomax and Delaney & Bonnie. He also kickstarted a successful solo career with the triple album *All Things Must Pass* and its global hit My Sweet Lord, and organised the first major charity concert, the Concert For Bangladesh at New York's Madison Square Garden. The dawn of the Seventies appeared to find him with new confidence in his abilities as a musician and songwriter, and brought critical and commercial acclaim.

Since the mid-Sixties Harrison had struggled to reconcile the spiritual and earthly, and at Friar Park he was often torn between his love of sex and drugs, and the search for enlightenment. His marriage to Pattie became strained by his infidelities, and she was courted by Eric Clapton, a friend of George who eventually confessed: 'I have to tell you, man, that I'm in love with your wife.' Pattie chose to remain with her husband, and the wounded Clapton retreated into heroin addiction.

The Harrisons, however, were in a slow decline. Pattie felt lonely in Friar Park, which lacked the intimacy and easy atmosphere of Kinfauns. She also found George increasingly distant. He became obsessive about chanting and meditation, and would spend long hours in the house's recording studio.

Drugs were commonplace – 'marijuana, uppers, downers and cocaine',[526] according to Pattie, but George bounced between extremes. 'He was either using it every day or not at all for months at a stretch,' she said of cocaine. 'Then he would be spiritual and clean and would meditate for hour after hour, with no chance of normality. During those periods he was totally withdrawn and I felt alone and isolated. Then, as if the pleasures of the flesh were too hard to resist, he would stop meditating, snort coke, have fun, flirting and partying. Although it was more companionable, there was no normality in that either.'[527]

Chris O'Dell, a former Apple employee who had become a trusted friend and assistant to the Harrisons, stayed at Friar Park for several months in 1970. She enjoyed the work, parties and company, although she soon became aware of George's changing moods. 'He never was much of a druggie,' O'Dell noted, 'although at times he drank plenty of alcohol. He'd go through these "clean" phases when he'd stop using any kind of drug but then, without warning, he'd join in and start drinking or using with us. Pattie and I used to joke that we didn't know if his hand was in the prayer bag or the coke bag.'[528] John Lennon came to a similar conclusion, telling *Double Fantasy* drummer Andy Newmark that 'George is just a frightened Catholic. God one day, coke the next.'[529]

O'Dell believed that Harrison had three personality types, which would emerge seemingly at random and would dominate the atmosphere in the house. 'The first George was great fun and loved to gossip, drink, smoke a little pot, and even, on rare occasions, snort a line or two of cocaine,' she said. 'This was my favourite George, the one I first got to know and love at Apple, and whenever he'd hang out with us, we were all happy. The second George was intense, sarcastic, and detached: he'd morph into this George when things were bothering him at Apple or with the other Beatles, or when something wasn't going quite right with the garden or the remodelling efforts. Little things would set him off at these times, and we'd all have to watch our step. The third George was the spiritual seeker, the one who would walk around with his hand inside his prayer bag and chant silently to himself. At these times he was peaceful and serene, totally absorbed in otherworldly thoughts. I had many amazing discussions with this third George and learned a lot from him, but truthfully, he wasn't a whole lot of fun for the rest of us who really preferred drinking, talking, laughing, and having fun.'[530]

O'Dell left Friar Park to go on tour with the Rolling Stones, and subsequently became a heavy user of cocaine and

Quaaludes. But she remained friendly with the Harrisons, and often returned to Friar Park. She also grew close to Ringo and Maureen Starkey, and was at their home in 1973 – Tittenhurst Park, recently purchased from Lennon and Ono – when George openly declared that he was in love with Maureen. They had become attracted to one another over some months, much to Pattie's distress, and Ringo took the news badly.

The affair with Maureen – one of several for George – was a key contributor to the break-up of the Harrisons' marriage, as was his drug use. 'George used coke excessively and I think it changed him,' Pattie recalled. 'I think it froze George's emotions and hardened his heart.'[531] Pattie left Friar Park in 1974 and took up with Eric Clapton – his love finally requited and heroin addiction conquered, but with a chronic alcohol problem that she was forced to accommodate.

ALTHOUGH he often claimed to be sanguine about Pattie's new relationship, Harrison's actions suggested otherwise. He adopted a heavy workload, setting up his Dark Horse label, recording the album of the same name, producing albums for Ravi Shankar and the group Splinter, overseeing the Music Festival from India at the Royal Albert Hall, and embarking on his first solo tour, all the while dealing with the fallout from a soured management deal with Allen Klein and a plagiarism suit for My Sweet Lord.

His drug and alcohol use also escalated, to the concern of those around him. While impressed with Harrison's energy within the studio, Splinter became worried by his gaunt appearance. And Klaus Voormann described it as 'a bad time for him. He became unreliable. It started when he was cutting the film for Bangladesh. I called and said I was coming up, and I heard him say, "Klaus is coming. Hide the dope." I appreciated George for his weaknesses as well as his strengths, and I could tell he was embarrassed. I didn't have much contact with him during that period. George, to me, was on a different plane.'[532]

In his autobiography Harrison described 1974 as 'a bad domestic year'. The turmoil was reflected in the music and lyrics of the *Dark Horse* album, released that December. One song in particular, Simply Shady, recounted a typical incident of the time: 'Somebody brought the juicer, I thought I'd take a sip,' it begins. 'Came off the rails so crazy, my senses took a dip.'

'After I split up from Pattie, I went on a bit of a bender to make up for all the years I'd been married,' Harrison said in 1979. 'If you listen to Simply Shady, on *Dark Horse*, it's all in there – my whole life at that time was a bit like [British radio soap opera] *Mrs Dale's Diary*. I wasn't ready to join Alcoholics Anonymous or anything – I don't think I was that far gone – but I could put back a bottle of brandy occasionally, plus all the other naughty things that fly around. I just went on a binge, went on the road... until it got to the point where I had no voice and almost no body at times.'[533]

Harrison's 1974 tour of the USA and Canada was hotly anticipated – the first by a Beatle in those countries since 1966. But he made it clear from the outset that this was no place for nostalgia, and that songs by his former band would be kept to a minimum. His co-billing with Ravi Shankar further tempered expectations. For Harrison, who had never relished touring, it often felt more like a test of mettle than an enjoyable enterprise.

Press conferences, interviews and on-stage pronouncements found Harrison tense, surly and abrasive – symptomatic of his poor health, high workload and a general distaste for being treated as public property. Although audiences were enthusiastic, music critics savaged the tour, finding Harrison dour and unwilling to play to the crowds.

Furthermore, his voice had become ravaged during pre-tour rehearsals, leading to 'Dark Hoarse' puns in the media, and he struggled to fulfil his duties as a frontman. One saving grace was his meeting Olivia Arias, a 25-year-old secretary working for

Dark Horse Records in America. The pair had already established a rapport on the telephone, and quickly fell in love after meeting in LA on the seventh date of the tour.

Harrison arrived back in England in January 1975 'shell-shocked' and in need of rest and recovery. 'When I got off the plane and back home I went into the garden and I was so relieved,' he said. 'That [tour] was the nearest I got to a nervous breakdown. I couldn't even go into the house.'[534]

The Dark Horse debacle marked the beginning of a long commercial and artistic decline, in which Harrison fell increasingly out of step with changes in the music industry. The career peaks of *All Things Must Pass* and *Living In The Material World* felt like distant memories, despite occasional new flashes of brilliance. He withdrew to Friar Park, immersing himself in domesticity, Formula One, a burgeoning interest in film production, and a coterie of close friends. A highlight of 1975's *Extra Texture (Read All About It)* was Tired Of Midnight Blue, written about a night out with music executives in Los Angeles. Depressed by having 'ended up in the back room with a lot of grey-haired naughty people',[535] he found comfort instead in home life. 'Don't know where I had been,' he sang, 'But I know what I have seen/Made me chill right to the bone/Made me wish that I'd stayed home with you.'

The years of stress and indulgence finally caught up with him in 1976. Shortly after beginning work on the *Thirty Three & ⅓* album, Harrison became jaundiced, lost weight and his energy levels plummeted. Initially thought to be food poisoning, the eventual diagnosis was hepatitis B. Harrison first attempted a cure through prayer, but when this failed to improve his condition his doctor prescribed vitamins and rest. He also consulted an LA acupuncturist who gave him herbal remedies, and gradually his health returned. The illness spurred Harrison into adopting a more abstemious lifestyle. 'I needed the hepatitis to quit drinking,' he told *Rolling Stone*.[536]

GEORGE AND OLIVIA married in Henley-on-Thames in September 1978, a month after the birth of their son Dhani. On his eponymous 1979 album, Harrison paid tribute to her in the song Dark Sweet Lady, describing how she took him from his personal nadir. The same album contained Soft-Hearted Hana, written about a magic mushroom experience on the island of Maui.

Harrison remained an advocate for the psychological benefits of LSD. Speaking of Madonna, with whom he had worked on the 1986 film *Shanghai Surprise*, he meditated on the pressures of fame.

'There's much more to life than just being a famous pop star,' he said. 'Unfortunately, a lot of them fall into the trap. They get surrounded by people saying how great they are, all these sycophants who surround them. And unfortunately, she has got all that going and she's fallen for it. But I think she has the ability to be a really nice person – you have to see it from the other side, which I can see too, which is that the pressure you're under when you are fab is tremendous. It sometimes does get you crazy when you can't write and can't do this when everybody's bugging you and shooting cameras in your face. So I sympathise from that point of view, too. But what she needs is just 500 milligrams of LSD!'[537]

Harrison's own drinking and drug use continued into the 1980s, and he had periods of heavy cocaine use. He also suffered mood swings and periods of depression. Olivia stood by him in the hope that he would eventually pull through, which he eventually did, finding contentment in music and spirituality. He even gave up smoking temporarily, after three decades of addiction, although the stress of making *Shanghai Surprise* led him to resume the habit.

He also renewed his belief in chanting and Transcendental Meditation. 'It took me years trying to figure out what's happening to me,' he said. 'I think it was just the accumulation of those years when there was drugs in my life and those years of staying up all night and partying and just being in recording studios and business problems and all these people I talked about earlier – the banks wanting their money and these other people not paying us and all that got me to the point where I said, "Jesus! I gotta do something here!" And I remembered, "What about meditation!" I had forgotten totally that that's what it was all about – to release the stress out of your system.'[538] His dedication to meditation even extended to him supporting the Natural Law Party in the 1992 UK general election, even suggesting to McCartney and Starr that the three of them should stand for parliament. Disappointingly, the idea came to nothing.

IN JULY 1997, while gardening at Friar Park, Harrison discovered a lump in his neck. The following month he had the tumour removed at the Princess Margaret Hospital in Windsor, and subsequently underwent radiation therapy at London's Royal Marsden Hospital. A series of check-ups followed at the Mayo Clinic in Minnesota, and it seemed as though he was in the clear.

News of the cancer broke in the media in May 1998. Speaking to reporters outside the gates of Friar Park, Harrison said: 'I'm not going to die on you, folks, just yet. I am very lucky. Sometimes, if you say the word "cancer" everybody automatically thinks it will end in misery, but it's not always the case. I was very lucky because it didn't go anywhere – all it was was a little red mark on my neck.

'I got it purely from smoking,' he continued. 'I gave up cigarettes many years ago but had started again for a while and then stopped in 1997. Luckily for me they found that this nodule was more of a warning than anything else. There are many different types of cancerous cells and this was a very basic type.'[539]

Harrison withdrew once again to convalesce. He worked sporadically, assembling a new edition of *All Things Must Pass* and planning reissues of his other works. But that all paled into insignificance when an intruder broke into Friar Park in December 1999, and stabbed Harrison multiple times in a frenzied and brutal attack. He and Olivia bravely fought off the man before police and paramedics arrived. Harrison sustained extensive physical injuries, which mercifully were not life-threatening, but the invasion of his home, the sanctuary he had held dear for three decades, was a deep psychological blow.

But bounce back he did, completing work on the *All Things Must Pass* reissue and making a series of new recordings at his home studio. Yet plans to record in 2001 with Jeff Lynne – his former bandmate in the Traveling Wilburys, and co-producer of the Beatles' Free As A Bird and Real Love – were put on hold when the cancer returned.

Part of Harrison's lung was removed, and statements were released to reassure the press and public, but behind the locked door the prognosis was poor. He underwent treatment in Switzerland, and flew to New York for radiation therapy after the cancer spread to his brain.

Knowing the end was near, Harrison made a final pilgrimage to India where he bathed in the Ganges and visited the Krishna temple in Varanasi, before flying to Beverly Hills. It was there on 29 November 2001 that he ended his days, in a house owned by Paul McCartney, surrounded by Olivia, Dhani and close friends.

To the end, Harrison remained convinced that LSD had provided a shortcut to a spiritual world that might otherwise have eluded him. 'I can't imagine, if I hadn't had it, how many years of normal life it would have taken to get me to the realisations: I might've never got them in this life,' he said. 'It just opened the door and I experienced really good things. I mean, I never doubted God after that. Before, I was a cynic. I didn't even say the word God; I thought "bullshit to all that stuff." But after that, I knew. It was not even a question of "Is there possibly a God?" – I knew absolutely. It's just that big light that goes off in your head.'[540]

11

IT DON'T COME EASY

Ringo Starr was the only member of the Beatles never to be involved in a police raid. More than the others, however, he struggled with excess and addiction before eventually finding redemption.

'Ringo's talent would have come out one way or the other,' John Lennon said in 1980. 'Whatever that spark is in Ringo, we all know it but we can't put our finger on it. Whether it's acting, drumming, or singing, I don't know. There's something in him that is projectable and [regardless of the Beatles] he would have surfaced as an individual.'[541]

That irrepressible star quality helped Ringo move on as the Beatles fell apart. The young man who had won over audiences in *A Hard Day's Night* had continued his acting sideline in 1968, appearing in the sex farce *Candy* and starring in the following year's *The Magic Christian*. He also made his directorial debut in 1972 with the T. Rex documentary *Born To Boogie*, showing that he was able to move with the times and embrace the new wave of glam rockers.

Starr became the first Beatle to release a non-experimental or soundtrack solo album. Released in the spring of 1970, *Senti-*

mental Journey was a collection of pre-rock standards, and provided a pleasant contrast to the Beatles' dark final months. He played on several early solo albums by Lennon and Harrison, including *John Lennon/Plastic Ono Band* and *All Things Must Pass*, and performed at the Concert For Bangladesh.

His early solo career took flight with a little help from his friends. A string of hits began with 1971's It Don't Come Easy, followed by Back Off Boogaloo and the US number ones Photograph and You're Sixteen. The 1973 album *Ringo* contained contributions from Lennon, McCartney and Harrison, while the follow-up, *Goodnight Vienna*, featured the likes of Lennon, Billy Preston, Klaus Voormann, Robbie Robertson, Harry Nilsson and Elton John.

Unlike the other former Beatles, Starr remained a frequent visitor to the Apple offices at 3 Savile Row. 'I was getting sucked into the decadence of the period,' recalled Dan Richter, who would also occasionally drop by. 'A typical day might include Cuban cigars from Mayfair, oysters for lunch at Pruniers, and a touch of coke. The coke seemed a natural part of the life I was living. I regularly relaxed with Ringo's financial guy, Hilary Gerrard, and Neil Aspinall. He always seemed to have lines of coke laid out on the glass coffee table in Ringo's office. Ringo was, as always, amiable and easy-going, but he was increasingly concerned by all the money Apple was spending on John and Yoko's film projects.'[542]

IN CONTRAST to his homebody reputation in the Sixties, Starr had become something of a party animal, perhaps the most outgoing of the Beatles. His taste for alcohol had not waned since his time as a boozing bar waiter in 1956, but with money, fame and freedom he became unstoppable. His friends, among them Marc Bolan, Harry Nilsson and Keith Moon, joined the hair-raising, high-octane wild ride to oblivion.

Starr's closest alliance was with Nilsson. The pair performed on each other's records, shared a similar sense of humour, and appeared together in several film and television projects including *The Point* and the unreleased *Harry And Ringo's Night Out*. They also collaborated on the horror musical *Son Of Dracula*, a chaotic disaster which was notable mainly for an enormous bar bill. 'I remember I did a movie with Harry Nilsson,' Starr said in 1998. 'He had all these players in the band, John Bonham, Keith Moon, Jim Price, and it was costing me just union rate, only about 30 quid a day. But it was costing £1,000 for booze! They were all gone by noon. It was funny. It was fun times, we were just out there playing and making stuff.

'Someone said, "We weren't musicians dabbling in drugs and alcohol; now we were junkies dabbling in music." I was sliding down, I wasn't taking enough interest. I was more interested in boogieing, just going out to parties and not doing what I did.'[543] One night in London, Starr and Moon went from the nightclub Tramp to the nearby Playboy Club, where they were thrown out for rowdiness – particularly Moon, who had been poking Playboy bunnies in the rear with a fork. The club later announced it was rescinding their membership 'because damage by Mr Starr and Mr Moon came to an amount totalling almost £30!'[544]

Cocaine had become ubiquitous in rock music by 1974, the year Starr arrived in Los Angeles during Lennon's Lost Weekend. During that period he made the *Goodnight Vienna* album, which included an ironic cover version of The No No Song. The lyrics describe various attempts to sell marijuana, cocaine and moonshine whiskey to a recovering addict who refuses each temptation.

Starr was a member of the Hollywood Vampires, a celebrity drinking fraternity which met upstairs at the Rainbow Bar and Grill on Sunset Boulevard. Formed by singer Alice Cooper, the principal members were Starr, Cooper, Moon, Nilsson and the Monkees' Micky Dolenz. 'It was that crowd, every night those same people,' said Cooper. 'Every once in a while John Lennon would come into town or Keith Emerson and they would be honourable members of the night.'[545] Those wishing to join were required to outdrink the other members, who also included John Belushi, Marc Bolan, Klaus Voormann and Mal Evans.

By this time Ringo's marriage to Maureen was all but over. 'It was the drugs that caused the breakup,' she told Chris O'Dell that December. 'I always thought Ritchie was strong enough to deal with any drug. All those years he never let any drug ever get hold of him and when he thought it was, he'd stop immediately. I always admired that about him. But cocaine changes your brain. It made him paranoid. God's honest truth. It changed his brain. I hate cocaine.'[546]

But his drinking was equally destructive. Maureen said he drank to cope with low self-esteem. 'I think he used it as a cloak to hide his weakness,' she told French magazine *Le Chroniqueur* in 1988. 'He would drink to get plastered to hide from it, but he knew that eventually he couldn't. I remember he even tried to commit suicide once. Well, I shouldn't say he did it intentionally because it took place when he was drunk, or at least I think so. He tried to cut his throat with his razor in the bathroom. He really frightened me at first, but I knew he wasn't conscious of it. It was something that he wouldn't have done if he was conscious and I knew it.'[547]

Their marriage ended in July 1975, the divorce papers citing his affair with American model Nancy Lee Andrews. Maureen was devastated at the failure of her marriage and sank into a deep depression, although she and Ringo later became close again.

Starr had other short-lived affairs with women during this time, including Chris O'Dell and singer Lynsey de Paul. But his relationship with Andrews grew serious. They were together for six years, and were engaged to be married, yet she increasingly had to contend with his drinking and drug-taking. 'I became a clown and wouldn't let him stay that way too long,' she said of his depressive tendencies. 'It took him a long time to come out of it.'[548]

Somewhere along the line the hits dried up and the film roles became fewer, but Starr showed little inclination to change his fortunes. 'I was taking less and less interest,' he said. 'I was more interested in just being out of my head.'[549] In contrast to the other Beatles, who were all domesticated and largely sober by the latter half of the Seventies, Starr remained the international playboy, with houses in Monaco, Amsterdam, Los Angeles and England. He frittered away much of his fortune while living the high life at film premieres, promotional tours, restaurants, casinos and nightclubs.

'I ended up as just some fucking celebrity. Someone in England put it so cruelly: They said if there's an opening of an envelope, he'll be there. That hit me. I thought, "Shit, yeah, this is what I'm doing now." I'd be at movie premieres in London with my bow tie on and a bottle of cognac in my pocket mixed with some Coca-Cola, so people would think it was just soda. It got really sad.'[550] He remained a warm and likeable character, although his behaviour was sometimes alarming – such as the time in the summer of 1976 when, 'feeling vaguely insane and drinking some new drink', he completely shaved his head and eyebrows. 'It was a time when you either cut your wrists or your hair,' he later explained, 'and I'm a coward.'[551]

In his childhood Starr had contracted peritonitis following a routine appendectomy. It had left him temporarily in a coma, and he spent many months recovering in hospital. A legacy of the disease was a sensitive stomach which left him unable to tolerate certain foods.

On 28 April 1979 he was rushed to Princess Grace Hospital in Monaco. 'Part of my intestines closed down and I was in a lot of pain,' he said. 'I got to the hospital finally and they gave me a shot of painkiller. Then, when I felt some relief I said, "Oh. I can go now." And Professor Chatalin, the doctor who was taking care of me, said, "Yes, you can go. And you can die!" So I said, "Well maybe we should have the operation".'[552]

Five feet of Starr's intestines were removed. He remained in intensive care for five days before being transferred to a recovery ward for a further week. Shortly afterwards he talked his way out of hospital and moved into Monte Carlo's Hôtel de Paris, where he passed the time at the bar. 'I couldn't drink because my intestines were healing but I could hang out with people so it helped get over that low passage,' he recalled. 'I'd given up cigarettes and I started lighting them for people because it gave me a buzz. One day I smoked a whole cigarette and within a week I'd bought a carton and was back on 60 a day.'[553] Soon he was drinking heavily again too.

Starr's relationship with Nancy Lee Andrews was floundering by the time he started work on the movie *Caveman* in February 1980. His head was turned by his co-star, the actor and model Barbara Bach, and their affair became an open secret on the film set. When he returned to Los Angeles Starr broke the news to a furious Andrews, who later filed an unsuccessful palimony lawsuit against him.

Ringo and Barbara married in April 1981 at Marylebone Register Office, where Paul and Linda McCartney had tied the knot 12 years before. During the reception, held at the Mayfair nightclub Rags, Starr shared a stage with McCartney and Harrison for the first time since 1969, knocking out some rock 'n' roll hits and ending the impromptu set with I Saw Her Standing There and Twist And Shout.

'If an actress doesn't have some kind of responsibility she can very easily go off the deep end,' Bach said. 'Ringo is part of my stability now. He has given me even more than I already had and that's what I want for our future.'[554] But stability was short-lived. Within a year of the wedding there were reports of violent arguments in which bottles and punches were thrown.

She too became a heavy drinker: 'Barbara fell into the trap because of me,' Starr said in 1989. 'She was an actress who used to go to bed at ten at night and get up at eight in the morning. Till we met. Then her career went the same way as mine. I did two records, a few shows. But working two days a year is not having a career.'[555] She did attempt to get their excesses under control, though with little success. 'Every couple of months she'd try and straighten us out,' Starr recalled, 'but then we'd fall right back into the trap.'[556]

By the mid-Eighties he was downing a bottle of champagne before midday, using cocaine, and drinking multiple bottles of wine a day. He was almost always seen wearing dark glasses, all the better to hide his bloodshot eyes. He made an exception, however, in a series of advertisements for Sun Country Classic Wine Coolers, with which he became the first Beatle to endorse a commercial product.

Having an alcoholic promote a wine product might seem inappropriate for all concerned, but the money was good – a reported $1 million – and the Canandaigua Wine Company initially seemed happy with the association. 'He fits the image of the product,' said chairman Marvin Sands. 'He's a classic with a dry and humorous sense that matches the dry, clear, happy taste of our new cooler.'[557] Yet the adverts were swiftly scrapped after failing to appeal to younger drinkers.

In 1986 Starr appeared on *It's A Live-In World*, the anti-drugs album to which Paul McCartney contributed Simple As That. Ringo's track You Know It Makes Sense was a spoken-word piece. 'Time passes so quickly but too quickly for some,' he intoned in his familiar sing-song Liverpudlian accent. 'You know what I'm talking about: it's the heroin problem, and it's a rapidly growing problem too, especially amongst today's kids.' As with McCartney's song, its well-intentioned message was nonetheless unlikely to dissuade anyone from drug-taking, and paid little heed to the complex reasons for addiction: 'So come on, don't be stupid. If you put a hole in your arm you must have a hole in your head.'

Starr had been an absent father for many years, and his relationships with his children had suffered. His musical career was in the doldrums too, as was his acting – his main success was narrating the children's TV animation *Thomas The Tank Engine And Friends*. His heavy drinking left him with little motivation anyway, and he sank into a period of stasis. 'I didn't work or do anything. I wouldn't go out, because you'd have to be in the car for 40 minutes without a drink.

'Drunks are great talkers. We'd sit around for nights on end and talk about what we were going to do. And of course I'd get so bleedin' drunk, I couldn't move. The result of being drunk was that nothing happened.'[558] When he did work, he was invariably so drunk he was barely able to remember what happened: 'I've got photographs of me playing all over the world but I've absolutely no memory of it. I played Washington with the Beach Boys [in 1984] – or so they tell me. But there's only a photo to prove it.'[559]

ON FRIDAY 7 OCTOBER 1988 STARR and Bach finally hit rock bottom. Their binges and blackouts had become public knowledge, as had their physical violence towards one another. But that afternoon Starr awoke to a scene of utter destruction. 'I came to one Friday afternoon and was told by the staff that I had trashed the house so badly they thought there had been burglars, and I'd trashed Barbara so badly they thought she was dead.'[560]

Hollywood actress Melody Stuart took a call from an anguished Starr at four o'clock the following morning. 'He told me he was scared he would kill his wife, Barbara, in their next drink-and-drug-fuelled fight,' she said. 'It's no secret that

Barbara and Ringo do cocaine now and again, but this time they had been drinking round the clock for three or four days. It was the usual pattern, drink, drugs, drink, drugs, followed by more drink. Ringo told me, "We had one motherfucker of a fight. Barbara started screaming and throwing things around the room." Barbara said vile things to him in drink, and Ringo shot back with some wisecrack comment. Then she went for him with an art deco lamp and cracked him across the head. He slapped her across the chops just to calm her down, but he split her lip and she started screaming the house down. Ringo told me he finished up with a bloody nose and half his hair torn out... The real horror was that neither could remember the fighting. Both had been in a blackout induced by a deadly cock-tail of drugs and booze.'[561]

Against the odds, the brutal incident did not spell the end of their marriage. Instead they both pledged to get help, a resolution which strengthened the bond between them. 'This was just the end of the line for me,' said Starr. 'I'd had enough and I'd caused a lot of damage. I had come out of a huge blackout. I said, "You've got to get us into one of the places. We need help." And she did.'[562]

Bach reportedly contacted a number of clinics which refused to allow her and Starr to remain together at the start of treatment. Eventually they were accepted by Sierra Tucson treatment centre in Arizona, and arrived early the following week. Starr 'drank all the way and got off the plane completely demented. I thought I was going to a lunatic asylum.'[563]

They remained in rehab for six weeks, at a reported cost of $35,000 each. After the introductory detoxification programme was complete they were given separate rooms without televisions, radios or telephones. They attended lectures, seminars and group therapy sessions, did their own laundry, and even cleaned the ashtrays, toilets and floors. Starr overcame his initial resistance and embraced the treatments: 'Eight days in, I decided, "I'm here to get help because I know I'm sick." And I just did whatever they asked me and, thank God, it pulled me through. I can never thank that clinic enough.'[564]

News of their stay reached the media midway through their time in Tucson. Although friends attempted to downplay the problems, confirmation eventually came from Starr's record company. The Beatles' former press secretary Derek Taylor, himself a recovering alcoholic, was asked to issue a statement on behalf of Starr and Bach, in an attempt to limit the media presence at the rehab facility.

'Undoubtedly, they came to the conclusion they couldn't handle their problems alone,' Taylor announced. 'They decided, over a time, there was something wrong and had to do something about it. That is the first step and it is a very brave one. I know he's doing OK. They are in a very convivial atmosphere. Fellow alcoholics who, by their very nature, are all very gregarious surround them. Every day for them is like being in a bar, with everyone sharing a joke and a laugh. The only difference is they don't have a drink in their hand. And that's a good thing. They all realise life can go on without alcohol. They can be just as funny, just as entertaining and just as capable. Ringo knows he wants to contain his problem and then he must take each day at a time. He will be with Barbara and I am sure they will beat it together.'[565]

The other former Beatles rallied too. George Harrison, who had spoken to Starr, made a brief statement of solidarity: 'I'm really glad he's sorting out his problems. Ringo's a lovely bloke and a great mate.' More loquacious was Linda McCartney, who said: 'They are both winners and will beat this together. There is no way a man of such wit and humour will let this beat him. Of course, it was obvious that they were drinking too much, but that is show business. It hits so many people but they can be cured... Barbara is a rather special friend of mine and I have spoken to her in the last few days. What she told me has given Paul and I every confidence that she and Ringo will come through this stronger than ever.'[566]

And so they did. Starr and Bach left Tucson on 25 November, returning to Tittenhurst Park. They were determined to remain sober, although that required some readjustment. 'If any of my friends can't deal with me being sober, then I just don't bother with them,' he said. 'Because for me to live is more important than a friend getting uptight because I won't have a drink. If we go to a party now, Barbara and I usually leave around about 11:30, when everyone else starts getting rocky. Your life is changed completely around.'[567]

STARR FOUND SALVATION IN WORK. In January 1989, just weeks after leaving the Tucson clinic, he embarked on a promotional tour for *Shining Time Station*, an American adaptation of *Thomas The Tank Engine*. His performance as Mr Conductor won him a Daytime Emmy nomination, and kickstarted a new chapter in his career. He appeared alongside George Harrison in the video for Tom Petty's I Won't Back Down, and released a single of his own, a duet of Act Naturally with Buck Owens recorded at Abbey Road Studios.

His return was truly cemented with a new band and tour in 1989. Ringo Starr & His All-Starr Band boasted a stellar line-up of performers who took turns at centre stage. The first incarnation featured Starr, Billy Preston, Joe Walsh, Nils Lofgren, Dr John, Clarence Clemons, Jim Keltner, and the Band's Rick Danko and Levon Helm.

The tour began in Dallas on 23 July and took in 30 US cities over 43 dates. Despite initial nerves Starr enjoyed the experience, as did the fans at each of the sold-out concerts. 'The first week was very strange at the end of the show,' he said, 'because my whole brain and body said, "Let's get messed up, let's party." This one voice of sanity, this spark of sanity, said, "We don't do that anymore," and we didn't. But it was hard. Just the first week. To do anything again, the first week, you have to really learn to do it again. And that's all it takes. I had some fears that sobering up, I wouldn't be humorous and I wouldn't be able to play. But they were just fears. They weren't true. So anyone out there who's thinking of getting straight, don't worry about it. You'll be just as loveable.'[568]

Numerous tours and live albums followed, with a revolving line-up. And although the venues became smaller over time, and the All-Starrs a little less dazzling, Ringo proved his worth as a touring musician who, more than five decades after the heyday of Beatlemania, could still pack a joint (a venue, that is).

Starr stopped eating meat, despite the occasional lapse, and in January 1990 gave up smoking cigarettes, a habit that had been with him since the early 1950s. He revelled in clean living, telling an interviewer: 'Three times they said to my mother, "He'll be dead in the morning." So what's that about? That's a little heavier than joining this band. But I feel I'm here for a purpose. I'm not quite sure what that is. God looks after me.'[569]

His relationship with his children improved too, after some rocky years, and his elder son Zak played drums with the All-Starrs on tour. In 1985 the first Beatle grandchild, Zak's daughter Tatia, was born. And in 2016 she had a baby boy of her own, making Ringo the first great-grandfather of the former Beatles.

'In my lost days,' Starr said in 1992, 'in the depths of fear, depression and loneliness, I used to tell my kids, "If you ever take drugs, let me get them for you." Now we sit and talk and I say, "You know, Daddy's changed." But I still tell them, if they get into trouble, at least they can come to me and I can take them to rehab. Because Daddy certainly knows where they are.'[570]

In October 1990 Ringo and Barbara were among 350 celebrity guests at the London Waldorf Hotel. The occasion was a fundraiser for the charity SHARP, the Self-Help Addiction Recovery Programme. The first SHARP clinic opened in London in 1992, and provided a free day programme for clients and their families with drug and alcohol problems. Barbara Bach and Pattie Clapton were members of its fundraising committee, and Ringo Starr was one of the Friends of SHARP.

The couple also contributed the foreword to *Getting Sober… And Loving It!*, a book by Derek and Joan Taylor which included testimonies from a number of recovering alcoholics. 'All the pain and wreckage of our past is now serving us well, standing us in good stead,' Starr and Bach wrote. 'It's hard for us to understand how people who haven't gone through that pain manage their lives because in recovery programmes you find you can manage your life, one day at a time. When things get really difficult you can think "It will pass today." If something happens that we really don't like, the bottom line is we won't feel like this forever.'[571]

Shortly after the release of his 1992 album *Time Takes Time*, Starr recorded several new songs. A visitor to the studio was the newly-sober Harry Nilsson. According to an observer at the session, Nilsson and Starr were unsure how to behave around one another now that their self-destructive days were behind them.

The new songs included Some Folks Do, effectively a follow-up to The No No Song. It featured the key line: 'Some folks do but I don't,' and was intended as a celebration of Starr's sobriety.

'Ringo had just given it all up,' co-writer Brian Cadd recalled. 'He was dry and clean and fabulous and just joyous about the whole thing. So, we wrote a song called Some Folks Do which was about drug taking and the fact that Ringo was now clean. Then he recorded it and we thought: "This is it. It is going to be the anthem for all drunks and druggies around the world."'[572] Some Folks Do was to have been the lead single from Starr's next album, yet the song was shelved and the project abandoned shortly afterwards.

Ringo's career and fortune were boosted by the success of the Beatles' *Live At The BBC* and *Anthology* projects in the 1990s, the Rock Band and Cirque du Soleil tie-ins, and the remasters, restorations and remixes that followed. He continued to tour and record, published books and held exhibitions with photographs and memorabilia from his past, supported charities including the David Lynch Foundation and his own Lotus Foundation, and was given an array of awards including his induction into the Rock & Roll Hall of Fame and being made a Commander of France's Order of Arts and Letters.

He practised meditation daily and worked out with a personal trainer three times a week, which left him looking slim and dapper. His fastidious clean-living extended to his diet which, apart from a Sunday cheat treat of oatmeal, a croissant and a cup of coffee, consisted almost entirely of vegetables and fruit juices. 'Every time I see Ringo, he smells of kale,' joked his brother-in-law, Joe Walsh of the Eagles.[573] Starr even adopted the germ-avoidance tactic of bumping elbows instead of shaking hands.

Ringo Starr was a man finally at peace with his past and in love with the present. Yet memories of his darkest of days were never far from the surface. At a Los Angeles dinner in 2015, Paul McCartney regretted making light of them. 'I know Ringo has been sober for years, so I joked, "C'mon, Ringo, have a whiskey." Ringo looked at me for a second and says, "What, and end up looking like you?" I deserved it.'[574]

HELP!

If you are struggling with substance abuse, or know someone who is, please know that help is out there. Support varies from country to country, and ranges from large organisations to local groups, and even online support.

It would be impossible to list anything but a fraction of the services available, but hopefully these will act as a starting point for further investigation. Do not be afraid to reach out.

Narcotics Anonymous: www.na.org
Alcoholics Anonymous: www.aa.org

Wikipedia has a section listing a number of other addiction and substance abuse organisations:

https://en.wikipedia.org/wiki/Category:Addiction_and_substance_abuse_organizations

There is also a page collating mental health groups:

https://en.wikipedia.org/wiki/Category:Mental_health_organizations

Finally, Release, the independent and registered charity founded in 1967 by Caroline Coon and Rufus Harris, is still going strong in the UK. Their website can be found at www.release.org.uk.

ACKNOWLEDGEMENTS

Special thanks to Maria Goodden.

Thanks also to:

Mark Amos, Drew Athans, Matt Bagnall, Cathy Blackman, Alex Cain, Francesca Donovan, Royston Ellis, Martin Fahie, Michael Gerber, Orlando Goodden, Ron Grelsamer, Kevin Harrington, Tracey Helton Mitchell, Mark Lewisohn, Katie Mac Aodhagáin, Barry Miles, Anita Ponne, Evan Scrimshaw, Eric Smith, Jude Southerland Kessler, Simon Wells, BBC Archives, the National Archives of the UK, and the good people of the Beatles Bible's fab forum.

Plus, of course, John, Paul, George and Ringo, and all who rode with them.

ABOUT THE AUTHOR

Joe Goodden is a journalist, blogger and paperback writer living in south Wales. Formerly a senior online producer at the BBC, he is a music lover and founder of the Beatles Bible website ('Not quite as popular as Jesus...'). *Riding So High – The Beatles and Drugs* is his first book.

beatlesbible.com
twitter.com/beatlesbible
facebook.com/beatlesbible

BIBLIOGRAPHY

Abel, EL. *Marihuana: The First Twelve Thousand Years* (Plenum Press, New York, 1980)

Aldridge, Alan (ed.). *The Beatles Illustrated Lyrics* (Macdonald Unit 75, London, 1969)

Ali, Tariq. *Street-Fighting Years: An Autobiography Of The Sixties* (Verso, London, 2005)

Aronowitz, Al. *Bob Dylan And The Beatles: Volume One Of The Best Of The Blacklisted Journalist* (1st Books Library, Bloomington, 2004)

Badman, Keith. *The Beatles Diary Volume 2: After The Break-Up 1970-2001* (Omnibus Press, London, 2001)

Badman, Keith. *The Beatles Off The Record* (Omnibus Press, London, 2000)

Badman, Keith. *The Beatles Off The Record Volume Two: The Dream Is Over* (Omnibus Press, London, 2002)

Baker, Chet. *As Though I Had Wings* (Indigo, London, 1998)

Barrow, Tony. *John, Paul, George, Ringo & Me* (André Deutsch, London, 2005)

Beatles, The. *Anthology* (Cassell & Co, London, 2000)

Best, Pete and Doncaster, Patrick. *Beatle! The Pete Best Story* (Plexus Publishing, London, 1985)

Bramwell, Tony with Kingsland, Rosemary. *Magical Mystery Tours: My Life With The Beatles* (Robson Books, London, 2005)

Boyd, Jenny and George-Warren, Holly. *It's Not Only Rock 'n' Roll – Iconic Musicians Reveal The Source Of Their Creativity* (John Blake, London, 2013)

Boyd, Pattie. *Wonderful Today* (Headline Review, London, 2008)

Brown, Peter and Gaines, Steven. *The Love You Make: An Insider's Story Of The Beatles* (McGraw-Hill, New York, 1983)

Butler, Dougal with Trengove, Chris and Lawrence, Peter. *Moon The Loon: The Amazing Rock And Roll Life Of Keith Moon* (Star, London, 1981)

Chapman, Rob. *Psychedelia And Other Colours* (Faber & Faber, London, 2015)

Clayson, Alan. *Ringo Starr* (Sanctuary Publishing, London, 2001)

Coleman, Ray. *Lennon: The Definitive Biography* (Pan Books, London, 2000)

Connolly, Ray. *The Ray Connolly Beatles Archive* (Plumray Books, Kindle Edition, 2011)

Cott, Jonathan. *Days That I'll Remember* (Doubleday, New York, 2013)

Cox, Barry, Shirley, John and Short, Martin. *The Fall Of Scotland Yard* (Penguin Books, Harmondsworth, 1977)

Davies, Hunter. *The Beatles: The Authorised Biography* (Heinemann, London, 1968)

Davies, Hunter. *The Beatles Lyrics* (Weidenfeld & Nicolson, London, 2014)

DiLello, Richard. *The Longest Cocktail Party* (Canongate, Edinburgh, 2000)

Doyle, Tom. *Man on the Run: Paul McCartney In The 1970s* (Polygon, Edinburgh, 2013)

Ellis, Geoffrey. *I Should Have Known Better: A Life In Pop Management* (Thorogood, London, 2005)

Emerick, Geoff and Massey, Howard. *Here, There And Every-where – My Life Recording The Music Of The Beatles* (Gotham Books, New York, 2006)

Epstein, Brian. *A Cellarful Of Noise* (Souvenir Press, London, 1964)

Faithfull, Marianne and Dalton, David. *Memories, Dreams And Reflections* (Harper Perennial, London, 2008)

Fields, Danny. *Linda McCartney: The Biography* (Little, Brown, London, 2000)

Fletcher, Tony. *Moon: The Life And Death Of A Rock Legend* (Omnibus Press, New York, 1998)

Geller, Deborah. *The Brian Epstein Story* (Faber and Faber, London, 1999)

Harrington, Kevin. *'Who's The Redhead On The Roof...?' My Life With The Beatles* (Kindle Edition, 2015)

Harrison, George. *I Me Mine* (First Chronicle, San Francisco, 2007)

Harrison, Olivia. *Living In The Material World* (Abrams, New York, 2011)

Hofmann, Albert (trans. Ott, Jonathan). *LSD: My Problem Child – Reflections On Sacred Drugs, Mysticism, And Science* (McGraw-Hill, New York, 1980)

Howlett, Kevin. *The Beatles: The BBC Archives 1962-1970* (BBC Books, London, 2013)

Howlett, Kevin and Lewisohn, Mark. *In My Life: John Lennon Remembered* (BBC Books, London, 1990)

Hutchins, Chris. *The Beatles: Messages From John, Paul, George And Ringo* (Neville Ness House, London, 2015)

Jones, Max and Chilton, John. *Louis – The Louis Armstrong Story* (Littlehampton Book Services, Worthing, 1976)

Kane, Larry. *Ticket To Ride* (Penguin Books, London, 2004)

Kessler, Jude Southerland. *She Loves You* (OnTheRock Books, Monroe, 2013)

Kirchherr, Astrid and Voormann, Klaus. *Hamburg Days* (Genesis

Publications, Guildford, 1999)

Leary, Timothy, Metzner, Ralph and Alpert, Richard. *The Psychedelic Experience: A Manual Based On The Tibetan Book Of The Dead* (Citadel Press, New York, 1992)

Leng, Simon. *While My Guitar Gently Weeps: The Music Of George Harrison* (Hal Leonard Corporation, Milwaukee, 2006)

Leigh, Spencer. *Love Me Do To Love Me Don't* (McNidder & Grace, Carmarthen, 2016)

Leigh, Spencer. *The Beatles In Hamburg* (Omnibus Press, London, 2011)

Leigh, Spencer. *The Best Of Fellas: The Story Of Bob Wooler* (Drivegreen, Liverpool, 2002)

Leigh, Spencer. *The Cavern: The Most Famous Club In The World* (SAF Publishing, London, 2008)

Lennon, Cynthia. *A Twist Of Lennon* (Star, London, 1980)

Lennon, Cynthia. *John* (Crown Publishers, New York, 2005)

Lewisohn, Mark. *The Complete Beatles Chronicle* (Pyramid Books, London, 1992)

Lewisohn, Mark. *The Complete Beatles Recording Sessions* (Hamlyn, London, 1988)

Lewisohn, Mark. *All These Years: Tune In – Extended Special Edition* (Little, Brown, London, 2013)

Lewisohn, Mark (ed.). *Wingspan: Paul McCartney's Band On The Run* (Little, Brown, London, 2002)

Madinger, Chip and Raile, Scott. *Lennonology – Strange Days Indeed* (Open Your Books, Chesterfield, 2015)

Martin, George and Hornsby, Jeremy. *All You Need Is Ears* (St Martin's Press, New York, 1979)

McCabe, Peter and Schonfeld, Robert D. *John Lennon: For The Record* (Bantam, New York, 1984)

McNab, Ken. *The Beatles In Scotland* (Polygon, Edinburgh, 2008)

Miles, Barry. *In The Sixties* (Jonathan Cape, London, 2002)

Miles, Barry. *Many Years From Now* (Secker & Warburg, London, 1997)

Miles, Barry. *The Beatles Diary Volume 1: The Beatles Years* (Omnibus Press, London, 2001)

Mold, Alex. *Illicit drugs and the rise of epidemiology during the 1960s* (Journal of Epidemiology and Community Health 61, 2007)

Norman, Philip. *John Lennon* (HarperCollins, London, 2008)

Norman, Philip. *Paul McCartney: The Biography* (Weidenfeld & Nicholson, London, 2016)

Norman, Philip. *Shout! The True Story Of The Beatles* (Pan Books, London, 2004)

O'Dell, Chris and Ketcham, Katherine. *Miss O'Dell: My Hard Days And Long Nights With The Beatles, The Stones, Bob Dylan, Eric Clapton, And The Women They Loved* (Touchstone, New York, 2009)

Pang, May and Edwards, Henry. *Loving John* (Corgi Books, London, 1983)

Peebles, Andy. *The Lennon Tapes* (BBC Publications, London, 1981)

Perasi, Luca. *Paul McCartney: Recording Sessions (1969-2013)* (L.I.L.Y Publishing, Milan, 2013)

Richards, Keith with Fox, James. *Life* (Weidenfeld & Nicholson, London, 2010)

Richter, Dan. *The Dream Is Over: London In The 60s, Heroin, And John And Yoko* (Quartet Books, London, 2012)

Roberts, Andy. *Albion Dreaming: A Popular History Of LSD In Britain* (Marshall Cavendish Editions, Singapore, 2012)

Sanchez, Tony. *Up And Down With The Rolling Stones – My Roller-coaster Ride With Keith Richards* (John Blake Publishing, Kindle Edition, 2011)

Schreuders, Piet, Lewisohn, Mark & Smith, Adam. *The Beatles' London* (Portico, London, 1994)

Schwartz, Francie. *Body Count* (Straight Arrow Books, San Francisco, 1972)

Shapiro, Mark. *All Things Must Pass: The Life Of George Harrison* (Virgin Books, London, 2002)

Sheff, David. *All We Are Saying* (St Martin's Griffin, New York, 2000)

Shipton, Alyn. *Nilsson: The Life Of A Singer-Songwriter* (Oxford University Press, Oxford, 2013)

Shotton, Pete and Schaffner, Nicholas. *John Lennon In My Life* (Coronet Books, London, 1983)

Sounes, Howard. *Fab: An Intimate Life Of Paul McCartney* (Harper-Collins, Kindle Edition, 2010)

Spitz, Bob. *The Beatles: The Biography* (Aurum Press, London, 2006)

Starr, Michael Seth. *Ringo: With A Little Help* (Backbeat Books, Milwaukee, 2015)

Starr, Ringo. *Postcards From The Boys* (Cassell Illustrated, London, 2004)

Strang, John and Gossop, Michael (ed.). *Heroin Addiction And The British System: Volume I – Origins And Evolution* (Routledge, Abingdon, 2005)

Sulpy, Doug with Schweighardt, Ray. *Drugs, Divorce And A Slipping Image* (The 910, Albrightsville, 2007)

Taylor, Derek and Harrison, George. *Fifty Years Adrift* (Genesis Publications, Guildford, 1984)

Taylor, Derek. *It Was Twenty Years Ago Today* (Fireside, New York, 1987)

Taylor, Joan and Taylor, Derek. *Getting Sober …And Loving It!* (Vermillion, London, 1992)

Thomson, Graeme. *George Harrison: Behind The Locked Door* (Omnibus Press, New York, 2013)

Turner, Steve. *Beatles '66: The Revolutionary Year* (HarperCollins, Kindle Edition, 2016)

Turner, Steve. *The Gospel According To The Beatles* (Westminster John Knox Press, Louisville, 2006)

Vyner, Harriet. *Groovy Bob – The Life And Times Of Robert Fraser* (Faber and Faber, London, 2001)

Wells, Simon. *Butterfly On A Wheel: The Great Rolling Stones Drugs Bust* (Omnibus Press, New York, 2011)

Wenner, Jann S. *Lennon Remembers* (Verso, London, 2000)

Williams, Allan and Marshall, William. *The Man Who Gave The Beatles Away* (Elm Tree Books, London, 1975)

Yule, Andrew. *The Man Who 'Framed' The Beatles: A Biography Of Richard Lester* (Donald I Fine, New York, 1994)

NOTES

[1] *Rolling Stone*, 11 September 1986.

[2] Connolly, *Beatles Archive*.

[3] McCabe and Schonfeld, *John Lennon: For The Record*.

[4] psychedelichippiemusic.blogspot.co.uk/2010/06/beatles-how-they-got-their-name.html

[5] *Ibid.*

[6] *Ibid.*

[7] Taylor, *Fifty Years Adrift*.

[8] roystonellisbeatpoet.blogspot.co.uk/2009/04/royston-ellis-with-jimmy-page-late-1960.html

[9] The Beatles, *Anthology*.

[10] Miles, *Many Years From Now*.

[11] *International Times*, 31 May 1973.

[12] roystonellisbeatpoet.blogspot.co.uk/2009/04/his-work.html

[13] Davies, *The Beatles*.

[14] Interview with BP Fallon, *Sunday Tribune*, 18 October 1987.

[15] Connolly, *Beatles Archive*.

[16] Barrow, *John, Paul, George, Ringo & Me*.

[17] Lewisohn, *All These Years: Tune In*.

[18] The Beatles, *Anthology*.

[19] Williams, *The Man Who Gave The Beatles Away*.

[20] *People*, 28 August 1989.

[21] Norman, *John Lennon*.

[22] The Beatles, *Anthology*.

[23] Williams, *The Man Who Gave The Beatles Away*.

[24] Miles, *Many Years From Now*.

[25] The Beatles, *Anthology*.

[26] *Ibid.*

[27] *Ibid.*

[28] McCabe and Schonfeld, *John Lennon: For The Record*.

[29] The Beatles, *Anthology*.

[30] Best and Doncaster, *Beatle!*

[31] *Ibid.*

[32] *Ibid.*

[33] Coleman, *Lennon*.

[34] The Beatles, *Anthology*.

[35] *Ibid.*

[36] Miles, *Many Years From Now*.

[37] The Beatles, *Anthology*.

[38] Best and Doncaster, *Beatle!*

[39] Leigh, *The Beatles In Hamburg*.

[40] Best and Doncaster, *Beatle!*

[41] The Beatles, *Anthology*.

[42] *Ibid.*

[43] *Ibid.*

[44] Wenner, *Lennon Remembers*.

[45] Coleman, *Lennon*.

[46] Lewisohn, *All These Years: Tune In*.

[47] Leigh, *The Beatles In Hamburg*.

[48] Lennon, *A Twist Of Lennon*.

[49] Lennon, *John*.

[50] Lennon, *A Twist Of Lennon*.

[51] Kessler, *She Loves You*.

[52] Lewisohn, *All These Years: Tune In.*

[53] Norman, *Paul McCartney.*

[54] Interview by Jean-François Vallée for French TV, 4 April 1975.

[55] Best and Doncaster, *Beatle!*

[56] Wenner, *Lennon Remembers.*

[57] Geller, *The Brian Epstein Story.*

[58] Lewisohn, *All These Years: Tune In.*

[59] *Ibid.*

[60] McCabe and Schonfeld, *John Lennon: For The Record.*

[61] The Beatles, *Anthology.*

[62] McCabe and Schonfeld, *John Lennon: For The Record.*

[63] Sheff, *All We Are Saying.*

[64] Lewisohn, *All These Years: Tune In.*

[65] *Piers Morgan's Life Stories*, 25 May 2012.

[66] Spitz, *The Beatles, The Biography.*

[67] Kessler, *She Loves You.*

[68] McCabe and Schonfeld, *John Lennon: For The Record.*

[69] Lennon, *John.*

[70] Miles, *Many Years From Now.*

[71] Purple Chick, *A/B Road* (8.107), 8 January 1969.

[72] Wenner, *Lennon Remembers.*

[73] *Beatlefan* issue 90, 1994.

[74] Wenner, *Lennon Remembers.*

[75] The Beatles, *Anthology.*

[76] Kane, *Ticket To Ride.*

[77] *NME*, 1 July 1966.

[78] Best and Doncaster, *Beatle!*

[79] Davies, *The Beatles.*

[80] Best and Doncaster, *Beatle!*

[81] The Beatles, *Anthology.*

[82] *Ibid.*

[83] *Ibid.*

[84] *Trinidad Express*, 5 May 1971.

[85] Leigh, *The Cavern*.

[86] Jones and Chilton, *Louis – The Louis Armstrong Story*.

[87] Taylor, *It Was Twenty Years Ago Today*.

[88] *The South Bank Show*, The Making Of Sgt Pepper.

[89] nostalgiacentral.com/pop-culture/fads/drugs-in-the-1960s/

[90] Taylor, *It Was Twenty Years Ago Today*.

[91] *Ibid*.

[92] Aronowitz, *Bob Dylan And The Beatles*.

[93] *Ibid*.

[94] *Ibid*.

[95] *Ibid*.

[96] Miles, *Many Years From Now*.

[97] Aronowitz, *Bob Dylan And The Beatles*.

[98] Geller, *The Brian Epstein Story*.

[99] Miles, *Many Years From Now*.

[100] *Ibid*.

[101] The Beatles, *Anthology*.

[102] Taylor, *Fifty Years Adrift*.

[103] *Ibid*.

[104] Kane, *Ticket To Ride*.

[105] Taylor, *Fifty Years Adrift*.

[106] Miles, *Many Years From Now*.

[107] Sheff, *All We Are Saying*.

[108] Wenner, *Lennon Remembers*.

[109] Sheff, *All We Are Saying*.

[110] The Beatles, *Anthology*.

[111] Barrow, *John, Paul, George, Ringo & Me*.

[112] Lennon, *A Twist Of Lennon*.

[113] The Beatles, *Anthology*.

[114] *Melody Maker*, 27 March 1965.

[115] The Beatles, *Anthology*.

[116] *Ibid*.

[117] *Ibid*.

[118] *L'Express*, 22 March 1970.

[119] The Beatles, *Anthology.*

[120] *Uncut,* July 2004.

[121] The Beatles, *Anthology.*

[122] Barrow, *John, Paul, George, Ringo & Me.*

[123] Lennon, *A Twist Of Lennon.*

[124] Lennon, *John.*

[125] Lennon, *A Twist Of Lennon.*

[126] Davies, *The Beatles.*

[127] Kane, *Ticket To Ride.*

[128] Taylor, *It Was Twenty Years Ago Today.*

[129] Barrow, *John, Paul, George, Ringo & Me.*

[130] Wenner, *Lennon Remembers.*

[131] Miles, *In The Sixties.*

[132] Sheff, *All We Are Saying.*

[133] The Beatles, *Anthology.*

[134] *Ibid.*

[135] Miles, *Many Years From Now.*

[136] *Observer* magazine, 26 November 1967.

[137] Miles, *Many Years From Now.*

[138] Cott, *Days That I'll Remember.*

[139] The Beatles, *Anthology.*

[140] *The South Bank Show*, The Making Of Sgt Pepper.

[141] Miles, *Many Years From Now.*

[142] Emerick and Massey, *Here, There And Everywhere.*

[143] Shotton and Schaffner, *John Lennon In My Life.*

[144] Martin and Hornsby, *All You Need Is Ears.*

[145] Miles, *Many Years From Now.*

[146] Taylor, *It Was Twenty Years Ago Today.*

[147] The Beatles, *Anthology.*

[148] Miles, *Many Years From Now.*

[149] Miles, *In The Sixties.*

[150] *Ibid.*

[151] *Melody Maker*, 5 August 1967.

[152] Vyner, *Groovy Bob.*

[153] Miles, *Many Years From Now*.

[154] *Melody Maker*, 2 December 1967.

[155] Boyd and Junor, *Wonderful Today*.

[156] The generally accepted date is 27 March, although some sources put it at 8 April.

[157] Turner, *The Gospel According To The Beatles*.

[158] *CREEM*, January 1988.

[159] The Beatles, *Anthology*.

[160] Wenner, *Lennon Remembers*.

[161] Boyd and Junor, *Wonderful Today*.

[162] *Ibid*.

[163] Wenner, *Lennon Remembers*.

[164] The Beatles, *Anthology*.

[165] *Ibid*.

[166] *Ibid*.

[167] Wenner, *Lennon Remembers*.

[168] *Ibid*.

[169] The Beatles, *Anthology*.

[170] Boyd and Junor, *Wonderful Today*.

[171] Lennon, *John*.

[172] Wenner, *Lennon Remembers*.

[173] The Beatles, *Anthology*.

[174] *West 57th*, CBS, 12 December 1987.

[175] Hofmann, *LSD: My Problem Child*.

[176] *Ibid*.

[177] *Wired*, 16 January 2006

[178] *New York Times*, 7 January 2006.

[179] Letter from Laura Huxley to Julian and Juliette Huxley, 8 December 1963.

[180] *CREEM*, January 1988.

[181] Davies, *The Beatles*.

[182] The Beatles, *Anthology*.

[183] *Rolling Stone*, 13 May 1971.

[184] *Daily Telegraph*, 19 April 2010.

[185] Wenner, *Lennon Remembers*.

[186] *Rolling Stone*, 11 September 1986.

[187] The Beatles, *Anthology*.

[188] *Ibid*.

[189] *Ibid*.

[190] Wenner, *Lennon Remembers*.

[191] The Beatles, *Anthology*.

[192] *Rolling Stone*, 13 May 1971.

[193] Sheff, *All We Are Saying*.

[194] The Beatles, *Anthology*.

[195] *Ibid*.

[196] Davies, *The Beatles*.

[197] Turner, *Beatles '66*.

[198] Miles, *Many Years From Now*.

[199] *Ibid*.

[200] *Ibid*.

[201] Vyner, *Groovy Bob*.

[202] Wenner, *Lennon Remembers*.

[203] Sheff, *All We Are Saying*.

[204] *Ibid*.

[205] The Beatles, *Anthology*.

[206] *Playboy*, December 1984.

[207] Leary, Metzner and Alpert, *The Psychedelic Experience*.

[208] *Ibid*.

[209] The Beatles, *Anthology*.

[210] Miles, *Many Years From Now*.

[211] Wenner, *Lennon Remembers*.

[212] *Evening Standard*, 4 March 1966.

[213] The Beatles, *Anthology*.

[214] Wenner, *Lennon Remembers*.

[215] Shotton and Schaffner, *John Lennon In My Life*.

[216] *Uncut*, October 1999.

[217] Wenner, *Lennon Remembers*.

[218] Shotton and Schaffner, *John Lennon In My Life*.

[219] *Ibid.*

[220] Miles, *In The Sixties.*

[221] The Beatles, *Anthology.*

[222] Vyner, *Groovy Bob.*

[223] *Ibid.*

[224] *Ibid.*

[225] *Ibid.*

[226] Miles, *Many Years From Now.*

[227] Davies, *The Beatles.*

[228] Taylor, *Fifty Years Adrift.*

[229] Coleman, *Lennon.*

[230] Lennon, *John.*

[231] *Ibid.*

[232] *Ibid.*

[233] *Ibid.*

[234] Lennon always maintained that he first met Ono on 9 November, prior to her exhibition opening. The number nine held deep personal significance to him, and recurred often in his life. However, advertisements for the exhibition and contemporary reports featured an opening date of 8 November. The *International Times* reported that the artworks were being installed until the early hours of that date, suggesting it was ready to be opened as planned later that morning. Lennon and Ono are known to have met the day before the opening, which would therefore most likely have been on 7 November.

[235] Sheff, *All We Are Saying.*

[236] *Ibid.*

[237] Aldridge, *The Beatles Illustrated Lyrics.*

[238] Leigh, *Love Me Do To Love Me Don't.*

[239] Wenner, *Lennon Remembers.*

[240] The Beatles, *Anthology.*

[241] Miles, *Many Years From Now.*

[242] *Ibid.*

[243] *Ibid.*

[244] Cott, *Days That I'll Remember*.

[245] Sheff, *All We Are Saying*.

[246] *Ibid.*

[247] Vyner, *Groovy Bob*.

[248] *Ibid.*

[249] Miles, *Many Years From Now*.

[250] The Beatles, *Anthology*.

[251] *In My Life: John Lennon Remembered*. BBC Radio 1, 8 December 1990.

[252] Wenner, *Lennon Remembers*.

[253] Martin, *All You Need Is Ears*.

[254] Davies, *The Beatles*.

[255] Martin, *All You Need Is Ears*.

[256] *In My Life: John Lennon Remembered*. BBC Radio 1, 8 December 1990.

[257] Martin, *All You Need Is Ears*.

[258] Miles, *Many Years From Now*.

[259] *Ibid.*

[260] Taylor, *Fifty Years Adrift*.

[261] *Ibid.*

[262] *Ibid.*

[263] *Ibid.*

[264] Lennon, *A Twist Of Lennon*.

[265] Taylor, *Fifty Years Adrift*.

[266] Lennon, *A Twist Of Lennon*.

[267] *Ibid.*

[268] Howlett, *The Beatles: The BBC Archives*.

[269] Chapman, *Psychedelia And Other Colours*.

[270] Howlett, *The Beatles: The BBC Archives*.

[271] Associated Press, 9 June 1967.

[272] Wenner, *Lennon Remembers*.

[273] Davies, *The Beatles Lyrics*.

[274] Brown and Gaines, *The Love You Make*.

[275] Norman, *Shout!*

[276] Miles, *Many Years From Now*.

[277] Miles, *The Beatles Diary*.

[278] Brown and Gaines, *The Love You Make*.

[279] The Beatles, *Anthology*.

[280] Miles, *Many Years From Now*.

[281] *Ibid*.

[282] Taylor, *It Was Twenty Years Ago Today*.

[283] *Life*, 16 June 1967.

[284] The Beatles, *Anthology*.

[285] Davies, *The Beatles*.

[286] Connolly, *Beatles Archive*.

[287] *Melody Maker*, 5 August 1967.

[288] The Beatles, *Anthology*.

[289] Hansard, vol 751 cc1148-65, 28 July 1967.

[290] *Sydney Morning Herald*. 22 June 1967.

[291] *Rolling Stone*, 5 November 1987.

[292] *Billboard*, December 1992.

[293] *Rolling Stone*, 22 October 1987.

[294] *CREEM*, January 1988.

[295] The Beatles, *Anthology*.

[296] *Rolling Stone*, 5 November 1987.

[297] Lennon, *A Twist Of Lennon*.

[298] *CREEM*, January 1988.

[299] Boyd and Junor, *Wonderful Today*.

[300] The Beatles, *Anthology*.

[301] Boyd and Junor, *Wonderful Today*.

[302] STP, standing for serenity, tranquility and peace, was the street name for 2,5-Dimethoxy-4-methylamphetamine, or DOM. The drug had first been synthesised in 1964 by American pharmacologist Alexander Shulgin, the so-called 'godfather of psychedelics', and was alluded to in Jimi Hendrix's 1967 song The Stars That Play With Laughing Sam's Dice. By including the names of two drugs, Hendrix's acronymic title went one step further than the Beatles were

believed to have done with Lucy In The Sky With Diamonds.

[303] The Beatles, *Anthology*.

[304] *Ibid.*

[305] *Ibid.*

[306] *Melody Maker*, 2 September 1967.

[307] Harrison, *I Me Mine*.

[308] Shotton and Schaffner, *John Lennon In My Life*.

[309] The Beatles, *Anthology*.

[310] *Innerview*, syndicated US radio, 29 August 1977.

[311] *Melody Maker*, 2 December 1967.

[312] Ellis, *I Should Have Known Better*.

[313] Shotton and Schaffner, *John Lennon In My Life*.

[314] Lennon, *John*.

[315] *In My Life: John Lennon Remembered*. BBC Radio 1, 8 December 1990.

[316] Wenner, *Lennon Remembers*.

[317] Sheff, *All We Are Saying*.

[318] *Trinidad Express*, 5 May 1971.

[319] Lennon, *John*.

[320] Taylor, *Fifty Years Adrift*.

[321] Shotton and Schaffner, *John Lennon In My Life*.

[322] Taylor, *Fifty Years Adrift*.

[323] Shotton and Schaffner, *John Lennon In My Life*.

[324] Taylor, *Fifty Years Adrift*.

[325] Wenner, *Lennon Remembers*.

[326] Lennon, *A Twist Of Lennon*.

[327] *Ibid.*

[328] Shotton and Schaffner, *John Lennon In My Life*.

[329] Sheff, *All We Are Saying*.

[330] McCabe and Schonfeld, *John Lennon: For The Record*.

[331] Geller, *The Brian Epstein Story*.

[332] *Ibid.*

[333] *Ibid.*

[334] Leigh, *The Best Of Fellas*.

[335] Geller, *The Brian Epstein Story*.

[336] Taylor, *Fifty Years Adrift*.

[337] Epstein, *A Cellarful Of Noise*.

[338] Geller, *The Brian Epstein Story*.

[339] Brown and Gaines, *The Love You Make*.

[340] Geller, *The Brian Epstein Story*.

[341] *Ibid.*

[342] *Ibid.*

[343] *Ibid.*

[344] *Daily Mail*, 26 April 2000.

[345] Davies, *The Beatles*.

[346] McCabe and Schonfeld, *John Lennon: For The Record*.

[347] Shotton and Schaffner, *John Lennon In My Life*.

[348] Hutchins, *The Beatles – Messages From John, Paul, George And Ringo*.

[349] Brown and Gaines, *The Love You Make*.

[350] *Ibid.*

[351] *Ibid.*

[352] Lewisohn, *Complete Beatles Recording Sessions*.

[353] Davies, *The Beatles*.

[354] Geller, *The Brian Epstein Story*.

[355] Wenner, *Lennon Remembers*.

[356] *Ibid.*

[357] McCabe and Schonfeld, *John Lennon: For The Record*.

[358] *The Times*, 9 September 1967.

[359] Geller, *The Brian Epstein Story*.

[360] The Beatles, *Anthology*.

[361] Geller, *The Brian Epstein Story*.

[362] Leigh, *The Cavern*.

[363] *Uncut*, July 2004.

[364] Vyner, *Groovy Bob*.

[365] *Ibid.*

[366] Miles, *Many Years From Now*.

367 *Ibid.*

368 *Ibid.*

369 *Ibid.*

370 *Ibid.*

371 Sounes, *Fab.*

372 *Playboy*, December 1984.

373 Miles, *Many Years From Now.*

374 *Ibid.*

375 groups.google.com/forum/#!topic/rec.music.beatles/9SuNGvusems

376 Schwartz, *Body Count.*

377 *Ibid.*

378 *Ibid.*

379 DiLello, *The Longest Cocktail Party.*

380 Badman, *The Beatles Off The Record.*

381 Taylor, *Fifty Years Adrift.*

382 Vyner, *Groovy Bob.*

383 Faithfull and Dalton, *Memories, Dreams And Reflections.*

384 Sanchez, *Up And Down With The Rolling Stones.*

385 *Ibid.*

386 Yule, *The Man Who 'Framed' The Beatles.*

387 Miles, *Many Years From Now.*

388 *Uncut*, July 2004.

389 Miles, *Many Years From Now.*

390 *Ibid.*

391 Vyner, *Groovy Bob.*

392 Strang and Gossop, *Heroin Addiction And The British System.*

393 Mold, *Illicit drugs and the rise of epidemiology during the 1960s.*

394 McCabe and Schonfeld, *John Lennon: For The Record.*

395 Richards and Fox, *Life.*

396 Strang and Gossop, *Heroin Addiction And The British System.*

397 Baker, *As Though I Had Wings.*

398 *Ibid.*

399 Vyner, *Groovy Bob.*

[400] *Observer* magazine, 26 November 1967.

[401] Sheff, *All We Are Saying.*

[402] *Rolling Stone*, 11 September 1986.

[403] Brown and Gaines, *The Love You Make.*

[404] Norman, *John Lennon.*

[405] Brown and Gaines, *The Love You Make.*

[406] Wenner, *Lennon Remembers.*

[407] Harrington, *Who's The Redhead On The Roof?*

[408] Author interview, 2015.

[409] Sanchez, *Up And Down With The Rolling Stones.*

[410] Cott, *Days That I'll Remember.*

[411] Miles, *Many Years From Now.*

[412] *Playboy*, December 1984.

[413] *Esquire*, December 1970.

[414] Miles, *Many Years From Now.*

[415] Schwartz, *Body Count.*

[416] *Ibid.*

[417] Lennon, *John.*

[418] *In My Life: John Lennon Remembered.* BBC Radio 1, 8 December 1990.

[419] Richards, and Fox, *Life.*

[420] *Desert Island Discs*, BBC Radio 4, 10 June 2007.

[421] Wenner, *Lennon Remembers.*

[422] Purple Chick, *A/B Road*, 14 January 1969.

[423] *Uncut*, 9 October 2015.

[424] McNab, *The Beatles In Scotland.*

[425] examiner.com/article/life-with-the-lennons-pt-1-john-yoko-s-love-affair-heroin-and-the-beatles

[426] Richter, *The Dream Is Over.*

[427] *Ibid.*

[428] Norman, *John Lennon.*

[429] Brown and Gaines, *The Love You Make.*

[430] Wenner, *Lennon Remembers.*

[431] *Ibid.*

[432] Richter, *The Dream Is Over*.

[433] Peebles, *The Lennon Tapes*.

[434] Connolly, *Beatles Archive*.

[435] *Toronto Daily Star*, 7 March 1970.

[436] *Uncut*, January 1998.

[437] Madinger and Raile, *Lennonology*.

[438] Richter, *The Dream Is Over*.

[439] examiner.com/article/life-with-the-lennons-pt-1-john-yoko-s-love-affair-heroin-and-the-beatles

[440] *Uncut*, September 2003.

[441] Taylor, *It Was Twenty Years Ago Today*.

[442] *Melody Maker*, 2 December 1967.

[443] Wells, *Butterfly On A Wheel*.

[444] *Glasgow Herald*, 21 June 1968.

[445] Schwartz, *Body Count*.

[446] Bramwell, *Magical Mystery Tours*.

[447] *Ibid*.

[448] Ali, *Street-Fighting Years*.

[449] Wenner, *Lennon Remembers*.

[450] Shotton and Schaffner, *John Lennon In My Life*.

[451] *NME*, 19 January 1974.

[452] The Beatles, *Anthology*.

[453] *Ibid*.

[454] *Ibid*.

[455] *Ibid*.

[456] Peebles, *The Lennon Tapes*.

[457] Brown and Gaines, *The Love You Make*.

[458] Madinger and Raile, *Lennonology*.

[459] *The Guardian*, 1 August 2005.

[460] Hansard, vol 772 c145W, 7 November 1968.

[461] *The Guardian*, 1 August 2005.

[462] Hansard, vol 772 c145W, 7 November 1968.

[463] Peebles, *The Lennon Tapes*.

[464] The Beatles, *Anthology*.

[465] *Ibid.*

[466] Peebles, *The Lennon Tapes.*

[467] uscis.gov/sites/default/files/USCIS/About Us/FOIA/John W. Lennon Pt.76.pdf

[468] Boyd and Junor, *Wonderful Today.*

[469] Shotton and Schaffner, *John Lennon In My Life.*

[470] Boyd and Junor, *Wonderful Today.*

[471] *Sunday Times*, 6 April 1969.

[472] Shotton and Schaffner, *John Lennon In My Life.*

[473] *Ibid.*

[474] *Sunday Times*, 6 April 1969.

[475] Boyd and Junor, *Wonderful Today.*

[476] Taylor, *Fifty Years Adrift.*

[477] *Sunday Times*, 6 April 1969.

[478] Emerick, *Here, There And Everywhere.*

[479] Cox, Shirley and Short, *The Fall Of Scotland Yard.*

[480] Peebles, *The Lennon Tapes.*

[481] FBI memo, 16 March 1972.

[482] *The Guardian*, 4 September 2014.

[483] Pang, *Loving John.*

[484] *Rolling Stone.* 14 February 1974.

[485] *Rolling Stone*, 25 April 1974.

[486] Shipton, *Nilsson: The Life Of A Singer-Songwriter.*

[487] *CREEM*, July 1975.

[488] Author interview, 2011.

[489] Doyle, *Man On The Run.*

[490] *Ibid.*

[491] *The Lost Lennon Tapes*, 91-20: *Milk And Honey* Outtakes/*Pussy Cats* Session, Westwood One, 13-19 May 1991.

[492] Author interview, 2011.

[493] *The Old Grey Whistle Test*, BBC, 18 April 1975.

[494] *Rolling Stone.* 5 June 1975.

[495] Sheff, *All We Are Saying.*

[496] *Beatlefan*, issue 116, January/February 1999.

[497] *Q,* issue 184.

[498] Doyle, *Man On The Run.*

[499] *Ibid.*

[500] *Daily Mail,* 11 August 1972.

[501] Sounes, *Fab.*

[502] Doyle, *Man On The Run.*

[503] Lewisohn, *Wingspan.*

[504] Doyle, *Man On The Run.*

[505] *Uncut,* July 2004.

[506] *Ibid.*

[507] Fields, *Linda McCartney.*

[508] *Playboy,* December 1984.

[509] Sounes, *Fab.*

[510] *Daily Telegraph,* 26 January 2014.

[511] Promotional interview for *Wingspan* documentary, 2001.

[512] Doyle, *Man On The Run.*

[513] *Daily Telegraph,* 26 January 2014.

[514] Flashback: Paul McCartney Busted in Tokyo. 93.3 WMMR – wmmr.com

[515] Badman, *The Beatles Diary Volume 2.*

[516] *Ibid.*

[517] *Ibid.*

[518] Associated Press, 18 January 1984.

[519] Badman, *The Dream Is Over.*

[520] *Playboy,* December 1984.

[521] Doyle, *Man On The Run.*

[522] *Uncut,* July 2004.

[523] *Daily Mirror,* 29 May 2015.

[524] Doyle, *Man On The Run.*

[525] Harrison, *Living In The Material World.*

[526] Boyd and Junor, *Wonderful Today.*

[527] *Ibid.*

[528] O'Dell and Ketcham, *Miss O'Dell.*

[529] Thomson, *Behind The Locked Door.*

[530] O'Dell and Ketcham, *Miss O'Dell*.

[531] Boyd and Junor, *Wonderful Today*.

[532] *Uncut*. August 2008.

[533] *Rolling Stone*. 19 April 1979.

[534] Harrison, *I Me Mine*.

[535] *Ibid.*

[536] *Rolling Stone*. 30 December 1976.

[537] *CREEM*, January 1988.

[538] Interview with Al Aronowitz, 1992.

[539] *The Independent*, 29 June 1998.

[540] *CREEM*, January 1988.

[541] Sheff, *All We Are Saying*.

[542] Richter, *The Dream Is Over*.

[543] *Mojo*, July 2001.

[544] Badman, *The Beatles Diary Volume 2*.

[545] *Prime Cuts – The Alice Cooper Story*, DVD, 2004.

[546] O'Dell and Ketcham, *Miss O'Dell*.

[547] Translated from *Le Chroniqueur*, July 1988.

[548] *People*, 17 January 1977.

[549] Starr, *Postcards From The Boys*.

[550] *Rolling Stone*, 7 October 1992.

[551] *People*, 17 January 1977.

[552] Starr, *Postcards From The Boys*.

[553] *Ibid.*

[554] *Woman*. 4 October 1980.

[555] *People*, 28 August 1989.

[556] *Ibid.*

[557] Associated Press, 12 December 1986.

[558] *People*, 28 August 1989.

[559] *Sunday Express*, 9 July 2010.

[560] *The Independent*, 28 October 1995.

[561] Badman, *The Dream Is Over*.

[562] *Orange Coast*, July 1992.

[563] *People*, 28 August 1989.

[564] *Ibid.*

[565] Badman, *The Dream Is Over*.

[566] *Ibid.*

[567] *People.* 28 August 1989

[568] *Orange Coast*, July 1992.

[569] *Ibid.*

[570] *Rolling Stone*, 7 October 1992.

[571] Taylor and Taylor, *Getting Sober… And Loving It!*

[572] undercover.fm/news/12856-brian-cadd-song-for-ringo-starr-remains-in-the-vault

[573] *Rolling Stone*, 15 April 2015.

[574] *Ibid.*

Printed in Great Britain
by Amazon

20052834R00210